PALLIATIVE **ford Branch**
NTY LIBRARY
IN IRE

KU-327-743

U

KIL

No. 219

WITHDRAWN

WITHDRAWN

FACING DEATH

Series editor: David Clark, Professor of Medical Sociology
University of Lancaster

The subject of death in late modern culture has become a rich field of theoretical, clinical and policy interest. Widely regarded as a taboo until recent times, death now engages a growing interest among social scientists, practitioners and those responsible for the organization and delivery of human services. Indeed, how we die has become a powerful commentary on how we live and the specialized care of dying people holds an important place within modern health and social care.

This series captures such developments. Among the contributors are leading experts in death studies, from sociology, anthropology, social psychology, ethics, nursing, medicine and pastoral care. A particular feature of the series is its attention to the developing field of palliative care, viewed from the perspectives of practitioners, planners and policy analysts; here several authors adopt a multi-disciplinary approach, drawing on recent research, policy and organizational commentary, and reviews of evidence-based practice. Written in a clear, accessible style, the entire series will be essential reading for students of death, dying and bereavement, and for anyone with an involvement in palliative care research, service delivery or policy-making.

PALLIATIVE CARE
IN IRELAND

Edited by Julie Ling and
Liam O'Síoráin

OPEN UNIVERSITY PRESS

Open University Press
McGraw-Hill Education
McGraw-Hill House
Shoppenhangers Road
Maidenhead
Berkshire
England
SL6 2QL

email: enquiries@openup.co.uk
world-wide web: www.openup.co.uk

and Two Penn Plaza, New York, NY 10121-2289, USA

First published 2005

A catalogue record of this book is available from the British Library

ISBN 0335 214932 (pb)   0335 214940 (hb)

Library of Congress Cataloging-in-Publication Data
CIP data applied for

Typeset by RefineCatch Ltd, Bungay, Suffolk
Printed in the UK by Bell and Bain Ltd, Glasgow

An Aran Prayer

Bás ola,	Death with anointing
Bás sona	Death with bliss
Bás solais	Death with illumination
Bás soláis	Death with consolation
Bás aithreachais	Death with repentance
Bás gan chrá	Death without torment
Bás gan scáth	Death without shadow
Bás gan bhás	Death without death
Bás gan scanradh	Death without dread
Bás gan dolás	Death without sorrow
Seacht n-aingeal an Spioraid Naoimh	Seven angels of the Blessed Spirit
Agus an dis aingeal coimhdeachta	And the twin guardian angels
Do m'dhionsa anocht agus gach oiche	Be around my roof tonight
Go dtig soils' is camhaoir	Until daybreak and the light

Contents

Notes on the contributors

Jide Afolabi is Senior Physiotherapist in Palliative Care at Our Lady's Hospice, Harold's Cross, where he has worked since 2003. Jide obtained a Bachelor of Medical Rehabilitation degree in Physiotherapy at the University of Nigeria in 1996. He worked in hospitals in Nigeria until moving to Ireland in 2002.

Maria Bailey is Education Coordinator at Milford Care Centre, Limerick. Maria spent many years as a community nursing sister in Birmingham before joining St Mary's Hospice Home Care Team in Birmingham as a home care sister. She completed a BSc (Hons) Palliative Care programme at the University of Central England, a PGDip. in Clinical Health Science Education and a Masters Degree in Nursing at Trinity College Dublin.

Frank Brennan is currently Staff Specialist in Palliative Medicine at St George and Calvary Hospitals, Sydney, Australia. He is a graduate in both medicine and law, and has worked at the St Luke's Hospital, Dublin; Our Lady's Hospital for Sick Children, Crumlin, and Milford Care Centre in Limerick.

David Clark is Professor of Medical Sociology and Director of the International Observatory on End of Life Care within the Institute for Health Research at Lancaster University. The author of many books and articles, he is the editor of the Facing Death series for Open University Press and has wide-ranging research interests in the global history, development and impact of hospice and palliative care.

Sinéad Donnelly is Consultant in Palliative Medicine for the Mid-Western Health Board, Ireland. Her research interests include MD on quality of life assessment; symptom assessment inpatients receiving palliative medicine;

qualitative research on the moment of death; documentary as an educational and research tool in palliative medicine; and art and medicine. She has published widely in the fields of cancer and palliative care, with a focus on Irish culture and philosophy, and has contributed to a variety of journals and edited collections.

Matthew Farrelly is a social worker and family therapist presently working at St Francis Hospice, Raheny. He has extensive experience of working with individuals and families dealing with loss as a result of terminal illness and bereavement. Prior to establishing the social work service at St Francis Hospice he worked with the hospice services in Sligo and at Our Lady's Hospice. Matthew has taught nationally and internationally in the area of bereavement and its impact on the family.

Stephen Higgins is Consultant in Palliative Medicine in St Joseph's Hospice, London. He trained in palliative medicine in Ireland and worked for a time as medical tutor in Our Lady's Hospice. His particular research interest is in the use of psychostimulants to treat fatigue.

Jacqueline Holmes is currently Assistant Director of Nursing for Palliative Care at Our Lady's Hospice and is an active member of the Nursing Advisory Forum of the Irish Association for Palliative Care. Jacqueline has worked within specialist palliative care settings in both the United Kingdom and the Republic of Ireland since 1997. She has considerable clinical experience within the in-patient and day care settings and management experience in in-patient, day care and home care settings.

Kaye Kealy is currently the team leader for the North 1 Home Care Team at Our Lady's Hospice. Kaye worked in oncology for five years before moving to palliative care in 1991. She has worked as a staff nurse and a manager in both in-patient and community specialist palliative care settings. Kaye is a long-standing member of the Irish Association for Palliative Care.

Michael Kearney is Visiting Professor at the Santa Barbara Graduate Institute, California, and at Santa Barbara Cottage Hospital, where he is helping to establish a hospital-based palliative care service. Michael is particularly interested in the area of integrated whole-person health care, and in psychological and existential aspects of end-of-life care. As an international lecturer and workshop leader he has taught throughout Europe, North and South America, Asia and Australia and has worked with Professor Balfour Mount as Visiting Professor at McGill Medical School, Montreal helping to develop teaching programmes on healing in medicine in the undergraduate curriculum.

Ann Keating is Principal Social Worker at Our Lady's Hospice. Ann has been a medical social worker for the past twenty years. She was the first hospice-based medical social worker in the Republic of Ireland. She recently completed a Masters in Social Work in her special interest area of bereavement and loss. Ann is a founder member of HEBER, a bereavement support network in the Republic of Ireland. In 2001 she published a story book on bereavement for children entitled *Best Friends*.

Orla Keegan has worked at the Irish Hospice Foundation since 1998. Her brief includes promotion and funding of research, the co-ordination of a Higher Diploma in Bereavement Studies and support of the foundation's development projects – including a care for patients dying in hospitals project. Her background is in psychology and health services research. She obtained a Masters in Social and Organisational Psychology from UCD and worked in Scotland and Ireland as a health services researcher, most recently at the Health Services Research Centre, Royal College of Surgeons in Ireland.

Christy Kenneally is a television presenter and author. His work includes an award-winning book of children's poetry, and two best-selling audiocassette tapes: *Communicating with the Sick and Dying* and *Sorry for your Trouble: Helping the Bereaved*. Christy has worked for a number of years with the terminally ill and their families, and in 1999 he published *Life after Loss; Helping the Bereaved*, which became a bestseller in Ireland and is used as a standard text in medical and counselling training facilities. Christy also runs a management training company and is an acclaimed after-dinner speaker.

Philip Larkin is College Lecturer in Nursing (Palliative Care) at The National University of Ireland, Galway. He has worked in a number of clinical and education posts in palliative care, in both Galway and Dublin, notably Nurse Tutor at Our Lady's Hospice, and Co-ordinator for Palliative Nursing Services for The Western Health Board. He is currently Vice-President of The European Association for Palliative Care, Milan, Italy, and holder of the 2003 Health Research Board Fellowship in Palliative Care.

Peter Lawlor is Consultant in Palliative Medicine at Our Lady's Hospice and St James's Hospital. He received his basic medical training in Dublin and completed a palliative medicine fellowship at the University of Alberta in 1997. He has subsequently worked in all parts of the Edmonton Palliative Care Program. Prior to returning to Dublin, Peter was Director of the University Hospital Palliative Care Program in Edmonton and Associate Professor in the Division of Palliative Care Medicine at the University of Alberta. He continues to hold an adjunct appointment with the University of Alberta as Associate Professor in the Department of Palliative Care Medicine. Peter's research interests include pain assessment and opioid side effects, especially opioid-related neurotoxicity. Currently he is completing a doctorate thesis on delirium inpatients with cancer.

Julie Ling is currently Nurse Advisor for Care of the Older Person and Palliative Care in the Department of Health and Children, Dublin. She started her career in palliative care at the Royal Marsden Hospital, London, in 1990 working as a staff nurse, primary nurse and latterly as a research nurse, before moving to Dublin in 1997. Working as a clinical nurse specialist she set up the palliative care team at St Luke's Hospital, Dublin before being appointed as the first Assistant Director of Nursing for Palliative Care at Our Lady's Hospice. She has written and published on various aspects of palliative care and is particularly interested in the provision of palliative care for older people.

Anna-Marie Lynch is a palliative care nurse specialist at James Connolly Memorial Hospital, Dublin. She has extensive experience in palliative care, particularly in hospital-based palliative care. She has worked in The Royal Marsden Hospital and St George's Hospital in London, and in St Vincent's University Hospital in Dublin, prior to her current position. Her areas of special interest include generic palliative care and palliative care ethics.

John McCormack was appointed CEO of the Irish Cancer Society in October 2002. The Society is the national charity for cancer care, dedicated to eliminating cancer as a major health problem and to improving the lives of those living with cancer. Two of John's key areas of interest are men's health and palliative care. In November 2003, he was instrumental in launching the first ever Men's Cancer Action Week. John is also involved in lobbying for the implementation of the recommendations of the 2001 Report of the National Advisory Committee on Palliative Care.

Regina McQuillan is currently Palliative Medicine Consultant at St Francis Hospice and Beaumont Hospital, Dublin. She graduated from University College Dublin in 1985 and trained in general medicine in Ireland and in palliative medicine in London and Cardiff. She developed the in-patient service at St Francis Hospice and the Palliative Care Service at Beaumont Hospital. She has a particular interest in palliative care education and palliative care for disadvantaged groups such as the mentally ill and those with learning disabilities. Regina is currently involved in two research projects; one on palliative care and learning disabilities and one that is an exploration of the end-of-life care needs of dementia patients.

Michael J. Murphy has held the position of Chief Executive Officer of Our Lady's Hospice since 1973. This role has been characterized by pro-active involvement in change management and development of services, particularly in the field of palliative care. Michael has worked in the health service for over 36 years and has extensive experience of health care strategic planning, management accounting and administrative systems. More recently he has guided the development and opening of the new Blackrock Hospice (December 2003) which is owned and managed by Our Lady's Hospice Ltd.

Tony O'Brien is Medical Director of Marymount Hospice and Consultant Physician in Palliative Medicine at Cork University Hospital. Over the past decade, Tony has promoted the appropriate development and active integration of specialist palliative care services in Ireland. He is a former Chairperson of the Irish Association for Palliative Care and more recently, served as Chairperson of the National Advisory Committee on Palliative Care. This committee prepared a report on the future development of palliative care services in Ireland, which was formally adopted in October 2001.

Eileen O'Leary is currently Regional Nurse Co-ordinator for Palliative Care Services on the South Eastern Health Board. She previously worked in community palliative care nursing in both urban and rural settings. She is a member of the Executive Committee of the Irish Association for Palliative Care (IAPC), and was involved in the compilation of *Going Home – Assisting a palliative care patient to travel home from the Republic of Ireland* by the IAPC. Eileen is also a member of a sub-committee involved in a project regarding nurse prescribing issues for palliative care nurses working in a community setting, and is book reviews publisher in the IAPC newsletters.

Liam O'Síoráin is Medical Director of Our Lady's Hospice in Dublin and a consultant at St James's Hospital, Dublin. He is interested in postgraduate training in palliative care and was the first National Specialty Director overseeing the setting up of the Royal College of Physician's higher training programme for specialist registrars. Research interests include outcome measures in palliative care and risk assessment in bereavement.

Maeve O'Reilly is Consultant in Palliative Medicine based at St Luke's Hospital, Our Lady's Hospice, and Our Lady's Hospital for Sick Children, Dublin. A graduate of University College Dublin, she trained in oncology before specializing in palliative medicine first at Our Lady's Hospice and subsequently at St Oswalds Hospice in Newcastle upon Tyne. As a registrar she conducted research into the palliative care needs of patients with HIV. Currently her main area of interest is in the development of paediatric palliative care services in Ireland and she is currently working with the national needs-assessment in palliative care for children.

Patrick J. Quinlan is currently Chief Executive of Milford Care Centre, a voluntary organization providing a range of specialist palliative care services, and services for older people within the Mid-Western Health Board region. Patrick has been working in the Irish Health Service for close to 30 years, the last fifteen years being spent in the field of specialist palliative care and services for older people. He has been associated with the work of the Irish Association for Palliative Care and the Irish Hospice Foundation. More recently he was a member of the working group that compiled the Report of the National Advisory Committee on Palliative Care (Oct 2001), which now represents the government's policy for specialist palliative care services in Ireland.

Deirdre Rowe is Occupational Therapist Manager in Our Lady's Hospice where she has worked for over twenty years. She developed the first occupational therapy service in specialist palliative care in the Republic of Ireland and worked as a clinician in hospice day care for a number of years. She is a regular guest presenter to students on the Higher Diploma in Nursing Studies (Palliative Nursing), a partnership between UCD, Our Lady's Hospice and St Francis Hospice.

Siobhan Sheehan is Clinical Nurse Manager (Ward Manager) of an 18-bed in-patient unit at Our Lady's Hospice. In 1997 she obtained a Diploma in Health and Social Welfare at the Open University and a BSc (Hons) in Palliative Care Nursing in 2002, at Kings College, London.

Geraldine Tracey is currently Day Hospice Manager at Our Lady's Hospice and is in the process of developing an advanced nurse practitioner post. Geraldine has worked in specialist palliative care since 1996. She has gained experience on the specialist palliative care in-patient unit, in palliative care education, policy and procedure development, community-based palliative care and day hospice. She is an active member of the executive and the Education and Research Forum within the Irish Association for Palliative Care.

Onja Van Doorslaer is a social researcher currently working as a freelance consultant lecturing and advising on qualitative research methods and analysis. Her background includes a BA in Anthropology and an MSc in Applied Social Research. She has carried out a number of qualitative research studies exploring areas such as: social networks among older people in Ireland; hospital staff retention and turnover; contemporary Irish attitudes towards death and dying; the use of health services by older people in Ireland; access to and use of health services by Travellers in Ireland. She has recently completed a Dublin-based study exploring the use of palliative care services by Irish Travellers.

Eithne Walsh is Physiotherapist Manager in Our Lady's Hospice where she has over 25 years clinical experience in multi-disciplinary teamwork. She was the first full-time physiotherapist in specialist palliative care in the Republic of Ireland. Eithne is a former chairperson of the *Irish Rheumatology Health Professionals Society*, which supports multi-disciplinary teamwork in rheumatology rehabilitation. Her special interest is the promotion of physiotherapy practice in palliative care nationally.

Series editor's preface

As the Facing Death series evolves, it is as if each new book has a story behind it; and that is certainly the case with this wonderfully rich collection on *Palliative Care in Ireland*. In June 2000, I travelled to Dublin to attend the Bas Solais ('Death with Illumination') conference that was organised by a group of colleagues based at Our Lady's Hospice. From the opening bars by the wonderful Irish Choir, Anuna, that opened the meeting the whole experience was one full of rich insight, practical wisdom and thoughtful reflection. Perhaps most striking of all was the real effort that was being made to put palliative care into a *cultural* context.

Not for the first time, I came back from Ireland replenished and refreshed with new ideas and thinking actively about the history and modern evolution of hospice and palliative care. A few weeks later I wrote to the conference organisers, suggesting that an edited book on palliative care in Ireland might be a worthy outcome of their meeting. I wanted them to test my hunch that there is a particular connection between Ireland's cultural landscape and the way in which it organises and delivers palliative care. I also thought that the experience of one country with a small population (less than four million) might have a great deal to teach other countries and regions of similar size about service and policy development and the relationship between state and voluntary sector provision in end of life care.

Almost five years later and now that the book is complete, I have not been disappointed. Julie Ling and Liam O'Síoráin have done a marvellous job in editing such a diverse and varied selection of chapters. Wisely, they have grouped them into particular themes. So parts of the book deal in turn with the history and development of Irish palliative care, the role of the voluntary sector and the challenges of management and policy integration. We see how hospice and palliative care services are delivered in urban and rural settings;

through inpatient units, hospital-based teams and day care services; and the special needs of children are highlighted. Faith, bereavement, and loss are brought together in a set of chapters that looks deep into the Irish tradition – and beyond – to find the essence of whole person care. Finally, a set of contributions focuses on challenges for the future – multi-culturalism, education and training, and further innovation.

I was delighted that Dame Cicely Saunders felt able to write the Foreword for the book; for it was she that gave the opening speech at the Bas Solais conference, and of course in her early work drew so deeply upon the work of the Irish Sisters of Charity, in developing her initial thinking at St Joseph's Hospice, Hackney.

This fascinating book marks a new departure for the Facing Death series. It is the first volume we have produced that concentrates on the development and delivery of palliative care in a single country. Of course, it builds on the contributions of earlier volumes. Certainly it takes a cue from the international concerns of *New Themes in Palliative Care*[1] and it is also influenced by the comparative approach of *The Ethics of Palliative Care: European Perspectives*.[2] The depth of in-country analysis is also reminiscent at times of *Transitions in End of Life Care: Hospice and related developments in Eastern Europe and Central Asia*.[3] Nevertheless, in its sole focus on the Irish scene, its comprehensive array of contributors from many disciplines and in the detailed representation it gives of the provision of palliative care in one country, it is quite unique in the series. I am delighted that we have been able to add it to our list of titles; I thank the editors and all who have written for it; and I commend the book to anyone with an interest in palliative care in Ireland, or indeed any other country.

David Clark

References

1 Clark, D Hockley, J and Ahemedzai, S *New Themes in Palliative Care*. Buckingham: Open University Press, 1997.

2 Ten Have, H and Clark, D *The Ethics of Palliative Care: European Perspectives*. Buckingham: Open University Press, 2002.

3 Clark, D and Wright M (2003) *Transitions in End of Life Care: Hospice and related developments in Eastern Europe and Central Asia*. Buckingham: Open University Press.

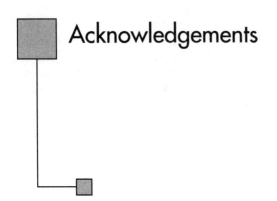

Acknowledgements

The catalyst for this book was the first international palliative care conference 'Bás Solais – Death with illumination' held in Ireland at Dublin Castle in June 2000. Anne Hayes chose the title of this conference and the poem from which it comes is reproduced in this book. Following this conference David Clark, the series editor, reflected that there was something different about Irish palliative care and we hope this book goes some way to proving this theory.

So many people have helped us in preparing this book, it is impossible to name them all but we would like to thank the following: all of the authors for their contributions given with such enthusiasm and commitment; our colleagues and friends in Our Lady's Hospice, St James's Hospital and the Department of Health and Children and finally: our families for their unending patience and support; Hugh and Joseph (JL) and Carol Ann, William, Cian, James and Ciara (LO'S).

Foreword

Dame Cicely Saunders

We are taught about death by the dying themselves and as they do so
they show us something of the meaning of life.

(Saunders, 1962)

In 1962 Mother Mary Paula of the Irish Sisters of Charity asked me to contribute to St Vincent's Annual report and write something of my experience
of working in St Joseph's Hospice, Hackney, which I had been doing since
1958. A tape-recorded conversation made the previous year illustrates how
important it is that adequate pain relief should be established as a first
priority:

Dr S: What was the pain like before you came here?

Mrs H: Well, it was ever so bad. It used to be just like a vice gripping
my spine – going like that and would then let go again – and I didn't
get my injections regularly – they used to leave me as long as they could
and if I asked for them sometimes, they used to say 'No, wait a bit
longer'. They didn't want me to rely on the drugs that were there, you
see. They used to try and see how long I could go without an injection
. . . I used to be pouring with sweat, you know, because of the pain . . .
I couldn't speak to anybody I was in such pain and I was having crying
fits – I mean I haven't cried, I think I've only cried once since I've been
here, that's all – well over a week. And I was crying every other day at
the other hospital. I was very depressed, ever so depressed; but I'm not
at all depressed here, not like I was there.

Dr S: Since you've been here and I put you on to regular injections,
what's the difference?

Mrs H: Well, the biggest difference is, of course, this feeling so calm.
I don't get worked up, I don't get upset, I don't cry, I don't get very,
very depressed – because I was getting awfully depressed – you know,

really black thoughts were going through me mind, and no matter how kind people were, and people were ever so kind – nothing would console me you see. But since I've been here, I feel more hopeful as well.

As I wrote for the Annual Report:

This was indeed a problem of drugs and medical care, but there was so much more to it than that. Mrs. H. was with us for nine months. She did a great deal to solve her difficult family situation (she was only 40), she entertained innumerable visitors, and she was busy all the time. Her family, her own vicar, all the nurses and, above all Sister herself, had very demanding parts to play as Mrs. H. gradually came through to understanding and acceptance and a greatly deepened faith. The work was that of St. Joseph's as a whole but the victory and final peace were Mrs. H's own. That is the kind of success that means the most to us.

What lies behind all this? Or rather, what do I believe I have seen here that I have not seen so clearly in any other hospital? I think the first and most important thing is that everyone who works here has accepted the fact of death and has the right attitude to it. Its discomforts and pain are faced and relieved without fear or bitterness. Faith is able to give to physical death positive value for it is seen as an offering of all we have to God. We are able to help the patients find this truth while we relieve their physical burdens, but all the time it is really they who are teaching us.

The whole approach to pain relief, which has proved to be such a catalyst in the development of hospice and palliative care around the world, has included many elements, above all attentive listening to patients. First of all came the moment in 1948 when David Tasma, a Jewish patient, asked me for comfort. So, respecting his Jewishness, I said the 23rd Psalm and one or two others I knew by heart. When I offered to read to him he said, 'I only want what is in your mind and in your heart'. It seemed to me, as I pondered this later over the years, that his request should be seen as a plea for all the science and learning of the mind, coupled with the vulnerability of one person with another. It looked to the bridge between love and science and, coupled with the advice of the surgeon I was then working for, impelled me to become a physician, entering St Thomas' Medical School in 1951 'in order to do something about pain'.

Once qualified, and on obtaining a Clinical Research Fellowship in order to study 'The Nature and Management of Terminal Pain', I applied to St Joseph's Hospice for the opportunity to spend some time there. I hoped to introduce the system of regular giving of oral morphine developed earlier by the nursing team at St Luke's Hospital, London, which had been founded in 1893 as a Home for the Dying Poor by the Methodist West London Mission.

I had spent the seven years from 1948 to 1955 there as an evening volunteer registered nurse. The regime of regular administration of morphine was observed as giving the best pain relief I had ever seen. I also knew, however, that this system was a complete contradiction of accepted clinical practice and teaching. I knew that only clinical research could challenge and change such teaching, healing people who had to suffer to 'earn' their pain relief, as illustrated in the tape recording of Mrs H's experience.

My time at St Joseph's resulted in a new confidence in what could be done to enable patients to face the end of their lives in peace. Pain relief has come a long way since then but that early work was essential. The evidence was as described in my chapter in St Vincent's Report. As I was able to write:

> To many visitors the most striking thing about St. Joseph's is that no one looks worried. The only thing that can really tell anyone about the work of St. Joseph's is the look on the patient's faces. They really do feel safe and happy, and if they are still finding the journey a hard one, they know it is being shared. We know that it is being shared by Our Lord and we have so often seen them come to realise this also, perhaps without any words of ours at all. We can take away pain, but not the whole hard thing that is happening, the weariness and the partings. But we see the sufferings assimilated so that the joy shines through. We see people either find meaning in suffering or else learn to accept it without understanding. It is wonderful to see questions die away as well as pain.
>
> (Saunders, 1962)

This is the 'whole person care' written of in Kearney's chapter. As an English Protestant before Vatican II I can only thank the Sisters for their welcome and for enabling me to practice at St Joseph's from 1958 to 1965. I then left to found St Christopher's Hospice in 1967, the first of the modern hospices that included care, research and teaching as well as home care and bereavement services.

The challenge now is to maintain what we can of the security of the older hospices as we see palliative care become linked to mainstream medicine. Clinical excellence can develop together with spiritual foundations and awareness of our common humanity. Only as this happens can we continue to offer the respect for each person that will enable them to end their lives in peace and dignity and find the key to their own situation and all it demands of them.

Reference

Saunders, C. (1962) 'Working at St. Joseph's Hospice, Hackney', from Annual Report of St Vincent's Hospital, Dublin.

Introduction

Julie Ling and Liam O'Síoráin

This book is an overview of palliative care services in the Republic of Ireland from a multi-professional viewpoint. It sets out to describe palliative care as it has developed and is practised in the Irish Republic. Palliative care services in Northern Ireland are part of the United Kingdom's National Health Service and thus differ from services in the Republic of Ireland. Some joint initiatives and links have been established between services north and south. For example a tripartite cancer care group was set up following the Good Friday Agreement. This group, the Ireland-Northern Ireland-National Cancer Institute (Washington, USA) Cancer Consortium was formed with the specific aim of reducing the incidence of cancer on the island of Ireland (Cancer Consortium, 2004). This group has strong links with palliative care in Ireland and this was reflected in the programme of a recent All Ireland Cancer Conference in Cork (2003).

To capture all of the colour and diversity of palliative care in Ireland in this slim volume is impossible and as such some areas of Irish palliative care have received less attention than they deserve. The book is divided into four parts.

The first is dedicated to the development of palliative care in the Republic of Ireland. It traces the origins of hospice care from the founding of Our Lady's Hospice, Dublin and Marymount Hospice, Cork in the 1800s to the publication of the government blueprint for palliative care services, the *Report of the National Advisory Committee on Palliative Care* (Department of Health and Children, 2001). This part of the book also acknowledges the role of the voluntary hospice movement in the Republic of Ireland which has been of vital importance in helping to establish specialist palliative care services nationwide. These groups and the two major national charities, the Irish Cancer Society and the Irish Hospice Foundation, have created a great awareness among the Irish public of the hospice/palliative care philosophy. It must be acknowledged that the generosity of the Irish public in supporting hospice care has been enormous. Perhaps this has to do with the fact that Irish people have an innate understanding and appreciation of the 'holism' that is so central to palliative care.

One of the main aims of the *Report of the National Advisory Committee on Palliative Care* was to ensure that core specialist palliative care services would become fully state funded in recognition of their importance as an essential part of health care. The management issues of implementing this report are also featured in this section. Funding of services in the Irish Republic varies greatly even within the same health board. Older, more established services have the majority of their core services funded by the state whereas some of the more recently developed services rely heavily on voluntary contributions from the public and charities. In the UK, palliative care services also vary in the amount of statutory funding that they receive with many services dependent for the majority of their funding on voluntary support.

While palliative care is available in every county of the Republic of Ireland (Irish Association for Palliative Care, 2001), currently there are inequities and inequalities in service provision and access. In some locations a specialist palliative care service is operational and in other areas one clinical nurse specialist working single-handed provides care for the population of a large geographical area. Part II of this book focuses on the delivery of palliative care services in a variety of settings, describing the development and provision of services in different settings including home care, hospice, hospital and day hospice. The development of palliative care services for children in the Republic of Ireland is also discussed.

The third part of this book perhaps more than any other captures the essence of Irish palliative care. Focusing on beliefs and bereavement, this section discusses the concept of whole-person care and the importance of maintaining the holistic approach in the face of the increasing medicalization of death and dying. The importance of language, heritage, religion and culture are also emphasized. The findings of original research conducted with the travelling community are also presented.

The final part of this book focuses on the future challenges and developments in palliative care in the Irish Republic in the twenty-first century. Ireland is a small country that has only recently experienced economic prosperity. Post-'Celtic Tiger' Ireland has seen substantial growth of and investment in the health services, which are currently in the process of major reform. Palliative care for the first time has a dedicated budget and has attained a critical mass in terms of development of services. With economic growth, emigration is at an all-time low and immigration at an all-time high. The arrival of multicultural Ireland brings with it challenges for health care professionals working in palliative care. The changing face of Ireland is not solely due to demographics. Many of the old taboo subjects, for example sex and death, are now discussed more openly. Some of this openness with regard to death and dying is due to the hospice movement, which has helped to create a shift in attitude and less fear of the dying process.

Education in health care is the key to developing the specialty of palliative care in the Irish Republic. In this section both medical and nurse education are discussed specifically from an Irish perspective. There then follows a selection of vignettes provided by health care professionals asked to reflect on what it is that is different about palliative care in Ireland. The final chapter attempts to define what 'Irish' palliative care is and focuses on the challenges ahead as palliative care becomes more integrated into the health services.

There is no doubting the impact that the publication of the *Report of the National Advisory Committee on Palliative Care* has had on this small and relatively new speciality. It is evident throughout this book that professionals of all disciplines working in palliative care in Ireland have enthusiastically embraced this strategy. While some aspects of the report have already been implemented, its full implementation remains the ultimate goal and will require a co-ordinated effort from all stakeholders to ensure that the model of excellence described becomes a reality.

There is no one Dame Cicely Saunders in the Republic of Ireland but there are many among the religious, volunteers and health care professionals, with her energy and vision, who have worked sometimes thanklessly over the years to bring the type of care hospice describes to their communities, families, friends and loved ones.

References

Cancer Consortium (2004) www.allirelandnci.org

Department of Health and Children (2001) *Report of the National Advisory Committee on Palliative Care*. Dublin: Stationery Office.

Irish Association for Palliative Care (2001) *Palliative Care Services in Ireland*. Dublin.

Part I

Palliative care development – the Irish experience

1 A national plan for palliative care – the Irish experience

Tony O'Brien and David Clark

Introduction

The name of Mary Aikenhead has come to be synonymous with the early history of hospice care in Ireland. Born in Cork in 1787, at age 25 she became Sister Mary Augustine and was established almost immediately as superior of a new order, known as the Irish Sisters of Charity, and the first of its kind in Ireland to be uncloistered. The Order made plans to establish a hospital and three of the sisters went to Paris to learn about the work of the Notre Dame de la Pitié Hospital. In Ireland they opened St Vincent's Hospital, Dublin, in 1834. Following many years of chronic illness, Mary Aikenhead died at Harold's Cross, Dublin, in 1858 but her influence continued to shape institutional approaches to the care of the dying in the Irish context over many years (Clark, 2004).

In September 1870 the Sisters founded St Patrick's Hospital for Incurables, made possible because of a generous bequest from Dr Patrick Murphy, a former Cork physician whose will entrusted his property to them on the condition that within two years of his death a hospital would be built to provide facilities for poor patients suffering from painful and incurable diseases, especially cancer. Dr Murphy's experience during his early medical career had made him aware of the dearth of medical facilities for the sick and poor in Cork and the Sisters of Charity had won his admiration through their dedicated work among the poor and, more particularly, their ministrations at the death-beds of his own father and sister.

Then in a ground-breaking move and fulfilling an ambition which she had long held, the convent where Mary Aikenhead spent her final years became Our Lady's Hospice for the Dying in 1879. Many consider this to be the first institutional provision of its kind beyond the mainland of Europe. The

Sisters' experience in visiting the sick poor in their homes, where they witnessed many death scenes, had convinced them of the great need that existed for a place where those with no hope of recovery could spend their last days. The lack of space in any of the Dublin convents, however, prevented the immediate commencement of such an apostolate and the opportunity did not occur until 1879 when circumstances arose which necessitated the removal of the motherhouse and noviciate from their former location in Harold's Cross to Milltown. With the help of a donation from two Dublin women, Mother Mary John Gaynor set about converting the old noviciate house into a home suitable for the reception of dying patients. The hospice provided accommodation for 27 patients. The Sisters were overwhelmed with referrals and in 1886, Mother John Gaynor and her community resolved to build a larger facility for 110 patients. In the early decades of Our Lady's Hospice for the Dying most of the patients suffered from tuberculosis. By the 1940s new treatments and better public health measures almost eliminated the disease. Our Lady's Hospice for the Dying then opened its wards to the chronically ill and elderly, and became simply 'Our Lady's Hospice'; a designation made official in 1964.

A less well-known Dublin home of this type is that named The Rest for the Dying, founded in 1904 for Protestants suffering from incurable diseases and established through the benevolence of a Col. F. C. Trench Gascoigne, who donated £5,000 towards its establishment. Its purpose was to provide for dying patients who were not suitable for admission to the general hospitals. In 1962 it changed its name to The Gascoigne Home in memory of its founder and subsequently was run as a nursing home.

Another early establishment with a similar focus was Milford House, founded in Limerick in 1928 by the Little Company of Mary, an Order with a specific mission to pray for, and where possible to care for, the sick and dying. As a Congregation committed to this apostolate, the Sisters became increasingly aware of the need for suitable facilities and began to develop ideas about the special care that could be given to dying patients.

From these institutions were to spring the first shoots of modern palliative care in the Republic of Ireland. In the following extract from an interview conducted in 1995, nurse and palliative care innovator, Sister Brigid Finucaine in speaking about the developments taking place in Limerick, captures some of the enthusiasm that was to be found in the emerging group of modern hospice enthusiasts:

> And from there we would have been hearing a lot about St Christopher's in London, and some of our Sisters in the English province would have worked there, so we would have a lot of information from them plus reading material. So it was decided that I would go and see. It was something I felt drawn to, there was something about the whole concept. It wouldn't have been called palliative care then; terminal

care we would have called it at that stage. I saw it as a challenge in going there and, I must say, in St Christopher's everything was way beyond my expectations. I thought that whole philosophy of care was just tremendous, in the whole personalised care. That would have been at the end of 1976 and the beginning of 1977, and I worked there for six months. As I said, I thought the individual care, the whole emphasis on the dignity of the person . . . I suppose the place was small and we, as staff, got a lot of personalised attention as well, and the whole emphasis then was on caring for yourself, too. You know, I can only deal with other people when I have already dealt with myself, that idea; dealt with it by looking at our own griefs and losses, and how we reacted and responded to sickness and to death, and to the many emotions that came up for other people. I thought that was fascinating. And also here, in the Midwest, there was a lot of requests for beds in Milford, to care for people who had terminal cancer. And the demand was growing and we were wondering; were we meeting that need or should we be meeting it? So we talked a lot about it and discussed it and deliberated about it, and then we said; we'd put aside nine beds in Milford House and look at it after a period of two years. So, that was following my return from St Christopher's. So three of us worked in that unit for two years. At the end of two years the demand was growing and growing. So the service we provided there was really the psychological, the spiritual, and emotional, and the physical aspects of caring for people in that situation. And news about the place grew and grew, and people became more interested and the beds were always full. And also I suppose the support grew. And it was something people talked a lot about. And a great interest grew amongst our staff and a number of staff went away and did further training in this area. And then, after the two years, we looked at it again, and then, in 1980, we decided about building a purpose-built hospice, which we have here now.

(Finucaine, 1995)

In 1977, nine beds in the Nursing Home at Milford House had been set aside to care for the terminally ill, an initiative that led in the next decade to the creation of a purpose-built hospice unit in the grounds of Milford House. At Harold's Cross, the rising incidence of cancer and the special acute needs of terminally ill patients led in 1979 to the opening of a 44-bed palliative care service. A home care service was added in 1985 and in 1990 it was decided to erect a new purpose-built palliative care complex; named CARITAS, it was officially opened on 10 June 1993 and a day care centre was added in 1995. Likewise, St Patrick's operated as a hospital for incurables for many years, but in 1980 a major development plan was launched to provide funds for a modern hospice within the existing hospital.

On 26 April 1984, Marymount Hospice, a purpose-built 25-bed unit was opened on the second floor of the hospital. From a focus on the long-term institutional care of the dying, a new emphasis on the palliative care of patients in all settings, according to their needs, was beginning to emerge.

Clare Humphreys (2003) has made a major contribution to our understanding of the care of patients in some of these early institutional settings. During the late nineteenth century, tuberculosis was the leading cause of death in Ireland, finally peaking in 1904, when the disease accounted for 16 per cent of all deaths. Dublin and Cork had particularly high mortality rates from the disease. Yet the voluntary hospitals were reluctant to accept those in the end stages of tuberculosis. Throughout Ireland there were only a handful of hospitals or sanitoria available to care for patients, and even these were reluctant to take advanced cases because of fears about infection. Of course, the rich were nursed at home, but for the majority of poor people suffering from the disease, the only option was the workhouse infirmary, with all its associated stigma. The facilities of the Irish Sisters of Charity in Dublin and Cork therefore played a special role in caring for patients with advanced tuberculosis, or phthisis as it was alternatively known. At Our Lady's the percentage of tuberculosis patients fluctuated between 68 and 74 per cent up to 1915, when it began to decline. But it was not until 1950 that cancer patients began to outnumber those with tuberculosis. Similarly at Cork, and despite the founding emphasis on cancer, the period throughout the 1930s saw a preponderance of tuberculosis patients. In the 1940s this began to change and by 1959, following the introduction of curative therapies, only a handful of patients were suffering from the disease.

Humphreys sees two principal factors accounting for the decline in numbers of tuberculosis patients in the two institutions after the mid-1940s. First, the Tuberculosis Bill of 1945 led to the reorganization and expansion of services throughout Ireland. Second, there was the influence of mass radiography and the discovery of antibiotic agents such as streptomycin. In the wake of these improvements in public health, however, came a growing transition to death from chronic, degenerative diseases and with it growing concerns about the care of the elderly and the dying as significant social groups in society. A 'space' was emerging for a new form of specialization which would soon be known as 'palliative care' and the ideas surrounding this quickly took off, leading to a huge upturn in service provision and professional interest.

The ideas and philosophies surrounding this new concept quickly developed during the 1980s. This increasing interest in the subject started to focus attention on the established units in Dublin, Cork and Limerick. These units were particularly associated with the 'care of the dying'. They were simultaneously revered and feared in equal measure. They were perceived as facilities where patients suffering from advanced cancer were sent to die. This care was typically described as 'terminal care'. The hospice units were all sited geographically separate from acute general hospitals. This isolation was not just a physical separation; it also reflected a fundamental attitudinal difference. Hospital care represented so-called 'active treatment' with the intention of achieving a cure. Hospice care was perceived as a more passive form of treatment where the sole outcome was inevitably death, albeit with enhanced pain and symptom management. Hospice care became relevant when 'there was nothing more to be done'. Not surprisingly, patients were often reluctant to consider admission to hospices as they represented an abandonment of all hope. This legacy is still in evidence today.

The term 'hospice' was employed to describe a building dedicated to a particular type of care for a select population of seriously ill patients, suffering from life-threatening disease. The concept of hospice as an approach to care with application in a variety of settings was yet to evolve. Community-based hospice care or 'home care' started to develop in the mid-1980s. In-patient units were prohibitively expensive to build and operate whereas mobile community-based teams had little if any capital costs. In a variety of settings across the country, local health care professionals and enthusiastic lay advocates alike started to identify and respond to the palliative care needs of patients in their local community. Inspired by a strong desire to make a difference and informed by developments in the United Kingdom, local hospice groups were established in various parts of the country. These services, appropriately termed the 'voluntary hospice movement', gained significant recognition and generated considerable interest and demand.

These newly established, voluntary hospice groups had a very clearly defined purpose, which was to improve the provision of palliative care services in their locality. Statutory involvement was limited, and consequently there was an excessive reliance on voluntary fund-raising efforts. However, with little or no bureaucracy, decisions were made quickly and implemented without delay. This relative independence meant that voluntary hospice groups were not constrained by the severe financial cutbacks that were applied to the health services in the late 1980s. Without exception, these hospice groups achieved a remarkable degree of success in a comparatively short period of time.

The Government's commitment to this area of care was first reflected in the National Health Strategy in 1994 (Department of Health, 1994). This document recognized the important role of palliative care services in terms of improving quality of life. It gave a commitment to the continued development of these services in a structured manner, in order to achieve the highest possible quality of life for patients and their families.

Palliative medicine was recognized as a medical specialty in the United Kingdom in 1987. In the mid-1990s, the Irish Medical Council was approached regarding the inclusion of palliative medicine in their list of recognized specialties. Having satisfied the various requirements, palliative medicine was approved for inclusion in June 1995.

If palliative care was to develop as an integral and vital part of health and social care services, there was an urgent need to develop policy that would support and foster this evolving specialty. Palliative care services could no longer rely solely on the generosity and goodwill of local communities and voluntary agencies. Equally, it was important not to alienate or disenfranchise those groups and individuals who had contributed so much to service development and provision. However, there was no agreed plan or strategy either locally or nationally.

In recognition of this deficiency, the Minister for Health and Children established the National Advisory Committee on Palliative Care in 1999. Membership of the committee caused much discussion and debate regarding appropriate representation of various professional interests. The overwhelming majority of health care professionals involved in palliative care in the Republic of Ireland are nurses – however, membership of the group did not include a palliative care nurse. Many nursing colleagues interpreted their lack of representation as insulting and felt that their contribution was not recognized, valued or appreciated. Representation was made to the Department of Health and Children and in due course two nurse advisors were appointed to support the committee in its work.

The following terms of reference were agreed:

With regard to

- The best interests of patients and their families
- Relevant national and international research, analysis and standards
- The principles set out in the National Cancer Strategy
- The policies and recommendations of the National Cancer Forum
- The palliative care requirements of persons with non-malignant diseases

To examine and make recommendations on:

- The principles underlying the development of specialist and non-specialist palliative care services nationally and regionally
- The organisation and development of an integrated palliative care service involving both statutory and voluntary providers, including the delivery of care in in-patient (hospital, hospice and nursing home), home care, day care out-patients and other appropriate settings
- Personnel, education and training standards
- Any other matters relating to palliative care, which the National Advisory Committee considers appropriate.
                     (Department of Health and Children, 2001)

It is often extremely difficult to achieve agreement and consensus on 'terms of reference' within a group. In this instance, the quality of the terms of reference laid the foundation for the production of a top-quality report. The key rests in the fact that the focus was placed primarily on the needs of patients and families. The opening line of the terms of reference required that the committee have 'due regard to the best interests of patients and families'. This element, more than any other consideration, set the tone and context for the discussions.

Further examination of the terms of reference identifies a number of other important principles. Recommendations of the committee were to be based on quality research evidence, where such evidence existed. This was important in terms of separating a culture of 'we want' from a culture of 'the patient needs'. The terms of reference also required the committee to address *palliative care needs of patients with non-malignant disease*. At this time, cancer patients comprised approximately 95 per cent of all palliative care activity and patients with non-malignant disease were largely excluded from accessing these services. In terms of the principle of equity, this position was difficult to justify.

Another important principle identified in the terms of reference relates to *the integration of services across various care settings*. The committee were not seeking to evaluate the relative merits of home care in comparison to in-patient hospice care. It was recognized that patients required care in a range of settings. Our function was to devise a strategy that would support patients in each and every setting.

The committee conducted its work with remarkable energy, enthusiasm and speed. Twelve meetings were convened over a 14-month period. An extensive consultative process was undertaken which included written submissions, oral presentations and a meeting with a group of internationally renowned experts at St Christopher's Hospice, London.

At the outset, the committee adopted the various relevant definitions as previously published by the World Health Organization (1990) and by the National Council for Hospice and Specialist Palliative Care Services (1995). These definitions focused attention on achieving and maintaining an optimal quality of life for patients and families. The committee also adopted a number of important principles of care as set out in previously published documents from the United Kingdom as follows:

- Palliative care is an important part of the work of most health care professionals, and all should have knowledge in this area, and feel confident in the core skills required.
- Primary health care providers in the community have a central role in and responsibility for the provision of palliative care, and accessing specialist palliative care services when required.
- Specialist palliative care should be seen as complementing and not replacing the care provided by other health care professionals in hospital and community settings.

- Specialist palliative care services should be available to all patients in need wherever they are and whatever their disease.
- Specialist palliative care services should be planned, integrated and co-ordinated, and assume responsibility for education, training and research.

In the Irish context, key palliative care principles were set out in the cancer strategy document (Department of Health, 1996), which identified principles of care in respect of palliative care services:

- Patients should be enabled and encouraged to express their preference about where they wished to be cared for, and where they wish to spend the last period of their life.
- Services should be sufficiently flexible and integrated as to allow movement of patients from one care setting to another, depending on their clinical situation and personal preferences.
- The ultimate aim should be for all patients to have access to specialist palliative care services where these are required.

These well-considered and highly laudable objectives presented an enormous challenge to service providers and health care planners alike. There was a requirement to develop programmes of care in every region of the country. A highly trained, adequately resourced, multi-professional, inter-disciplinary team must staff each programme. Each team must provide care in an integrated fashion, and embrace all care settings, including in-patient hospice units, community-based settings and hospital care. The objectives were clear but a detailed strategy was needed that would give direction and guidance. The remainder of this chapter considers some of the recommendations of the *Report of the National Advisory Committee on Palliative Care* published by the Department of Health and Children in 2001.

Recommendations of the *Report of the National Advisory Committee on Palliative Care*

At the outset, the committee was aware of the patchy distribution of specialist services. The various elements necessary for the provision of services needed to be considered. During the course of initial deliberations, a number of vitally important principles were agreed:

- Palliative care is a vital and integral part of our health service.
- The Department of Health and Children must support the appropriate development of palliative care services in all regions.
- There is no one place of care that is inherently superior to all other areas of care, and is applicable to all patients and at all times, regardless of their individual needs and preferences. Consequently, patients must have

choice, real choice, regarding their preferred place of care and place of death.

- Services must be patient-focused, sensitive and responsive to patients' changing needs.

The chief executive officer of each health board (authority area) has a statutory responsibility for the planning and delivery of palliative care services in their region. In view of the important role already established by various voluntary agencies in service provision, the potential for developing services in a spirit of partnership between the statutory and voluntary agencies was identified.

Quantifying the scale of unmet need

It is anticipated that the need for palliative care services will increase significantly in coming years. Population projections indicate a significant increase in those aged 65 years or older. This has implications for palliative care services as ageing increases the risk of becoming patients or carers. Currently, over 95 per cent of all patients availing of palliative care services have cancer. In the coming years the number of people dying from cancer is expected to rise. Concerns about equity have fuelled the debate regarding the extension of specialist palliative care services to include patients with life-limiting illnesses other than cancer, such as advanced and progressive cardiovascular, neurological, rheumatological and respiratory diseases. The committee estimated that the extension of palliative care services to include patients with non-malignant disease would require current service levels to double.

The need for specialist palliative care services will increase significantly over the coming decades. Factors governing this increasing demand include the following:

- Increased proportion of elderly in our communities;
- Inclusion of patients with progressive and advanced disease of a non-malignant aetiology;
- The involvement and integration of specialist palliative care services at an earlier stage in the disease trajectory;
- Increased awareness of the role and value of specialist palliative care services, among health care professionals and the general public.

Settings for palliative care

No single care setting is inherently better than another. Services must be provided in the full range of settings. The National Advisory Committee

Report on Palliative Care (Department of Health and Children, 2001) identified the importance of the specialist palliative care unit as the focal point for all specialist palliative care activity in a region. It is envisaged that each health board (authority area) will develop a fully comprehensive specialist palliative care unit, capable of supporting service provision, education, training and research. Informed by a detailed needs-assessment, each region must plan the development of services in a comprehensive range of settings to include an integrated model of care, providing services in specialist in-patient beds, in community settings (patients' homes, nursing homes, hospitals for the elderly), acute general hospitals, day care and out-patient services.

Structure of palliative care settings

The structure and environment of a specialist palliative care in-patient unit should be appropriate to the needs of patients and staff, and should also be sensitive to the needs of families and friends. Fundamentally, all specialist palliative care units must be capable of supporting and facilitating the range of functions required of them. The National Advisory Committee recommended that an Expert Group on Design Guides for Specialist Palliative Care Settings be established. The report of this committee is currently in press.

Levels of specialization

The committee recommended that palliative care services should be structured in three levels of ascending specialization. These levels refer to the training and expertise of the staff providing the service:

Level one – palliative care approach:
All health care professionals should apply basic palliative care principles as appropriate. Some patients with advanced and progressive disease will have their palliative care needs satisfactorily addressed at this level of expertise.

Level two – general palliative care:
At an intermediate level, a proportion of patients and families will benefit from the expertise of health care professionals who, although not engaged full time in palliative care, have undertaken additional approved training and have gained additional expertise in palliative care.

Level three – specialist palliative care:
Specialist palliative care services are those services whose core activity is limited to the provision of palliative care.

All three levels of service provision should be available and all patients should be able to engage easily with the level of expertise most appropriate to their needs at any point in time. Palliative care services, both specialist and non-specialist, should be available in all care settings.

Specialist palliative care services

Specialist palliative care services are those services with palliative care as their core specialty and are analogous to secondary or tertiary health care services. The committee recommended that all specialist palliative care services should have an essential minimum core of professionally trained staff with recognized post-registration specialist training and clinical experience in palliative care. In addition to nursing and medical personnel, a specialist palliative care team should include the following disciplines: physiotherapy, occupational therapy, social work, speech and language therapy, pharmacy and clinical nutrition.

Specialist palliative care services also require staff specifically trained to meet the psycho-social needs of the patient, family and carers, and suitably trained and experienced members of staff who will be responsible for bereavement support. Other requirements include a co-ordinator of spiritual care and a volunteer co-ordinator. Equally, specialist palliative care services must be supported by an informed, supportive and capable administrative structure with available expertise in finance, strategy and planning, human resources and information technology. The importance of developing appropriate risk management structures is self-evident. Additional support needed includes catering, property management, maintenance, portering, and security.

Bereavement support

Bereavement support is an integral part of palliative care and should be incorporated into all specialist palliative care programmes. Prevention of complex bereavement problems is an important component of specialist palliative care services and the committee recommended that bereavement support should begin early in the disease process, long before the death of the patient. The single most important factor in reducing the burden of complex grief reactions is to ensure that each patient and family is offered an optimal level of care and support while the patient is alive.

The aim of bereavement support is to rehabilitate individuals and families before and after the death of a loved one. Not every family member or friend of a deceased person needs bereavement counselling. The majority of bereaved people successfully complete the task of grieving in their own way, and at their own pace, with the help of family and friends. It is important to develop appropriate screening tools capable of identifying those family members at increased risk in their bereavement.

All specialist palliative care staff offer a general level of bereavement support to individuals and families. Specialist palliative care nurses play an important role in bereavement support in the community. Volunteers may be trained to provide general bereavement support to family and carers. For those who require extra support, appropriately trained staff such as social workers, psychologists or professional counsellors should be available. An appropriate member of staff should be nominated as bereavement service co-ordinator.

Education, training and research

Education is a core component of specialist palliative care. The committee recommended that the culture of continuing professional education and development should be promoted among health care professionals in all disciplines involved in the delivery of palliative care. Currently, there is no academic department of palliative care in the Irish Republic. Medical schools should develop an academic department and introduce accredited training opportunities for all disciplines and levels of expertise. A core curriculum for medical undergraduates should be developed and introduced in all medical schools with similar programmes incorporated into the under-graduate curricula for nursing and allied health care professionals. Each specialist palliative care unit should set up a nursing practice development unit to develop, implement, and monitor nursing practice in the unit. A clinical practice development co-ordinator should be employed in each specialist palliative care unit.

The application of research findings encourages the growth and develop-ment of a specialty and is a critical element in defining a specialist palliative care service. All health care professionals working in palliative care should have the opportunity to engage in research. We wish to foster a culture of critical review and questioning. Specific training in research methodology and interpretation of research data will be required. Adequate funding should be identified to support quality palliative care research in the Republic of Ireland. This will require significant investment in infrastructure.

Communication

Failure by health service staff to communicate effectively has been identified as a major impediment to quality care (Addington-Hall and McCarthy, 1995; Seale and Kelly, 1997; Higginson *et al.*, 1990). This failure to communicate occurs at several levels in different care settings; with patients and their families, within the hospital services, within community services, and between hospital and community health care professionals.

All staff involved in the care of patients with progressive disease and their families should receive specific training in communication skills. Structures should be put in place to support this recommendation. Suitable space and facilities to allow privacy during conversations between doctors and patients and their families should also be provided. Discharge planning, including early communication with health care professionals in the community, should be encouraged in all hospitals to facilitate the seamless transfer of patients to the community.

Standards in palliative care

Increasing emphasis is placed on the importance of evaluating health care services. It is now recognized that a systematic approach to evaluating and improving quality of care should be central to any service. The committee recommended that every specialist palliative care service should have an explicit commitment to quality improvement ensuring that a culture of delivering the best possible quality of care is promoted in all disciplines. Standards should be set in all dimensions of service provision in relation to the structure, process and outcome of care. These should also encompass aspects of training and development of services. Systems should be developed to evaluate the quality of specialist palliative care services.

A key recommendation of the committee was the development of a National Minimum Data Set, which should provide standardized information on all patients of the specialist palliative care services. Standardized performance indicators and outcome measures should be utilized in specialist palliative care services in order to evaluate and maintain quality standards.

Funding and accountability

The level of financial support available from individual health boards for palliative care services varies between health board areas. This has arisen mainly due to the absence of a policy on palliative care services at national level. The future development of specialist palliative care services requires a commitment to the ongoing provision of an adequate level of public funding, with a corresponding commitment to quality and accountability from service providers.

Statutory funding should be made available on a phased basis to meet the core running costs of all specialist palliative care services, and in all care settings. All proposals for specialist palliative care services, including capital developments, should be prepared within the context of national policy, regional plans, agreed priorities and local needs.

There should be a separate protected budget for specialist palliative care services, administered by a senior officer of the health board. The funding priorities for specialist palliative care services should be determined at health board level. All day-to-day expenditure should be met by the health board palliative care budget.

Health boards should work in partnership with the voluntary service providers in their areas. Partnerships should be formalized by way of service agreements. The process should respect the independent identity and operational autonomy of individual voluntary service providers. However, the process should also respect the statutory, regulatory and public accountability responsibilities of the health boards, the Department of Health and Children, and the Minister for Health and Children.

Planning and development

The Minister for Health and Children should establish a National Council for Specialist Palliative Care with a view to advising the Minister on national policy. The National Council should be broadly based and have representatives from the appropriate statutory and voluntary agencies. In addition, each health board should establish two regional committees on palliative care – a Regional Consultative Committee and a Regional Development Committee.

The Regional Consultative Committee should be an advisory committee. It should provide a broadly based forum for the exchange of information and ideas on all matters pertaining to palliative care, both specialist and non-specialist, in the region. It should advise the Regional Development Committee on any matters relating to the provision of palliative care services in the region, including new developments.

The Regional Development Committee should prepare an agreed development plan for the region, within the policy guidelines issued by the Department of Health and Children, and having regard to the recommendations of the National Council and the Regional Consultative Committee. It should advise the Chief Executive Officer on the allocation of all statutory resources, both capital and revenue, provided for new and developing services.

Priorities, timeframes and costs

Palliative medicine is a new and developing specialty. The National Report described the various elements and structures necessary to support a comprehensive palliative care service.

It is recommended that all health boards should undertake a detailed needs assessment study, to inform the most appropriate approach to service development in each region. At a regional level, all health boards should undertake a needs-assessment study to define the palliative care needs in their area. Priorities for the development of a specialist palliative care service should be based on national policy and should be decided by health boards at regional level, based on the need for services, as defined by the recommended needs assessment, and also taking account of advice provided by the regional committees on palliative care. The implementation of the recommendations contained in the National Report should occur over a five- to seven-year period.

Conclusion

The Minister for Health and Children, Mr Micháel Martin launched the report in October 2001. Prior to its launch, the report was considered and approved by government. On the occasion of the launch, Minister Martin gave an undertaking to implement the Report over a five- to seven-year timeframe. Each health board was asked to establish two committees. They were also required to undertake a needs assessment study within a nine-month timeframe. At the time of writing only half of these needs assessments have been presented to the Department of Health and Children.

The Department started the work of establishing the national council as recommended and indeed invited nominations from relevant groups. However, despite this initial enthusiasm, the Department has not convened a meeting of the council. Currently the Department of Health and Children is undergoing a restructuring and the role and relevance of a wide range of councils and advisory committees is being assessed. This process has resulted in a significant delay in establishing the National Council for Specialist Palliative Care and has resulted in much confusion and disappointment. The council is a vital element in supporting the evolving specialty of palliative care. Hopefully, we will see definitive action on this matter in the very near future.

The Department established a committee which has produced 'Design guidelines for specialist palliative care' (Department of Health and Children, 2004). This report will offer valuable guidance to teams who are preparing a design brief for a new specialist palliative care unit. It is noteworthy that while the National Report formally attempted to estimate revenue costs, no such exercise was undertaken in respect of capital costs.

The *Report of the National Advisory Committee* (Department of Health and Children, 2001) has attracted favourable comment in Ireland and abroad. The Irish report was critically important when the Council of Europe established a committee of experts to examine and report on palliative care developments across Europe. We have travelled a long way and in partnership we have achieved a great deal. We have a clear strategy for future development and we must remain committed and focused. We are determined to provide a level of care that both defines and reflects best international practice. Our patients and their families require and deserve nothing less.

References

Addington-Hall, J. and McCarthy, M. (1995) Dying from cancer: results of a national population based investigation, *Palliative Medicine*, 9:295–305.

Clark, D. (2004) History, gender and culture in the rise of palliative care, in S. Payne, J. Seymour, C. Ingleton (eds) *Palliative Care Nursing. Principles and Evidence for Practice*. Maidenhead: Open University Press, pp. 39–54.

Department of Health (1994) *Shaping a Healthier Future: A Strategy for Effective Healthcare in the 1990s*. Dublin: Stationery Office.

Department of Health (1996) *Cancer Services in Ireland: A National Strategy*. Dublin: Stationery Office.

Department of Health and Children (2001) *Report of the National Advisory Committee on Palliative Care*. Dublin: Stationery Office.

Department of Health and Children (2004) *Design Guidelines for Specialist Palliative Care Settings*. Dublin: Stationery Office (In Press).

Finucaine, B. (1995) Oral history interview with David Clark for the Hospice History Programme of the International Observatory on End of Life Care, Lancaster University, UK.

Higginson, I., Wade, A. and McCarthy, M. (1990) Palliative care: views of patients and their families, *BMJ*, 301:277–81.

Humphreys, C. (2003) Tuberculosis; poverty and the first 'hospices' in Ireland, *European Journal of Palliative Care*, 10(4):164–7.

Keegan, O., McGee, H., Brady, T. *et al.* (1999) *Care of the Dying – Experiences and Challenges. A study of health service care during the last year of life of patients at St. James' Hospital*, Dublin.

National Council for Hospice and Specialist Palliative Care Services (1995) *A Statement of Definitions*. London.

Seale, C. and Kelly, M. (1997) A comparison of hospice and hospital care for people who die: views of the surviving spouse, *Palliative Medicine*, 11:93–100.

World Health Organization (1990) *Cancer Pain Relief and Palliative Care: Report of a WHO Expert Committee*. Geneva.

2 The voluntary sector

Liam O'Síoráin, Orla Keegan and John McCormack

Introduction

This chapter describes the important role charities and voluntary agencies have played in developing hospice and palliative care services in the Republic of Ireland. It focuses on the two main national charities, the Irish Cancer Society and the Irish Hospice Foundation, which have supported hospice care. These two major national charities have had a critical catalytic effect in helping services to become established although there are significant differences in how the charities operate, fund raise and prioritize areas for development, and in their respective core activities. The chapter will also focus on one voluntary organization, North West Hospice, as an example of a voluntary hospice group.

The Voluntary Movement

The origin of modern hospice and palliative care is in Dame Cicely Saunder's response to the very human request for help through 'what is in your mind and in your heart'. For those who have had contact with the hospice model of care in any of its locations, the core of the message is enthusiastic giving – of self and of skill. It is not surprising then that the hospice movement has strong roots in the voluntary sector and the ethos of community.

The voluntary movement is party to nuances of vocabulary, 'terminological tempest' was a 1990 description of the sector (Anheier and Knapp, 1990). The voluntary hospice movement has become shorthand for an exhausting list of activities, responsibilities, planning and services conducted in the name of hospice care all over Ireland.

Within the hospice movement there are large, non-statutory and not-for-profit organizations engaged in a range of clinical, support and fund-raising activities in order to provide hospice and palliative care services. There are voluntary hospice groups providing hospice home care in rural and urban communities, managed by voluntary boards of community members and supported through the financial contributions of the community. There are other smaller community groups which do not provide a direct client service but provide fund-raising support for hospice. Some of these community groups may be involved in a limited number of non-clinical services in support of hospice – for example, providing or arranging transport.

The voluntary sector in Ireland refers to a range of concepts:

The concept of reciprocity, collective give and take: The voluntary sector often provides a strong manifestation of community. We see hospice movements initiated by local people to respond to observed need and building on real experiences.

The concept of independence: Voluntary services, organizations and committees are independently constituted; they therefore have a flexibility in their ability to provide ranges of support in responsive timescales.

The concepts of advocacy and voice: Voluntary efforts provide a focus and a mechanism for local and special interests – these may be represented to local statutory and national government in an effort to shape policy.

The concept of not-for-profit: Organizations encompassing paid professional administrative and clinical staff employed to provide hospice care.

The concept of volunteering: Volunteers may be involved in a range of activities, e.g. befriending patients, supporting, driving, fund-raising, bereavement support. In in-patient hospices there may be a paid volunteer co-ordinator.

The case study of the North West Hospice is an example of all of these features and core concepts – particularly the flexibility of approach allowed by independence, community links and creative lobbying.

Contemporary context

With the exception of the larger in-patient units and religious-founded hospices the voluntary hospice movement is a relatively recent phenomenon dating from the late 1980s in Ireland. This period in Ireland is also characterized by societal change on a large scale. Among these changes is an increase in the statutory allocation of funds to support core services –

including palliative care. The *Report of the National Advisory Committee on Palliative Care* (Department of Health and Children, 2001) delivers a blueprint for the organization of professional services in an equitable and sustainable fashion. This document recommends the creation of structures at regional level which will encourage voluntary hospice groups to take part in consultation and development activities relative to palliative care. Importantly, it also recommends the establishment of a National Council for Palliative Care, a focus and a forum for statutory and voluntary voice. Unfortunately this has yet to come into being some three years after publication of the plan.

Today, voluntary groups organized at town and county level are faced with a very different set of problems from the pioneering spirit of set-up. Among these are navigating relationships with statutory health boards and increasing administrative loads relating to issues such as partnership, service agreements, and maintaining a professional/voluntary balance.

Donnelly-Cox and Jaffro (1999) in detailing the voluntary sector ethos in Ireland describe a similar dynamic in the *third sector* (the third sector reflects an economic entity, relative to the traditional sectors of the statutory and private sector). The traditional voluntary organization has mostly given way to professional or social service voluntary organizations and these bodies exist alongside community development organizations with an even stronger emphasis on community participation and empowerment. Donnelly-Cox and Jaffro (1999) suggest in looking for a way forward for the voluntary sector that '*each organization type needs to integrate characteristics typical of the other*', so recommending more emphasis on empowerment in the typical voluntary organizations and more emphasis on professional service in the community development arena.

Voluntary activity specifically in health care has a long history in Ireland and the voluntary–statutory relationship has been played out over centuries. Barrington (1986, cited in O'Ferrall, 2000) detail the history of the voluntary hospitals, originating in religious philanthropy and educational imperative but giving way to state subvention for a number of reasons – among them a lack of coherence and policy around a role for the voluntary sector in Irish health care. Formalization of the relationship has been approached through a number of strategic and legal directives, with a move towards regional and local contracting of services from voluntary organizations – through service planning and agreements and a move away from unconditional grant aiding of services (O'Ferrall, 2000).

A 1997 survey examining voluntary–statutory partnerships in palliative care identified a relatively *ad hoc* approach to partnership (Haslett, 1998). A shorter replication of the survey shows some improvement such as more identifiable contacts in health boards (Irish Hospice Foundation, 2003). However, a cause for concern was a decrease in the 'tone' of relationship with health authorities – 62 per cent of respondents felt 'welcomed and supported' by health authorities in 1997, while only 31 per cent used the same descriptor in 2003.

The uncritical adoption of partnership is seen as a threat to the independence of the voluntary sector and hence *actual* partnership (Donnelly-Cox and Jaffro, 1999). O'Ferrall's (2000) analysis of the service planning approach as it operates in Ireland is one of 'dependent partnership', where voluntary agencies are not partners in the negotiation of process, goals, and service provision but rather are party to a deterministic and power-imbalanced relationship. Optimal partnership or co-operative models are based on equality; the rationale for partnership should be value-driven and underpinned by the belief that the value added by voluntary agencies is preserved in the process, and not bureaucratized (O'Ferrall, 2000). Similarly, independence in and of itself does not merit guarding; rather a balanced co-operation is required to develop equitable local access to hospice services, and to provide the structure for the development of standards and guides to practice.

Individual voluntary groups traditionally relate to each other and communicate in a range of informal and *ad hoc* ways. The publication of the *Report of the National Advisory Committee on Palliative Care* (Department of Health and Children, 2001) and the increased financial contributions towards palliative care from the statutory sector have been a precursor to the development of more formal links between groups on a regional basis. Voluntary hospice groups from one health authority area for example have formed an alliance; a forum to share information and explore strategic directions.

The North West Hospice

Before health boards were prepared to become involved in funding or managing palliative care services, individuals in communities recognized the need for these specialist services. Throughout the Republic of Ireland, in the late 1980s and early 1990s, voluntary hospice groups both urban and rural were established, sought charitable status and employed nurses to provide a home care service. The energy and enthusiasm of these voluntary groups were central in bringing hospice into public awareness. Many of these voluntary groups are community-based and work essentially within community boundaries (county, county-wide or more regional). Most home care services in rural Ireland owe their origins to this effort established largely because families wanted an excellence of care delivered locally for those in their communities who were dying of cancer.

Many people in rural areas who suffered from cancer faced the prospect of travelling many miles from their homes to either Dublin or Cork for their radiation therapy. The radiation oncologists held peripheral clinics in the major regional hospitals where new patients were seen and old patients reviewed. Until very recently medical oncologists were based in Dublin and Cork, again necessitating travelling long distances for specialist care. This lack of locally developed oncology services created a vacuum and it allowed hospice services to grow as the only local specialist cancer care provider. This of course challenged the home care teams to define their boundaries and to be aware of their limitations.

Each of these hospice groups has their own unique history of the local, regional and indeed national battles that were fought to establish their services. North West Hospice is one such group which, since its establishment, has been at the forefront of voluntary hospice groups nationally. While this cannot be as comprehensive a description as desired given the space limitations, it endeavours to give a flavour of some of the challenges faced by such a voluntary organization.

The original impetus to setting up a hospice service in the north-west, was the perception that existing services for patients with cancer were limited. The initial energy and vision came from Clare Campbell, a social worker employed by the North Western Health Board at Sligo General Hospital. A small group of volunteers came together in 1986 and a number of public meetings were held to create awareness, raise the profile and harness some of the obvious energy and enthusiasm. A small executive committee was formed with interested business people, health care professionals and clergy.

Fund-raising was critical and it was recognized that charitable status and a fund-raising strategy would be essential. North West Hospice became a limited company and employed its first nurses, Carmel Tunney and Ann-Marie McCafferty, in 1989. As with many of the home care nurse pioneers, both nurses received further training at Our Lady's Hospice, Dublin, before starting their work in the community. Their humanity, professionalism and excellence in care established a strong foundation for the service. By 1990 the team had grown with the addition of a medical director Dr Liam O'Síoráin and a social worker, Eva Duffy. North West Hospice was one of the first services to have a truly multi-professional approach to patient and family care.

With the arrival of a doctor with palliative care experience and building on the existing strong foundations, links were established with all the hospitals in the region and a consult service developed. A joint out-patient clinic with the visiting radiation oncologist from St Lukes, the major cancer treatment centre in the Republic of Ireland, was also pioneering at the time. These bridge-building exercises were critical and gave credibility to the hospice at a time when palliative medicine was not a recognized medical specialty.

In tandem with increasing referrals came greater public awareness. One of the major reasons for this was the setting up of a network of regional support groups. Meetings were held usually in the evening and attended by the local community. Numbers varied from half a dozen to up to a hundred and the group usually had a brief talk from the chairperson of fund-raising, Noreen McGloin, and the medical director, followed by a video on hospice services. These groups worked tirelessly over the ensuing years to raise awareness and much needed funds. Without their efforts the hospice would not have survived and attained the necessary critical mass.

While this approach was hugely successful in embedding the hospice philosophy and giving a certain ownership of the service to the community, it created a pressure to perform on the team: 'you are only as good as your last patient'. The team were also relatively identifiable as being the 'face of hospice' and team members would certainly have been conscious of the public relations element to their work.

This local support also created a political awareness among TDs (members of parliament) and councillors who were keen to see that hospice services continued to grow locally. Accessibility to politicians is a feature of Irish life and local politicians paying their respects to the family of the deceased would attend many funerals. Given that over one in four of their constituents were dying of cancer, awareness of hospice was inevitable. The use of carefully worded 'Parliamentary Questions' (PQs) raised by opposition TDs was a useful way of both obtaining information about the location of funding and of keeping the Department of Health aware of the political lobbying in place. Inevitably, questions raised were channelled back to the health board, sometimes with helpful outcomes.

While there was growing public support, the local health board were very slow to embrace this new service. There was no government money available and the North Western Health Board, who at that time were among the most forward looking and innovative in the country, were close to obstructive in their dealings with hospice.

The Irish Cancer Society were hugely supportive and their grant aid towards a 'Daffodil Nurse', a specialist palliative care nurse funded by the proceeds of Daffodil Day, was an endorsement of the whole service. The Irish Hospice Foundation, through both 'Sunflower Day' and the national 'Coffee Morning,' was of vital importance in both providing funds and continuing the media publicity drive. The local weekly paper, the *Sligo Champion*, played a critical role in these early days and also at a later date, when two sequential editorials pinned the North Western Health Board on a funding issue. Use of local radio stations was also important and all contributed to the increasing public and political awareness.

Direct political lobbying also played a part and the very first 'state approved' funding was given through the National Lottery fund in 1992. This came about through direct lobbying of the Minister of Finance, Mr Albert Reynolds, whose wife Kathleen is a native of Ballymote, County Sligo.

In 1991 North West Hospice hosted 'Progress in Palliative Care', a multi-professional conference at which Dr Declan Walsh, Director of Palliative Care Services at the Cleveland Clinic, gave the keynote address. This was a hugely ambitious undertaking for a small hospice but was very well attended and succeeded in drawing in many local health care professionals. The conference was held again in 1993 and Dr Jan Sjernsward, Director of Cancer and Palliative Care at the World Health Organization, gave the keynote speech.

At this time in the Republic of Ireland the government was drawing up a national health strategy document called 'Shaping a Healthier Future' (Department of Health, 1994). Sligo was the epicentre of medical and nursing politics with the presidents of the Irish Medical Organisation (IMO), The Irish Hospital Consultant's Association (IHCA) and The Irish Nursing Organisation (INO) all working in Sligo General Hospital. Dr Seamus Healy, a hospice board member, as president of the IMO, was aware of the current initiatives in the Department of Health. At his suggestion Dr Tim Collins, a native of Sligo who was working as a special advisor to the then minister of health Mr Brendan Howlin, was invited to Markree Castle to meet with Dr Sjernsward. This informal meeting was also attended by Drs Liam O'Síoráin, Michael Kearney and Tony O'Brien.

Dr Collins was supportive in wanting to see hospice and palliative care included in the new strategy and shortly afterwards the Department of Health invited some of the key people to a meeting in Dublin at which senior departmental members had a broad ranging discussion about palliative care services. When *Shaping a Healthier Future* was published in 1994, there was half a page on developing palliative care. For the first time palliative care was officially in print and was here to stay.

Much has happened in North West Hospice since 1994. The service has now grown with a larger home care team and an eight-bed in-patient unit and day hospice facilities. A heated debate took place on locating the in-patient unit. Many felt an existing site in scenic Rosses Point should be developed as a tranquil location. In the end the hospice board opted for developing on site directly linked to Sligo General Hospital. This decision allowed more opportunities for integrating the service and is also the recommended option for specialist palliative care units in the National Advisory committee report (Department of Health and Children, 2001).

Funding from the North Western Health Board is in place for the North West Hospice but there is still a significant shortfall every year, which has to be met by the charity. This is in contrast to Our Lady's Hospice, Dublin, which receives essentially 100 per cent funding to provide similar specialist palliative care services. Much of the hospice's energy is still consumed by fund-raising and whereas this gives some independence and, as detailed earlier, improved responsiveness, it is a huge effort for a relatively small charity with a small catchment population.

The future brings uncertainty. It is vital to secure a second consultant for the region to support the existing post and to work closely with the new oncologist appointments brought about through the National Cancer Strategy (Department of Health, 1996). The National Advisory Committee's recommendations on regional committees and a national council have been slow to be implemented. The current process of restructuring of health boards and the subsequent loss of the local councillors' voices may also be detrimental. The support and goodwill of the people of the region remains essential.

The Irish Cancer Society

The Irish Cancer Society (ICS) is the major national cancer charity whose remit includes all cancer care from screening programmes to hospice home care. The ICS's interest and support for palliative care services is evident in the establishment of the first home care service at Our Lady's Hospice in 1985. Funding from its annual Daffodil Day is largely spent on palliative care services. Funds raised during the nationwide Daffodil Day campaign are collected centrally and then allocated throughout the country depending on where support is sought and needs identified.

The board of the ICS is dominated by senior consultants, mainly in oncology rather than palliative care. The ICS receives requests from many sources for grant aid. The medical committee, which is made up of health care professionals directly involved in patient care, considers these applications at a monthly meeting effectively functioning as an executive committee.

It is now nearly 20 years since palliative home care services first began in the Irish Republic. In that time the service has sought to ensure the best quality of life for those dying with cancer in their homes. This is in keeping with the ethos of the Irish Cancer Society as the national charity for cancer care. The philosophy of the ICS since 1963 has been to eliminate cancer as a major health problem and to improve the lives of those living with the disease. Through research, education and patient care the ICS strives to achieve these goals. Over the years, the picture of cancer in Ireland has changed. With advances in early diagnosis and treatment, survival rates continue to rise. However, for those patients whose cancer is not curable, the ICS places great importance on its role in palliative care. Here the aim is to provide the best possible quality of life, not only for patients but also for their families. Care for the dying, as all those involved in palliative care will attest, is a time when respect for the human spirit is paramount. Certainly this principle has guided the Society in the development of palliative home care services.

Involvement in palliative home care services first began in 1985 when Our Lady's Hospice approached the ICS for funding to set up a home care service. It was a significant moment in the history of the ICS at a time when 'quality of life' for patients with advanced cancer was undergoing radical change. The ICS supported the concept of caring for people in their place of preference and was aware that many of those with terminal cancer preferred to live their final days at home surrounded by loved ones. A greater demand for a very limited supply of hospice beds was putting pressure on in-patient services. But perhaps more crucially, advances in pain and symptom control were making it possible for patients to be cared for in their homes.

With a long tradition in establishing hospices, the Irish Sisters of Charity set up Our Lady's Hospice in Dublin in 1879 and then St Joseph's Hospice in Hackney, London in 1905. In 1985 the sisters' more recent experiences in England gave them first-hand knowledge of how patients could be cared for in their own homes. St Joseph's Hospice community palliative care team had been set up in 1975 and was successfully serving a number of London boroughs.

In Dublin, starting a specialist service from scratch presented an enormous challenge. Drawing on their experiences, Sister Francis Rose O'Flynn, Matron, and Sister Ignatius Phelan, Director of Home Care, rose to the challenge. The service was designed, organized, and planned by Our Lady's Hospice, while funding was provided by the ICS. Many obstacles were overcome in true pioneering spirit. Spearheading the initiative on behalf of the society were Tom Hudson, then CEO, along with Maura McDonnell, patient services manager and Vincent Koziell, board member.

Thus began the first home care service in the Irish Republic, provided by a specialist team, consisting of a doctor and four nurses trained in symptom control and family support. The society agreed to fund this service as a pilot scheme for three years. Dr Veronie Hanley provided medical leadership and expertise. The team's emphasis on quality care and its philosophy of supporting GPs and the community team proved very successful with 193 patients availing of the service during the first year and 260 patients by the third year. Initially the team worked within a six-mile radius of the hospice in the urban community.

The success of this project led to other communities around the country seeking a similar service. Coinciding with the public requests for a home care service, the first Daffodil Day was held by the society in 1988. This resulted in extra funds being available. In response to the demands of the public for a better service for people with advanced cancer who wished to remain at home these funds were used to support home care teams. Essentially, the funds paid the salaries of nurses employed full-time either by their local health board or hospice committee.

From this evolved a growth in services developed jointly by the ICS, health boards and local communities. The ICS covered the length and breadth of the country as negotiations between the various groups continued. The society's actions always came at the request of the local community, whether health professionals, local people or a combination of both. The success of the services rested entirely on obtaining the full co-operation of the medical and nursing professions already working in the community such as GPs and public heath nurses, in addition to the relevant health board.

In order to advance the setting up of services, the ICS worked closely with community services, particularly local hospice groups. Traditionally, the fundamental philosophy of palliative care has been holistic, based on the development of a 'team'. At times, this working together was a source of great stress and yet, when approached with openness and honesty, it was the greatest area of success. The ICS provided guidance and recommendations during these initial negotiations, but was careful not to interfere in local structures and systems of care. In 1986 another community-based nursing service was established; the home care service was extended into a night nursing service, recognizing that caring for someone with advanced cancer at home can be very difficult, particularly at night. At first the service was offered to families in difficult financial circumstances but this was extended to all in 2000. This service has continued to grow with 1,032 patients availing of it during 2003.

The ongoing success of home care teams depended on the availability of essential funds. Today the ICS provides grants of over €1 million towards the salaries of specialist palliative care nurses working in home care services throughout the Irish Republic.

The ICS also recognized the importance of education for nurses employed in home care services. Regular workshops were established and ran throughout the year. The purpose of these workshops was to allow nurses to meet and gain mutual support, share knowledge and grow in awareness of their need for ongoing support and development. The need for extra skills, particularly in communication, became evident. Support for these workshops was widespread and they successfully continue today. In 2000 the ICS supported Bás Solais, a major international palliative care conference hosted by Our Lady's Hospice in Dublin Castle.

The Irish Cancer Society is very proud of its association with the voluntary hospice movement in Ireland. The society's core values of serving people and communities, leadership, teamwork, respect for the individual, responsibility, accountability, and stewardship have found echoes in their values. Their experiences have deepened ours. But most importantly in developing palliative home care services, the patient has guided us. Only by respecting the dignity of those dying from cancer have we learnt to serve them better. Out of this comes the ability to respond to new challenges and be innovative in cancer care.

The Irish Hospice Foundation

The Irish Hospice Foundation was founded in 1986 and has itself evolved in function and form. Like so many voluntary organizations, it was founded by someone who benefited from a service and saw the need to do so much more.

Her father's illness, over a period of many months, brought Mary Redmond, a young Irish woman not long returned from Cambridge, England, into contact with Our Lady's Hospice, Dublin. Mary Redmond fast became an advocate for hospice and specialist palliative care, recognizing that these models of care needed to be extended to wider groups of people and not limited to those who had a cancer diagnosis.

The 'Hospice Foundation' was launched in a 'blaze of publicity' connected to the 1986 *Today Tonight* television programme which focused on the care provided at Our Lady's Hospice. Moreover, the programme highlighted the need for expanded care for dying patients and those facing death. Irish people responded to the challenge and the fund-raising machine ground into action. The Foundation began its life very closely aligned to Our Lady's Hospice; appropriately, a major project for the Foundation was a focus on education. The donated time, effort and ideas of many well-known Irish people, mobilized by the Foundation, resulted in a £1.6 million donation for the Education and Training Centre at the hospice.

A second hospice and the provision of more beds for the Dublin area was a vision of the founder of the Foundation. By February 1989, the fruits of meetings, negotiations, toil and fund-raising began to appear with the initiation of a home care service in Raheny on Dublin's north side. St Francis Hospice was born with £1.3 million raised during the first three years.

The 'Hospice Foundation' became the 'Irish Hospice Foundation' in function and in name by developing a country-wide structure of networked fund-raising to support hospice nationally. Each year it co-ordinates two national fund-raising events on behalf of hospice groups all over Ireland – Sunflower Days, which began in June 1992 and Ireland's Biggest Coffee Morning, which began in September 1993.

The co-ordination of Sunflower Days involves the delivery of over 320,000 sunflowers together with promotional material to hospice groups all over the country. The Foundation also produces and broadcasts radio advertisements and co-ordinates the national PR activity in the lead-up to this event.

For the past 11 years Bewley's, the well-know Irish home of coffee, have been the generous sponsors for 'Ireland's Biggest Coffee Morning'. They supply in excess of 25,000 packets of coffee for the event each year. Once again the Irish Hospice Foundation (IHF) co-ordinates the production of all print and promotional material for this event as well as all national PR and promotional activity. Marian Finucane, a radio host on the national broadcaster RTE, has been the face of 'Ireland's Biggest Coffee Morning' since the beginning and lends her voice to the radio advertisements for the same. The key to both these ventures is the guiding principle that 'money raised locally stays locally'. These annual fund-raising events are now well established and help, in no small way, to raise awareness about hospice and hospice services among the general public.

The IHF support for voluntary hospice manifests in different ways – fund-raising, education and awareness, research grants and commissioning, consultation, lobbying and advocacy and service development through pioneering projects. The IHF acts as a support to the voluntary movement, it is not however a membership organization and representation on national issues is prefaced by this caveat. A direct form of service and a clinical link to hospice was developed early in the Foundation's existence by the late Thérèse Brady, a clinical psychologist and educator at University College Dublin. As both academic and practitioner, Thérèse was able to match theory and practice not only in the development of volunteer bereavement services following on from the research of Colin Murray Parkes, but also in the design of training programmes in loss and bereavement.

Most recently the IHF has consolidated its presence and services by acquiring new premises and a home for training and information, particularly in relation to bereavement. This initiative demonstrates two more dimensions of the voluntary sector – namely, the influence and legacy of pioneers on the one hand (in this case the groundwork laid by Thérèse Brady in the bereavement area) and the response to central palliative care policy on the other (the noted lack of formal bereavement support protocol in the *Report of the National Advisory Committee on Palliative Care*, 2001).

The mission of the Foundation remains essentially the same – to support the development of hospice and palliative care through fund-raising, capacity building, advocacy, education and training, lobbying, information dissemination, innovative projects, and research support. The vision is that no one should have to face death without appropriate care and support, including support for the family extending into bereavement. The aim is to support the philosophy and the specialty of palliative care.

The IHF supported the initiation of specialist palliative care teams in acute hospital settings during the 1990s by seed-funding clinical nurse specialist in palliative care posts in a number of hospitals. From close contact with the teams and through local research on the area the Foundation is convinced that in a very practical way the hospice/palliative care philosophy should permeate the hospital setting where most people die, and most families encounter death. The IHF has recently launched a pilot project, 'Care for people dying in Hospitals Project,' situated in Our Lady of Lourdes Hospital, Drogheda, in the north east of Ireland, to focus on all elements of care and encounters in a hospital setting. This project is in line with the aspiration of the *Report of the National Advisory Committee on Palliative Care* (Department of Health of Children, 2001) to develop services and to meet the needs of patients with illnesses other than cancer.

The special case of children with life-threatening conditions in need of palliative care has also been a focus for the IHF for a number of years. Among the fund-raising initiatives is an annual walk by the lady captains of the Dublin golf clubs which has consistently raised funds directly for the provision of paediatric oncology liaison nurses based in a tertiary paediatric hospital, in Crumlin, Dublin, but with a remit to travel the country. Recently the IHF has funded a specialist palliative care nurse for the same hospital and has partnered the Department of Health and Children in funding a national needs assessment to quantify and describe children's palliative care needs in order to work to the provision of appropriate and accessible services.

The changing and evolving landscape for voluntary–statutory relationships forms the immediate focus of the IHF's support of the voluntary hospice movement, therefore lobbying, advocating and examining methods of fostering true co-operative partnership will be our priority for the years ahead. The challenge will be to maintain the richness of the hospice legacy, handed down through visionary individuals and community initiatives, which provides a multi-disciplinary, multi-faceted service based on the complex needs of each human being. Those needs – physical, emotional, psychological, spiritual, social – are well expressed in the inspirational phrase of Dame Cicely Saunders when she says: 'You matter because you are you and you matter all the days of your life.' Her phrase has also acted as a catalyst to permeate, at the level of national policy, the values that flow from a human rights approach to the care of the dying.

Conclusion

The impact of the voluntary sector on palliative care services has been enormous. Both the ICS and the IHF have each contributed greatly to patient and family care throughout the country. Both differ in their structure and governing bodies with the ICS having predominantly an oncology medical presence on its board and the IHF a greater business and legal presence. At this stage in the development of palliative care services and with the existence of a formal consultant in palliative medicine group and the well-established Irish Association for Palliative Care, greater collaboration is needed between all interested parties to ensure the opportunity of implementing the National Advisory plan fully is not lost.

References

Anheier, H. and Knapp, M. (1990) Voluntas: an editorial statement, *Voluntas*, 1(1): 1–12.

Department of Health (1994) *Shaping a Healthier Future: A Strategy for Effective Healthcare in the 1990s*. Dublin: Stationery Office.

Department of Health (1996) *Cancer Services in Ireland: A National Strategy*. Dublin: Stationery Office.

Department of Health and Children (2001) *Report of the National Advisory Committee on Palliative Care*. Dublin: Stationery Office.

Donnelly-Cox, G. and Jaffro, G. (1999) *The Voluntary Sector in the Republic of Ireland: into the Twenty-First Century*. Coleraine: University of Ulster.

Haslett, D. (1998) *A Study of Partnership between Voluntary and Statutory Sectors in Palliative Care in Ireland*. Dublin: Irish Hospice Foundation.

Irish Hospice Foundation (2003) *Irish Voluntary Hospice Groups – The Picture in the Wake of the Report of the National Advisory Committee on Palliative Care*. Internal report. Dublin: Irish Hospice Foundation.

O'Ferrall, F. (2000) *Citizenship and Public Service: Voluntary and Statutory Relationships in Irish Healthcare*. Dublin: The Adelaide Hospital Society in association with Dundalgan Press.

3 | Managing palliative care services in the Irish Republic

Michael Murphy and Pat Quinlan

Introduction

Historically the foundations of palliative care services in the Republic of Ireland are closely linked with religious orders. Developments in the health system have resulted in the evolution of a modern health service. In line with these changes palliative care services have developed and have been guided and influenced by the publication of several key documents. For the first time palliative care now has a strategy at national level to guide developments. At the centre of government policy in Ireland is the development of a 'people-centred' approach to care (Department of Health and Children, 2001). This sits well with the ethos of palliative care where quality of life is a central issue. Managing palliative care services in the Republic of Ireland presents a challenge in a constantly changing health service which is currently undergoing a large scale reform.

The existence of hospitals and particularly hospices is evidence of a progressive civilization in which people are interested not only in their own well-being but also that of the community. The holistic approach of fostering co-operation and co-ordination among caregivers is not an innovation. As early as 4000 BC, religions identified certain of their deities with healing. Doctors were frequently priest physicians and administered both drugs and healing suggestions.

In the Middle Ages, both on the Continent and in England, there were numerous hospices run by religious communities and lay people. Hospice means literally 'a shelter for travellers'. The establishment of voluntary hospitals in Ireland took place in the early decades of the eighteenth century with the establishment of, for example, the Rotunda hospital and the Royal Hospital in Donnybrook. The voluntary hospital movement was still the main force in providing for the sick poor during the first half of the nineteenth century.

The growth of more liberal political attitudes and the lifting of restrictions on the Catholic community was a significant influence on the development of voluntary hospitals. This allowed the foundation of a number of new Irish congregations of religious, in particular the Irish Sisters of Charity and the Sisters of Mercy, dedicated to the care of the sick poor. Hospice care in Ireland originated in the late nineteenth century, with the establishment of Our Lady's Hospice in Dublin and St Patrick's Hospital / Marymount Hospice in Cork.

Modern palliative care is concerned with improving quality of life by treating distressing symptoms and offering psychological, social and spiritual support in different care settings. An essential component of managing services is providing a pleasing environment for patients, staff and visitors. However, it was not until the passing of the Public Hospitals Act in 1933 that steps were taken to build modern hospitals. The hospital building programmes of the 1930s and 1950s were major undertakings in Ireland at that time.

The great catalyst for this wave of construction was the establishment of the Hospitals' Sweepstakes in 1930 under the terms of the Public Charitable Hospitals (temporary provisions) Act. This was intended to provide a source of funding for some of the voluntary hospitals in Dublin which were in financial difficulties. Subsequent legislation provided for the setting up of the Hospitals' Commission which surveyed and identified the categories of hospitals required.

The Department of Health was established in 1947 and became the Department of Health and Children in 1997. The Department's primary role is to support the government and the Minister for Health and Children in formulating, implementing and evaluating policies for the health services. The Department also has a role in the strategic planning of health services in consultation with health boards, the voluntary sector and other government departments. Each year the Department of Health and Children allocates funding to the health boards which, in turn makes decisions on the distribution of available resources to the agencies in their area.

The Health Boards were set up under the Health Act, 1970 and came into being in April 1971. They have a statutory responsibility for administering the health and personal social services provided in health legislation and by ministerial initiatives. Currently there are seven health boards and an additional three area health boards (set up within the Eastern Regional Health Authority). Each health board is regionally based and varies in size depending on the population it serves.

The further development of specialist palliative care in-patient units and community-based home care teams has been taking place since the mid-1970s, catalysed by the growth of the hospice movement in the United

Kingdom and as part of what has become an international health care movement.

Palliative care services in the Republic of Ireland

In the Republic of Ireland today there are six dedicated specialist palliative care in-patient units, and 28 home care teams. There have also been significant developments and improvements in the delivery of specialist palliative care within acute hospitals, with many of them now having dedicated consultant input and directly employing trained palliative care staff. In addition many district hospitals and community and nursing units throughout the country have dedicated palliative care beds that are available to local home care teams and general practitioners. A common thread running through all of these developments has been the principle of developing services to complement rather than supplant existing services in community and hospital settings.

The voluntary sector in Ireland has been to the forefront in the development of specialist palliative care services over the past 15 years. Much of this development has taken place in co-operation and partnership with local health boards. Both health strategies (Department of Health, 1994; Department of Health and Children, 2001) acknowledged the major contribution played by the voluntary sector in general in Irish health care service provision, and as such recommended the ongoing involvement of the voluntary sector in the future planning and delivery of specialist palliative care services.

The health boards have statutory responsibility for planning and commissioning health services within their region. Funding is provided by the health board for services, and monitoring takes place in accordance with approved governance structures. In most cases the statutory and voluntary sectors work well together and the 'ethos' of the hospice is maintained and respected. One of the key strengths in this area is good collaboration between the statutory and voluntary sectors in an effort to provide 'best practice' in palliative care and in putting patients/carers first. The hospice movement also has an important role in fostering the hospice ethos and in shaping that ethos in the service in general.

Service providers have the opportunity to engage with their local health board in order to influence the funding, developments and monitoring of services by developing a yearly service plan. An annual service plan is produced in each health board and its implementation is monitored by the Department of Health and Children. Within each health board there is a service planner who is specifically assigned to palliative care.

Government recognition of the valuable role played by palliative care has led to the provision of a significantly increased level of public funding (see

Figure 3.1, p. 39) and the further development of palliative care in all its facets. This recognition has been incorporated into four key policy reports as follows:

1) Health Strategy – *Shaping a Healthier Future* (Department of Health, 1994)
2) Health Strategy – *Quality and Fairness* (Department of Health and Children, 2001)
3) *Cancer Services in Ireland: A National Strategy* (Department of Health, 1996)
4) *Report of the National Advisory Committee on Palliative Care* (Department of Health and Children, 2001a)

1. The health strategy – *Shaping a Healthier Future* (1994)

The health strategy, *Shaping a Healthier Future* (Department of Health, 1994), was the first strategy document to feature palliative care and suggested that palliative care services be developed in a structured manner.

2. The health strategy – *Quality and Fairness* (2001)

In the latest health strategy, *Quality and Fairness* (Department of Health and Children, 2001), the Government has agreed to develop a national palliative care service. This strategy undertakes to develop palliative care services through structured planning in all health board areas throughout Ireland. Furthermore it confirms that a palliative care approach should be an integral part of all clinical practice and services should also be available to those dying of diseases other than cancer.

The health strategy (Department of Health and Children, 2001a) also places 'people-centred' care as a high priority in achieving quality in health care. Surveying patients regarding their satisfaction with the services provided and the way in which services are delivered leads to patient involvement in planning and evaluation of health care (McGee, 1998). A recent national survey of patients' perceptions of the health services in the Republic of Ireland (Irish Society for Quality and Safety in Healthcare, 2002) concludes that patients in acute hospitals felt that the standard of care they received in hospital was high. In the present climate of patient-focused health service provision, the quality of palliative care services must also be open to assessment and evaluation.

Leahy (1998) refers to a number of headings under which quality in health care could be considered:

1) Effectiveness or technical competence, which is an area often emphasized by the doctor;

2) Social acceptability, which is of particular concern to the patients and their relatives;
3) Efficiency, or the ability to deliver a service for the lowest unit cost;
4) Accessibility, which defines the availability of a service to the individual;
5) Relevance, which indicates that the service is that which is required by the individual and/or society;
6) Equity, indicating the equality of access to services.

These general principles underpinning quality in health care equally apply to palliative care and should form a cornerstone for service providers to evaluate the services they provide.

According to the National Council for Hospice and Specialist Palliative Care Services (1996), all palliative care services should have an explicit commitment to improve the quality of the care delivered. This should include making the most appropriate use of resources and providing equity in terms of accessibility and the provision of service. Quality improvement initiatives including audit should be led by senior managers and clinicians and should be part of every-day practice throughout organizations. Audit should not be confined to health care professionals but should include all personnel and should focus on all aspects of the service provided in order to promote research-based practice.

Assessment of a patient's quality of life is assuming increasing importance in medicine and health care (Spilker, 1990). In the United Kingdom quality of life, health status and the experiences of patients and carers are explicitly identified among significant indicators of health gain. In palliative care, quality of life is considered to be the *raison d'être* (Cohen and Mount, 1992). Most authors who have considered palliative care have placed quality of life as the primary outcome to be assessed (O'Boyle, 1998). However, while many definitions of palliative care include quality of life as a central theme, there is little evidence to support the effectiveness of palliative care in improving quality of life for patients with life-limiting illnesses (O'Boyle and Waldron, 1997). It is also difficult to translate research findings regarding quality of life into practical decisions regarding patient care (Skeel, 1997).

3. The cancer strategy

The Cancer Strategy (Department of Health, 1996) and its subsequent implementation stressed the importance of organizing cancer services to provide care across the continuum of cancer from screening through to palliative care services. Furthermore the concept of patient choice for location of care was also emphasized. Emphasis was placed on the need for the emergence of a more structured and formalized arrangement between the voluntary sector and the health boards in order to provide optimum palliative care. The aim of the cancer strategy (Department of Health, 1996) was to ensure that those who develop cancer receive efficient, timely care and treatment while maintaining quality of life to the greatest extent possible. The subsequent evaluation of this strategy (Deloitte, 2003) reports considerable progress in the development of palliative care services in the Irish Republic.

In 2000, the National Council for Hospice and Specialist Palliative Care in its Draft National Plan and Strategic Framework for Palliative Care, proposed a set of national standards and performance indicators that would apply to both the National Health Service (NHS) and voluntary sector providers. Within this recommended framework, there were seven domains or areas of assessment identified as follows:

1. Fair access – to recognize that access to palliative care services should be in relation to patient and carer needs irrespective of geography, socio-economic group, ethnicity, age or sex;
2. Timeliness – to recognize that timeliness of access for those with palliative care needs is important: there are often no second chances for this group of patients;
3. Effectiveness – to recognize that access must be to care which is effective, that is which meets the assessed needs of patients and carers;
4. Patient/carer experience – to ensure that the delivery of care is sensitive to individual needs, to assess the way in which patients and their carers experience and view the quality of care they receive;
5. Communication between professionals – to ensure that effective communication between professionals within and between providers in both the NHS and voluntary sector facilitates continuity of care;
6. Efficiency – to ensure that care is provided without waste of resources, for example through having clear palliative care strategies in place locally which avoid duplication of services;
7. Health outcomes of palliative care – to assess the contribution of palliative care to improvements in overall health of the population.

4. *Report of the National Advisory Committee for Palliative Care* (2001a): A summary of key findings from a manager's perspective

The *Report of the National Advisory Committee for Palliative Care* (Department of Health and Children, 2001a) was launched by the Minister for Health and Children in October 2001. This report was approved by government and as such is recognized by all key stakeholders as national policy. Publication of this report has led to further investment in and development of palliative care services in the Republic of Ireland (Figure 3.1) with palliative care now receiving a dedicated budget for the first time.

Additional Funding for palliative care (2002–2004)			
Health Board	2002	2003	2004
Eastern Regional Health Authority	€1.930 m	€0.701 m	€0.340 m
Midland Health Board	€0.330 m	€0.122 m	€0.065 m
Mid-Western Health Board	€0.748 m	€0.257 m	€0.125 m
North Eastern Health Board	€0.590 m	€0.217 m	€0.105 m
North Western Health Board	€0.787 m	€0.290 m	€0.145 m
South Eastern Health Board	€0.578 m	€0.213 m	€0.175 m
Southern Health Board	€1.072 m	€0.376 m	€0.105 m
Western Health Board	€0.892 m	€0.280 m	€0.140 m
Total	€6.927 m	€2.456 m	€1.2 m

(* Funding provided in addition to base funding. Source: Department of Health and Children, 2004)

Figure 3.1 Additional funding for palliative care in Ireland*

Many of the recommendations have implications for managers of palliative care services:

1. growing demand for palliative care
2. recommendations for staffing levels
3. quality of service
4. funding of services including:

- New development monies allocated must tie in with both national and regional policy for palliative care, and should be prioritized in accordance with assessed need.
- The respective roles and requirements of both statutory and voluntary organizations involved in the provision should be set out and signed off in formal service agreements between the parties.
- There should be greater accountability for the use of funds generated through fund-raising and funded projects should be based on overall regional and national policy for the operation and further development of specialist palliative care.
- The establishment of a National Council for Specialist Palliative Care as an ongoing advisory body to the Minister for Health and Children.
- At regional level, health boards are required to establish regional consultative committees and regional development committees in palliative care, responsible for planning / policy formulation and resource allocation, respectively. The recommended composition for membership of these committees is outlined in the report.

One of the recommendations of the *Report of the National Advisory Committee for Palliative Care* (Department of Health and Children, 2001a) was that a needs assessment be carried out in each of the eight health boards areas. This process involved all stakeholders, including service providers. The needs of the local population were prioritized in relation to palliative care requirements for in-patient, day care, out-patient and home care service. The process also took into account service users' views. On the basis of this process, service commissioning and planning will be prioritized on a needs basis.

Structure of the health care system in the Irish Republic

The Irish health care system is currently undergoing major structural reform. However, this reform programme is not yet complete. The key elements of the proposed reform programme are outlined below.

Key elements of the current health care structural reform programme

In 2003, a number of major decisions were taken by government relating to the reform of the health service. The key elements of this change programme include:

- A major rationalization of existing health service agencies to reduce fragmentation, including the abolition of existing health board/authority structures;
- The reorganization of the Department of Health and Children, to ensure improved policy development;
- The establishment of a Health Services Executive (HSE) which will be the first body ever to be charged with health service as a single national entity. The HSE is to be organized on the basis of three core divisions:

  1) National Hospitals Office (NHO)
  2) Primary, Community and Continuing Care Directorate (PCCC)
  3) National Shared Services Centre (NSSC)

- The establishment of a Health Information and Quality Authority (HIQA) to ensure that quality of care is promoted throughout the system;
- The modernization of supporting processes (service planning; management reporting, etc.) in line with recognized best practice;
- The strengthening of governance and accountability across the system.

Future challenges

For palliative care the process of transforming our health care system requires innovation and vision. Innovation will demonstrate the benefits of integration and co-ordination of services, and vision will provide us with an overall unified framework as outlined in the National Advisory Committee Report (Department of Health of Children, 2001). As people live longer their needs change and with an ageing population chronic illness is more common. More is known about healthy living and improvements in medical technology and treatments has resulted in longevity for greater numbers of people.

New developments in palliative care directly improve the care of patients with life-limiting illness and implicitly educating and influencing others to adopt these values into routine practice indirectly leads to improvements in care. In essence, the main challenge for palliative care services is to develop an accessible, person-centred system that ensures effective professional and institutional resources are available to assist people requiring palliative care services. The system should embrace and promote the principle of person-centredness (Department of Health and Children, 2001a) while accepting the responsibility of using resources appropriately and efficiently.

Conclusion

The need and demand for palliative care will increase significantly over the next five years. There are a number of reasons for this:

- The incidence of cancer is increasing.
- The demand for palliative care for patients with non-cancer conditions is also increasing, for example, respiratory and neurological conditions.
- The reorganization of the health service may be viewed as an opportunity to establish palliative care services on a more equitable basis.

Some of the challenges that may arise in the next five years are:

- There is a possibility of reduced service developments in the context of general budgetary constraints.
- Paediatric and adult services may not become properly integrated. It is essential that a seamless transmission is made from the childhood service into the adult service in relation to conditions such as cystic fibrosis and neurological disorders.
- In the new, reformed health service the specialty of palliative care could be placed in either the NHO or the PCCC pillar. It is therefore important that a structural 'home' be found for palliative care.

The National Advisory Committee *Report* (Department of Health of Children, 2001) is the most important development for palliative care service provision in the Irish Republic in recent times. The recommendations of the report have now been adopted as national policy, a move that should ensure that palliative care will have higher priority in relation to public funding in the years ahead. This report sets out national standards and as such offers clear and welcome guidelines to service providers and managers which will ensure that all such services operate in accordance with best practice.

References

Cohen, R. and Mount, B. M. (1992) Quality of Life in terminal illness: defining and measuring subjective well being in the dying, *Journal of Palliative Care*, 8:40–45.

Deloitte (2003) *An Evaluation of 'Cancer Services in Ireland: A National Strategy 1996'* on behalf of The National Cancer Forum. Dublin: Stationery Office.

Department of Health (1994) *Shaping a Healthier Future: A Strategy for Effective Healthcare in the 1990s.* Dublin: Stationery Office.

Department of Health (1996) *Cancer Services in Ireland: A National Strategy.* Dublin: Stationery Office.

Department of Health and Children (2001), *Quality and Fairness a Health System for You, Health Strategy.* Dublin: Stationery Office.

Department of Health and Children (2001a) *Report of the National Advisory Committee for Palliative Care.* Dublin: Stationery Office.

Department of Health and Children (2004) www.healthnet.ie

Donabedian, A. (1985) *Explorations in Quality Assessment and Monitoring.* Vols 1–3, Ann Arbor: MI Health, Administration Press.

Irish Society for Quality and Safety in Healthcare (2002) *National Patient Perception of the Quality of Healthcare 2002.* Dublin.

Leahy, A. L. (1998) *Moving to a Quality Culture. The Irish Health System in the 21st Century.* Dublin: Oak Tree Press.

MacEachern, M. (1957) *Hospital Organisation and Management.* Chicago: Physicians' Record Company.

McGee, H. M. (1998) Patient Satisfaction Surveys: Are they useful as indicators of Quality of Care?, *Journal of Health Gain*, 2:5–8.

National Council for Hospice and Specialist Palliative Care Services (1996) Occasional paper on *Making Palliative Care Better – Quality improvement, Multi-Professional Audit and Standards.* London.

National Council for Hospice and Specialist Palliative Care Services (2000) *Draft National Plan and Strategic Framework for Palliative Care.* London.

O'Boyle, C. A. (1998) *Quality of Life Assessment: An Important Indicator of Health Gain: The Irish Healthcare System in the 21st Century.* Dublin: Oak Tree Press.

O'Boyle, C. A. and Waldron, D. (1997) Quality of Life issues in Palliative Medicine, *Journal of Neurology*, 244:18–24.

O'Dwyer, F. (1997) *Irish Hospital Architecture – A Pictorial History.* Dublin: Department of Health and Children.

Skeel, R. T. (1997) Quality of life dimensions that are most important to cancer patients, *Oncology*, 7:55–61.

Spilker, B. (ed.) (1990) *Quality of Life Assessments in Clinical Trials.* New York: Raven Press.

Part II

Service delivery

4 Urban home care in the Republic of Ireland

Kaye Kealy and Geraldine Tracey

Introduction

Our Lady's Hospice has a long tradition of caring for the sick of Dublin and celebrated 125 years of existence in 2004. Through the 1970s and early 80s the modern hospice movement world-wide recognized and promoted the concept of caring for terminally ill patients in their own homes. In response to this, the Republic of Ireland's first palliative home care service was established in 1985 at Our Lady's Hospice with support from the Irish Cancer Society. The initial team consisted of a nurse manager, a medical director and one staff nurse. They provided a 24-hour, 7-day service for terminally ill cancer patients, covering a 10-mile radius from Our Lady's Hospice. Demand for the service was instant and in the space of one year three more nurses were added to the team. In 1989 the Daughters of Charity established a second home care team in north County Dublin. This team is now attached to St Francis Hospice, Raheny.

The focus of home care in its early days was on care of terminally ill cancer patients and their families. The admission criteria for home care included the necessity of having a family member committed to the full-time care of the dying patient. This excluded patients who lived at home and who had no identifiable carer, leading to a relatively high rate of death at home. The team also acted as pioneers in promoting the concept of hospice care nationwide. Initially many of the home care teams around the country were nurse-led. Many of these nurses attended the 'six week palliative care course' (later extended to eight weeks) and then went on to spend time at Our Lady's Hospice, gaining experience in both in-patient and home care settings.

Social and demographic changes influenced the evolving role of the home care team. One significant change was the acknowledgement of the need for earlier palliative care involvement in the patient's disease trajectory. The advent of hospital-based palliative care teams facilitated access to palliative care services for a significantly greater number of patients at an earlier stage in their disease trajectory. These teams have played a significant role in disseminating the knowledge and skills of palliative care to other health care professionals. This in turn has had a direct impact on the number and type of patients being referred to home care. It has also changed the referral pattern from a majority of GP-initiated referrals in the earlier years to a majority of consultant referrals in recent years.

In October 1991, in response to the AIDS epidemic in Dublin, a separate home care team was established to meet the needs of this patient population. At its peak this team was seeing over 60 new AIDS patients each year and worked closely with Department of Genito-urinary Medicine at St James's Hospital. With the advent of new therapies, the needs of these patients changed and the number of deaths greatly declined. Subsequently the AIDS and cancer home care teams amalgamated in 1997.

In 1994 the first lay nurse manager was appointed to the home care team. The number of palliative care nurses on the team continued to grow (Figure 4.1). Planning for the future has led to a number of structural changes in home care over time. In the late 1990s it was envisaged that two satellite teams would be created, one based in Blackrock and the second in Tallaght, in the Adelaide Meath incorporating the National Children's Hospital. In February 2000, in preparation for this move, the service was formally divided into three teams, covering different geographical areas. Two additional clinical nurse managers were appointed to lead and support the newly created teams. In September 2003, phase two of these plans reached fruition when one of the home care teams moved from Our Lady's Hospice to the newly opened Blackrock Hospice. This team is now known as the Blackrock Home Care Team.

A recommendation of the *Report on the Commission on Nursing*

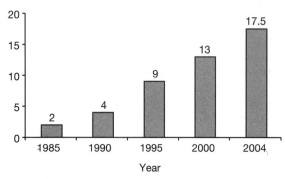

Figure 4.1 Number of home care nurses in Our Lady's Hospice, Dublin

(Department of Health and Children, 1998) led to the development of a clinical career pathway for nurses in the Republic of Ireland. The National Council for Professional Development of Nursing and Midwifery (NCNM) was established to undertake this brief and in 2001 the status of clinical nurse specialist (CNS) was granted to many of those working in home care, in recognition of their substantial experience. Those currently applying for posts on the intermediate pathway must provide evidence of both clinical experience and postgraduate educational qualifications in palliative nursing before being granted clinical nurse specialist status (NCNM, 2001). Not all nurses working in home care are clinical nurse specialists.

Medical support to home care is currently provided at consultant, medical director and registrar level. This is an evolving area as the traditional model of doctors carrying out all first visits and thereafter having only occasional contact with the patient is changing.

> The myriad of issues faced by a patient with a life threatening illness, and a family, who must adapt to illness, and eventual death of one of its members, exceeds the expertise of any one caregiver. The inter-disciplinary team bringing together individuals with a diversity of training, who share the goal of improving the quality of life of the patient, is best equipped to provide a nurturing environment for patients and family.
>
> (Cummings, 1998)

In keeping with the ethos of palliative care, the home care team has evolved into a multi-professional service. Yet another milestone was reached in 2003 when a medical social worker was appointed to each home care team. This has greatly enhanced the multi-professional team's ability to meet the complex needs of patients and their families, thus fulfilling another of the National Advisory Committee on Palliative Care's recommendations (Department of Health and Children, 2001).

The current home care team aims to work with existing community care services to help patients spend as much time as possible at home during their illness. At present the service is available to patients with a cancer diagnosis and those with other specific diseases such as AIDS or motor neurone disease, in south Dublin city and county. The patient's General Practitioner (GP), public health nurse (PHN), hospital team, the patient themselves or their families, may initiate referrals. The GP must give permission for the home care team to be involved, as he/she remains the patient's primary carer in the community.

The home care team currently provides a seven-day service, which operates Monday to Friday between 08.00 hrs and 18.30 hrs, with a limited service at weekends and on public holidays. Outside working hours there is a telephone advisory service for patients under the care of the home care team. Other services available to home care patients include:

- Day hospice
  - physiotherapy
  - occupational therapy
  - chaplaincy
  - nursing
  - palliative care medical clinic
  - complementary and creative arts therapies
- Admission to the palliative care unit

Education

The first dedicated centre for palliative care education was opened at Our Lady's Hospice in 1986. Through the years, team members have participated in both in-house and external education programmes promoting high quality palliative care. In 2001 an education and training co-ordinator was appointed to home care on a part-time basis. The aim of this post was to promote best practice, assist with clinical placements for students and promote and assist nursing staff with audit and research. The role also included the provision of palliative care education to the wider primary health care team.

Challenges

There is a growing body of evidence that the majority of patients would choose to die at home (Karlsen and Addington-Hall, 1998; Wilkinson et al., 1999). A prospective study by Tiernan et al. (2002) based at Our Lady's Hospice found that 81.7 per cent of patients referred to the home care team expressed a preference to be cared for at home during the final stages of their illness. This figure is higher than in studies carried out in the UK. One of the greatest challenges for the home care team is the ever-increasing demand for the service where new patients have increased from 273 annually in 1988 to 595 in 2003 (Figure 4.2). This is influenced by a number of factors, which include

- The growing number of hospital-based palliative care teams and the ongoing development of the oncology services;
- The concept of earlier referral to the palliative services;
- Older age groups tend to be the greatest users of the service with an increasing life expectancy and a growing elderly population has significant implications for the delivery of palliative care services (Department of Health and Children, 2001).

The National Advisory Committee on Palliative Care (Department of

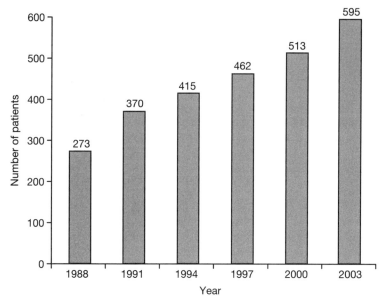

Figure 4.2 Number of patients visited

Health and Children, 2001) recommended that there should be at least one whole-time equivalent (WTE) specialist palliative care nurse per 25,000 population. This would mean a minimum of 24.5 WTE home care nurses on the team compared to 17.5 as it stands. The simple solution to meeting this challenge is to provide more resources in terms of personnel. In the interim, Our Lady's Hospice endeavours to find creative solutions to meet patient needs. This issue is compounded by difficult driving conditions and long travelling times which limit the amount of visits a home care nurse can achieve on a daily basis as identified in a recent review of the Our Lady's Hospice home care service (Hopkins, 2004). However, there are also wider issues regarding staff recruitment to all nursing posts but to home care in particular where experience and qualifications are essential. Living expenses and the ever increasing price of houses in Dublin has resulted in many such nurses choosing to relocate to areas outside the capital.

Traditionally in the Republic of Ireland the majority of palliative care has been provided in the patient's home (Department of Health, 1996). The development of specialist palliative day hospice has resulted in an increasing number of patients receiving multi-professional palliative care on an out-patient basis where appropriate. The relationship between the home care team and day hospice team continues to evolve and develop to the benefit of the patients and their family. Patients who are fit to travel can avail themselves of this service and at a later stage perhaps of the home care service.

Social and demographic changes in recent years have resulted in a smaller pool of available carers at home. Many women work outside the home and for some who have migrated to the city, they have little back up. Support at home produced the strongest influence on place of death (Addington-Hall and McCarthy, 1995). Deficits have been highlighted in relation to domestic and practical help, and lack of information on the resources available outside the health care system (Jones *et al.*, 1993). Studies have also shown that the difficulties of relatives were more often the cause of hospital admission than those of the patient (Wilkes, 1984). Support from nursing (Thorpe, 1993), social services access to specialist equipment and receipt of an attendance allowance all showed statistically significant effects in enabling patients to remain at home (Karlsen and Addington-Hall, 1998). Other Irish studies have highlighted the difficulties for carers in the community. These included emotional difficulties in coping with the terminal illness of their relative, the time needed for caring, problems with night nursing, and ensuing exhaustion and social isolation (Riper, 1995).

The National Advisory Committee on Palliative Care (Department of Health and Children, 2001) recommended that the following supports be put in place to make care at home an easier option, thereby reducing unnecessary hospital admissions (Wiles *et al.*, 1999):

- Access to palliative care advice: palliative care nurses should provide a seven-day service.
- Access to paramedical services in the community: each palliative care unit should develop its own physiotherapy, occupational therapy and social work departments, which should also meet the needs for palliative care patients in the community.
- Aids and appliances in the community: each health board should have a sufficient bank of equipment to meet the needs of palliative care patients in the community.
- Access to medicines in the community.
- Care attendants should be available to support families of patients in the community.
- All patients should have adequate access to respite in a setting of their choice.

It has been acknowledged that palliative care is a 'stressful' area to work in (Vachon, 1995). Many initiatives are in place within the organization to address this issue. Clinical supervision was introduced for home care nurses in 2003 in response to the changing role, the individual nature of the work, as both a method of support and learning and to some extent audit. Harkin-Kirwan (2000) highlights that nurses in high-stress areas with much autonomy and close dealings with confidential issues particularly require clinical supervision. Financial support for the pilot was secured from the NCNM. Following a favourable review of the initiative, it was deemed a valuable asset and continues to be supported by the organization.

Good communication is the cornerstone for delivering palliative care. It requires an appreciable amount of time to keep in close contact with both our primary care colleagues and those who are hospital-based (Department of Health and Children, 2001). Home care as a secondary service depends on gaining information from both the patient's general practitioner (GP) and public health nurse and their hospitals.

Quality

The quest to achieve quality of care continues to challenge the Health Service. The home care team struggles to meet their audit and research remit. While one main objective is to help more patients to die in their place of preference, increasing this number doesn't necessarily equate with high-quality care (Hinton, 1996). In 1996 an external organizational audit was carried out. It was felt that it offered a useful approach to the setting and monitoring of standards relating to the structure of palliative care services. It enabled good practice to be identified and reinforced, and highlighted areas for improvement.

Some other examples of strategies to evaluate our current service are:

Time and motion study of clinical nurse specialists in home care (Ling, 2001)
This time and motion study showed that home care nurses spend more time in administrative tasks and driving than actually seeing patients. Satellite teams geographically based but linked to the hospice would help to change this pattern.

GP satisfaction questionnaire (Tracey, 2003)
In 2003, a questionnaire was sent out to the GPs in the Our Lady's Hospice catchment area (n = 379). This study was designed to assess family doctors' level of understanding and satisfaction with the home care service and also to identify their learning needs in relation to palliative care and estimate the number of non-malignant referrals that might be made. Family doctors generally had a good understanding of the role of palliative care but most responded that they would appreciate further education and training in this area. Family doctors on average estimated that they would refer twice as many patients to the service, if it were offered to people with non-malignant disease. This was recognized in the National Advisory Committee Report (DOHC, 2001) and has implications for future planning of the service.

Audit of the Home Care Out of Hours Service (Hale, 2003)

Prior to 1998 the home care service provide round-the-clock cover; outside normal working hours, a nurse on call gave telephone advice or visited as appropriate. Due to a number of factors it became increasingly difficult to sustain a 24-hour on-call service. In July 1998 the service changed, and domiciliary visits by the team were restricted to between 08.00 hrs and 18.30 hrs, with a telephone advisory service provided by experienced ward staff out of hours. This service was audited in 2003 and the following conclusions were made: Patients, families and the home care teams all agreed that it was beneficial to provide some form of 24-hour service. The study suggests that the majority of problems were easily and rapidly solved during these night calls, restoring the family's sense of security. Since the conclusion of this study we have changed the method of recording out-of-hours calls so that audit can take place on an annual basis, and revised support and training available for ward staff to manage the out-of-hours calls.

Home care review (Hopkins, 2004)

This review was commissioned in order to respond to both local and national initiatives, including the comprehensive *Report of the National Advisory Committee on Palliative Care* (Department of Health and Children, 2001). The aim of the review was to:

• Examine areas of current service provision;
• Highlight local and national policy on palliative care;
• Make recommendations for the continued development and direction of the service in the light of that policy.

This document is one of several strategic initiatives undertaken in the past year by Our Lady's Hospice, which will help shape the future development of the home care service.

Conclusion

There is a growing body of evidence demonstrating that involving home care services increases the likelihood of the patient dying at home (Tiernan *et al.*, 2002). Home care services in the Republic of Ireland have developed at a relatively rapid pace; however, many challenges lie ahead.

References

Addington-Hall, J. and McCarthy, M. (1995) Regional study of care of the dying: methods and sample characteristics, *Palliative Medicine*, 9:27–35.

Cummings, I. (1998) The interdisciplinary team, in D. Doyle, G. Hanks, Ch. 2 The challenge of palliative medicine, in D. Doyle, G. W. Hanks and N. MacDonald, *Oxford Textbook of Palliative Medicine*, 2nd edn. Oxford: Oxford Medical Publications, pp. 19–30.

Department of Health (1996) *Cancer Services in Ireland: A National Strategy.* Dublin: The Stationery Office.

Department of Health and Children (1998) *Report of the Commission on Nursing. A Blueprint for the Future.* Dublin: The Stationery Office.

Department of Health and Children (2001) *Report of the National Advisory Committee on Palliative Care.* Dublin: The Stationery Office.

Hale, A. (2003) Audit of the Home Care Out of Hours Service at Our Lady's Hospice, Harolds Cross. (Unpublished)

Harkin-Kirwan, P. (2000) Unravelling the confusion of clinical supervision, *An Bord Altranais News*, Summer, pp. 3–5.

Hinton, J. (1996) Services given and help perceived during home care for terminal cancer, *Palliative Medicine*, 10:125–34.

Hopkins, K. (2004) Home Care Service Review. Building on the Past to Look to the Future. Our Lady's Hospice, Harolds Cross. (Unpublished)

Jones, R., Hansford, J. and Fiske, J. (1993) Death from cancer at home; the carer's perspective, *British Medical Journal*, 306: 249–51.

Karlsen, S. and Addington-Hall, J. (1998) How do cancer patients who die at home differ from those who die elsewhere? *Palliative Medicine*, 12(4):279–86.

Ling, J. (2001) Palliative Home Care Nurses Time and Motion Study, Our Lady's Hospice, Harolds Cross. (Unpublished)

National Council for the Professional Development of Nursing and Midwifery (2001) *Clinical Nurse/Midwife Specialists: Intermediate Pathway*, Dublin.

Riper, H. (1995) Palliative care in the Mid-Western Region: A Multidisciplinary approach, Mid-Western Health Board, Milford Hospice, University of Limerick. (Unpublished)

Thorpe, G. (1993) Enabling more dying people to remain at home, *BMJ*, 307:93–100.

Tiernan, E., O'Connor, M., O'Síoráin, L. and Kearney, M. (2002) A prospective study of preferred versus actual place of death among patients referred to a palliative care home-care service, *Irish Medical Journal*, September, 95(8):232–5.

Tracey, G. (2003) Primary Carers' Impressions of the Palliative Home Care Service Provided from Our Lady's Hospice, Harolds Cross and Their Education Needs. (Unpublished)

Vachon, M. L. (1995) Staff stress in hospice/palliative care: a review, *Palliative Medicine*, April, 9(2):91–122.

Wiles, R., Payne, S. and Jarnett, N. (1999) Improving palliative care services: a pragmatic model for evaluating services and assessing unmet need, *Palliative Medicine*, 13:131–7.

Wilkes, E. (1984) Dying now, *Lancet*, 28 (1): pp. 950–2.

Wilkinson, E. K., Salisbury, C., Bosanquet, N., Franks, P. J., Kite, S., Lorentzon, M. and Naysmith, A. (1999) Patient and carer preference for, and satisfaction with, specialist models of palliative care: a systematic literature review, *Palliative Medicine*, 13(3):197–216.

5 | Home care in rural Ireland

Eileen O'Leary

Introduction

There are currently up to 150 home care nurses working in the Republic of Ireland and many of these are clinical nurse specialists. Approximately 50 per cent of these nurses work in rural Ireland, a quarter cover both urban and rural with the remaining quarter covering urban alone. Home care in rural Ireland can be traced back to the 1980s. Since this time palliative care services have developed considerably and the *Report of the National Advisory Committee in Palliative Care* (Department of Health and Children, 2001) has assisted in focusing both the statutory and voluntary groups in the further development of specialist palliative care services throughout Ireland.

Development of rural home care services

Following the establishment of the first home care team in Dublin, home care teams developed in Cork in 1986 and in Limerick in 1988. These home care teams provided care to patients who resided in both urban and rural settings. Consequently, home care nurses often travelled many miles daily from their urban base. These teams in Dublin, Cork and Limerick had access to medical support and in-patient care. In 1988 the first rural, nurse-led home care team was established in Kilkenny in the south east of Ireland. This service covered Carlow and Kilkenny with a population of 100,000. In the intervening years services have developed throughout the country.

The *Report of the National Advisory Committee on Palliative Care* noted that palliative care services were established in the Republic of Ireland due largely to the strong and determined efforts of various voluntary organizations. Currently, funding of home care nursing posts in the Irish Republic is complicated. Posts are derived from a combination of statutory funding (Health Board) and voluntary funding (for example, Irish Cancer Society and local voluntary groups). Amounts contributed by each group to each post vary throughout the country.

Home care nurses in rural Ireland may work as part of the multidisciplinary team based in a specialist in-patient unit in an urban site although some are based in local hospitals, local health centres or an independent site in rural Ireland. These nurses may have contact with the specialist palliative care service in their local region. However, there is huge geographical variation in the services provided across Ireland. Many nurses work as part of a team but there are also areas where home care nurses work single-handed serving a large geographical area.

The *Report of the National Advisory Committee on Palliative Care* recommended that all home care teams be based in a specialist palliative care unit. Where this is not possible home care teams should be based in satellite palliative care units. These satellite bases function as an extension of the lead specialist palliative care unit for the region and would have close clinical, educational and administrative links. An example of a satellite home care team was established in September 2003 in Bantry, West Cork. Four clinical nurse specialists in palliative care (home care nurses) now provide a seven-days-a-week service to a population of over 50,000 people in the rural community, community hospital and acute general hospital from this town in West Cork. The team are part of the multi-disciplinary team based at the Specialist Palliative Care Unit in Cork city nearly 60 miles away. This service developed through the collaboration of both the voluntary and statutory sector.

Patient profile in rural Ireland

The population of the Republic of Ireland is almost four million (Central Statistics Office, 2002) of these approximately 40 per cent (one and a half million) reside in rural Ireland. Nearly 13 per cent of this rural population are aged over 65 years of age (see Figure 5.1). Population projections indicate that between 1996 and 2031 the number of people aged 65 years and over is expected to double. The largest increase is expected to be in those aged over 80 years. Currently there are more women than men over 65 years of age, double the number of single men and four times the number of widowed females live in rural as opposed to urban Ireland.

The majority of patients cared for by home care teams have a diagnosis of cancer. The National Cancer Registry Ireland (2002) reported that older people were much more likely to develop cancer, with the risk doubling in

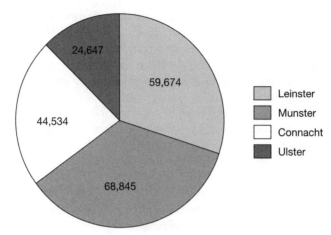

Figure 5.1 Rural population over 65yrs per province

every successive decade of life. Most patients, (60%) were aged over 65 years at the time of diagnosis and the majority (72 per cent) of cancer deaths also occur in those over 65.

The *Report of the National Advisory Committee on Palliative Care* noted that population projections have significant implications for palliative care services as older age groups tend to be the major users of palliative care services. The demand for these services can be expected to rise in parallel with the rising numbers and proportion of this age cohort. Also of significance are the socio-economic and demographic changes such as more women working outside the home and ageing family carers.

The largest rural population in Ireland is located in Munster. Many rural areas of Ireland have low-density populations, in isolated areas with poor transport infrastructure. The palliative care patient's main carer is often an elderly spouse or perhaps a bachelor brother. Many patients live alone with only local neighbours as the main carers. Mobile and ambulant patients provide less of a challenge to home care nurses. However, when the patient's condition deteriorates, it may necessitate admission to the local hospital or, in some situations, the designated specialist in-patient unit in the region. This can result in much distress for the dying patient and their carer.

Role of the rural home care nurse

The role of the home care nurse involves providing specialist nursing advice and support to patients and families in their place of care, that is home, nursing home or community hospital. In the community the home care nurse works with the patient's own general practitioner and public health nurse who continue to be the patient's primary carers. The work of home care nurses does not aim to replace existing services but to compliment them by providing support and advice.

Good communication prevents the team from becoming fragmented and provides a source of emotional support not only to patients but also to health care professionals. This is particularly important for home care nurses working in isolation in rural Ireland.

Support structure for the rural home care nurse

Home care nurses working from a specialist in-patient unit have the support of colleagues on the palliative care team. Each nurse is unique and each person has something different to offer to the team. The team is also there as a resource to discuss problems and options and to assess and evaluate care strategies. Nurses working alone in rural Ireland may lack this support and advice and the facility of keeping things in perspective through coming together, talking, sharing and supporting one another. This facility assists in bringing richness to the team that can only benefit those for whom they care. The nurses support may be derived from her own nursing colleagues in the team if she or he is fortunate enough to have such a network. Alternatively, she may receive her support from the primary care team. When the nurse works alone in home care she has greater responsibility for her actions or interventions.

Infrastructure of rural Ireland

Rural Ireland may be very attractive to relax and visit, particularly when on holidays. While beautiful, the landscape of rural Ireland can also be isolating. Invariably this creates an impact on the home care nurse's daily work. Many miles may have to be travelled to visit one patient. In summer, picturesque scenery attracts many tourists to Ireland, which is great for the economy; however, nurses travelling on these roads are delayed by tour buses viewing the countryside, resulting in longer journey times. Journeys are also hampered by animals such as sheep wandering off the sides of ditches and mountains and making sudden decisions to cross the road.

Access to patients is also particularly difficult in winter. Nurses' journeys may be delayed by frosty roads, floods and in some areas snow. On these occasions wellingtons and rainwear are a must. Patients and families fear that during the bad winter weather neither the primary care team nor home care nurse will be able to visit. This can be a very distressing and worrying time for both the patient and their family or carer.

Off the coast of Ireland there are many islands still inhabited by a dwindling population. Transport to these islands is not for the faint-hearted. Access can be by passenger boat, car-ferry or cable-car. One such cable-car providing access to Dursey Island in West Cork was erected in the 1950s. It is used for all journeys to and from the island for people and farm animals alike. Passenger boats providing access to most islands can take anything up to one hour. In rough weather these are not for the seasick passenger. On arrival at a patient's home the nurse may require agility on her side. On occasion, if access is not possible through opening the gate, climbing may be the only option. This is all in a day's work!

Any challenge experienced by the nurse in travelling to or from the patient's location must also be encountered by the patient and their family or carer. Some patients may live alone and are dependent on neighbours for transport. Families or carers may be without transport and are dependent on the family member working in the local town or city to access the necessary provisions.

First visit

The home care team's first visit provides the challenge of locating the patient's house. Initially directions are received by telephone. Accuracy is everything! When stranded at a four-way crossroad contemplating which to take nurses may soon realize that good listening skills are essential. If lost, home care nurses can often rely on the local population to provide directions. However, this information often comes at a price, since locals go to great lengths to determine the identity of the nurse and the reason for visiting which can cause difficulty in terms of patient confidentiality and anonymity. On arrival at the patient's house many home care nurses working in the rural setting are reluctant to leave the car as they are greeted by a 'friendly' dog. Many patients' charts carry a warning 'Beware of dog'! On assessment, further issues may come to light such as the fact that some patients living in rural Ireland have no running water, often having lived this way for many years. Obviously the nurse has to be non-judgemental and consider the alternatives for accessing and heating running water.

During this first visit the patient or family gives an account of their illness to date. This usually includes details of travelling to the nearest specialist oncology centre for treatment. As these are located in the largest cities around Ireland, rural patients describe the difficulties they have experienced in getting to the oncology centre. These often include busy roundabouts and different lanes of traffic to traverse. This can prove extremely traumatic for the elderly carer driving.

Communicating with patients

Davies and Oberle (1990) described the supportive role of the nurse in palliative care. One such dimension was identified as making the connection. This is described as getting to know another in a much deeper sense. Furthermore it identified as spending time with the other, finding a common bond and establishing rapport. The home care nurse needs to be a skilful communicator and receptive to what the patient's and family/carer's needs are. Connecting with patients includes knowledge of what is important to the patient and this may require home care nurses working in rural Ireland to be knowledgeable in local sporting interests such as Gaelic games, thus demonstrating interest in the patient and the community. Depending on the base of the rural home care nurse, she may be required to communicate through the Irish language. The Irish language may also be used to greet and welcome the nurse on her arrival. While many home care nurses would be able to communicate through Irish, the population of rural Ireland is changing. Many inhabitants are non-nationals such as Europeans with origins in Germany and Holland who have moved to particular areas in rural Ireland. However, some of these people speak little English. On occasions an interpreter is required.

Access to medication

Patients living in rural Ireland have some difficulty in accessing medications. In some cases the pharmacist may not have the prescribed medication in stock and delivery from the distributor to the pharmacist may take up to 48 hours. Once the drugs have arrived at the pharmacy, a family member or carer has to arrange collection of the drugs. Some drugs require specific documentation from the Department of Health and Children before they can be distributed to the pharmacist (for example, Methadone). All lead to undue stress for the patient, family and carers.

A must for every home care nurse working in rural Ireland is a sense of humour!

Conclusion

Working in rural Ireland presents the home care nurse with many challenges. Working in this environment, home care nurses lack the level of support and advice from the specialist palliative care team to which her colleagues in the urban setting have access. This position can be very isolating; however, it also provides opportunities and challenges and results in much job satisfaction.

References

Central Statistics Office (2002) *Census 2002 – Ages and Marital Status, Volume 2.* Cork: Central Statistics Office.

Davies, B. and Oberle, K. (1990) Dimensions of the supportive role of the nurse in palliative care, *Oncology Nursing Forum,* 17(1):87–94.

Department of Health and Children (2001) *Report of the National Advisory Committee on Palliative Care.* Dublin: The Stationery Office.

National Cancer Registry Ireland (2002) *Cancer in Ireland 1994–2002: Incidence, Mortality, Treatment and Survival.* Cork: National Cancer Registry.

In-patient palliative care units

Regina McQuillan

Introduction

The tradition of caring for the dying in special, set-aside in-patient units started in Ireland in Cork with the founding of St Patrick's Hospital for the care of patients with cancer in 1870 and in Dublin in Our Lady's Hospice in Harold's Cross in 1879 (McCarthy, 2004). Both were set up by the Congregation of the Religious Sisters of Charity (known as the Sisters of Charity or the Irish Sisters of Charity). Over the next one hundred years, these were the two in-patient facilities in Ireland. They cared principally for patients with tuberculosis, which was widespread in Ireland. By the 1950s, more effective TB treatment was available and fatalities reduced. The hospice cared for frail elderly with chronic illnesses.

Cancer prevalence increased in the 1960s with a rise in demand for care of these patients. In 1979, two wards (44 beds) in Our Lady's Hospice were designated for care of patients with advanced cancer. The first specially designed palliative care unit in the Republic of Ireland was opened at the hospice in 1993. In 2004, Our Lady's Hospice opened a second, 12-bedded, specialist palliative care unit in Blackrock, Co. Dublin. Our Lady's Hospice cared for patients with cancer and motor neurone disease, and in response to the developing AIDS crisis, extended care to AIDS patients in the 1990s.

Marymount Hospice, the dedicated specialist palliative care unit in Cork, was established on the middle floor of St Patrick's Hospital in 1984. A consultant in palliative medicine was appointed in 1991. Plans for a new purpose built 44-bedded specialist palliative care unit in Cork are now at an advanced stage.

In the 1970s an in-patient hospice service was developed by the Little Company of Mary in Limerick, in a nine-bedded unit attached to Milford

House, an existing nursing home (Mid-Western Health Board, Milford Hospice, Irish Cancer Society, 1991). In 1983 a purpose-built 20-bedded unit was opened. Milford Hospice from its inception, although principally for patients with cancer, also cared for patients with other illnesses. In 1999, a new palliative care unit was opened with a capacity for 30 beds. The first consultant in palliative medicine was appointed in January 2000.

The 1980s and 1990s saw further development of palliative care services driven in part by the growing voluntary hospice movement. In 1989, St Francis Hospice was founded in Raheny on the north side of Dublin. This was the result of collaboration between the Daughters of Charity of St Vincent de Paul (a religious community, sometimes referred to in Ireland as the French Sisters of Charity) and the Irish Hospice Foundation. A home care team was established in 1989, followed by a day care service in 1993 and an in-patient unit in 1995. The 19-bedded in-patient unit set new design standards for a specialist palliative care unit in Ireland. An important part of this plan was early and close involvement with the state agencies, at that time the Eastern Health Board, to ensure as much co-operation and revenue funding as possible.

The Letterkenny Hospice, an eight-bedded unit, serving part of the north west of the country, opened in 2003. This operates under a partnership arrangement between the North Western Health Board and the Donegal Hospice, a voluntary hospice group. A palliative medicine consultant was appointed in 2002.

The Galway Hospice Foundation followed a similar pattern to St Francis Hospice establishing a home care service, followed by a day care service and then an in-patient unit. The in-patient unit opened in 1997. A palliative medicine consultant was appointed in 2000. Despite some significant difficulties in relation to concerns about medication management all services at Galway Hospice are now in operation (Galway Hospice Foundation, 2004).

These units offer specialist palliative care, are consultant-led and staffed by health care professionals with additional specialist palliative care skills. Other in-patient hospice services exist but do not currently meet criteria defining a specialist palliative care unit (Department of Health and Children, 2001).

The North West Hospice was founded in 1986 and developed a home care service in 1989 (North West Hospice, 2004). An eight-bedded unit was opened in 1998 adjacent to Sligo General Hospital. This was the first and is currently the only unit located on the same site as an acute hospital, benefiting from closer integration with acute services. Patients admitted here are under the care of medical officers, not a palliative medicine consultant. The North West Hospice, in conjunction with the North Western Health Board, plans to appoint a second consultant for the region enabling full development of a specialist palliative care service.

St Brigid's Hospice, a six-bedded unit in the Drogheda Memorial Hospital in County Kildare admits patients with terminal illness, mainly cancer. There are plans to develop this unit with the appointment of specialist palliative care staff.

St Christopher's Hospice in Cavan was built by a charitable organization. Although the charity hoped this would be a hospice unit, no agreement was made between the charity and the North Eastern Health Board to provide revenue funding. A service agreement allowed the opening of seven beds in 1998 – five beds for patients with sensory/motor disabilities and two as general palliative care beds. It is hoped to open the remaining six beds by the end of 2004 with a total of three general palliative care beds.

Specialist in-patient palliative care units are expensive to build and to run, involving high staff costs and high staff-to-patient ratios. Not all patients either need or wish to be admitted and research suggests most patients indicate a preference for care at home (Tiernan *et al.*, 2002). However, for difficult and complex cases, the specialist environment is absolutely necessary and the skill mix and holistic care cannot be replicated in any other setting. These units also serve as essential training environments for staff. The *Report of the National Advisory Committee on Palliative Care* (Department of Health and Children, 2001) makes clear recommendations for the development of specialist palliative care units in all health board regions. Design guidelines for specialist palliative care settings have been developed and aim to ensure that patients and families enjoy a high standard of accommodation and comfort (Department of Health and Children, 2004). Currently there are no in-patient palliative care units in three health board areas (north east, midland and south east).

Conclusion

There is increasing demand for in-patient specialist palliative care beds. As the population ages and palliative care extends its services to meet the needs of patients with diseases other than cancer, increasingly demand will outstrip supply. It is essential that existing specialist units increase bed capacity and develop satellite facilities where necessary to meet the needs of patients and families in the future.

It is also desirable that units, which currently practice general palliative care, for example the North West Hospice, should also develop as specialist palliative care services with the appointment of appropriate specialist staff and development of facilities. Further developments of these units demands appropriate partnerships between the voluntary bodies who founded them, and statutory services. Clear management and organizational structures with administrative and clinical governance is essential to ensure excellent specialist palliative care, good use of resources and protection of the ethos of voluntary agencies.

Further opportunity to develop both in staff education and training is necessary. Academic palliative care with an emphasis on postgraduate and undergraduate education is essential. The development of palliative care will be influenced by government policies, including, for example, the Health Service Reform Programme, the current embargo on recruiting additional public service employees and the National Cancer Strategy (Dept of Health, 1996).

There is a need to address the issue of inequities in funding. Historically in the Republic of Ireland, the Catholic religious orders and the voluntary hospice sector have been the main drivers and funders of specialist palliative care services. This is gradually changing as the state recognizes the importance of palliative care and begins to share in its responsibility to ensure that all its citizens will be able to avail themselves of these services when and if they need them.

References

Department of Health and Children (2001) *Report of the National Advisory Committee on Palliative Care*. Dublin: Stationery Office.

Department of Health and Children (2004) *Design Guidelines for Specialist Palliative Care Settings*. Dublin: Stationery Office (in press).

Galway Hospice Foundation (2004) *Review of Medication Management Practices at Galway Hospice by an Independent Expert Review Group*. Galway Hospice, Ireland.

McCarthy, Kieran (2004), *A Dream Unfolding: A Portrait of St. Patrick's Hospital and Marymount Hospice*. St. Patrick's Hospital/Marymount Hospice.

Mid-Western Health Board, Milford Hospice, Irish Cancer Society (1991) Report of Working Party on Hospice Care.

North West Hospice (2004) http://www.iol.ie/nwhospice

Tiernan, E., O'Connor, M., O'Síoráin, L. and Kearney, M. (2002) A prospective study of preferred versus actual place of death among patients referred to a palliative care home-care service, *Irish Medical Journal*, 95(8):232–5.

7 Hospital-based palliative care teams

Anna-Marie Lynch

Introduction

Over 60 per cent of deaths in the Irish Republic take place in hospitals or institutions (Keegan *et al.*, 1999). It is estimated that 7500 cancer related deaths occur each year (National Cancer Registry, 2003) and this accounts for over 20 per cent of the total number of deaths in the Irish Republic (Central Statistics Office, 2003). In the UK it is reported that over 90 per cent of cancer patients are admitted to hospital at some stage during the last year of their life (Addington-Hall and McCarthy, 1995) and there is no evidence to suggest that the situation is any different in Ireland. The importance of providing specialist palliative care in acute hospitals cannot be underestimated.

Hospital-based palliative care teams

The Irish Sisters of Charity were influential in establishing the first hospital-based palliative care team, when in 1989 St Vincent's University Hospital and Our Lady's Hospice, Dublin appointed a consultant in palliative medicine. The aim was to make specialist palliative care available to patients dying in the hospital. In 1991, initially with the help of funding from the Irish Cancer Society, the first palliative care nurse post was sanctioned in the hospital. This was followed in 1993 by the appointment of a palliative care nurse to St Vincent's Private Hospital.

The appointment of a palliative care consultant between Marymount Hospice and Cork University Hospital, and the subsequent appointment of a palliative care nurse in 1995 led to the establishment of the first hospital-based team outside Dublin. Also in 1995 the Irish Hospice Foundation became involved in the funding of hospital palliative care posts, when they seed-funded the salaries of two palliative care nurses in St James's Hospital, Dublin. The Foundation went on to fund a second nurse post in St Vincent's University Hospital, as well as nurses in Beaumont Hospital, Dublin, St Luke's Hospital (The National Radiotherapy Centre of Ireland) and a second post in Cork. Funding from the Foundation was provided to 'pump-prime' posts for the first two years after which time funding was taken over by the hospital or health board.

The majority of patients dying from cancer are admitted to hospital in the last year of life. Many of these patients and others with active progressive non-malignant disease benefit from the advice and support of specialist palliative care services. Specialist palliative care services in acute general hospitals are at an early stage of development in Ireland. A number of hospitals have consultant-led teams while others develop links with local palliative care units and home care services.

The publication of the *Report of the National Advisory Committee on Palliative Care* (Department of Health and Children, 2001) led to an increase in the number of hospital-based teams throughout the country. Currently there are 28 teams in the Republic of Ireland, including one in a paediatric hospital. There are a number of variations in the structure of these teams.

The well-established multi-disciplinary palliative care teams are usually consultant-led. Consultants are often employed on a sessional basis between hospital and the local palliative care unit. These teams consist of at least one nurse specialist, a social worker, a registrar in palliative medicine and a secretary. In other hospitals, for example in the smaller hospitals in the Mid-Western Health Board, the service is provided by a nurse specialist, who meets regularly with the consultant in the region to discuss the patient caseload. In the Midland Health Board, where there is no consultant, the local community-based nurse specialists provide a service to the hospitals when requested. In more rural areas, such as Bantry Hospital, West Cork, which has less than 100 beds, one of the local community palliative care nurses rotates into the hospital every six months. In hospitals where there is no palliative care team, advice and support for patients with advanced cancer is sometimes provided by an oncology nurse specialist or a cancer nurse co-ordinator.

Development of the hospital-based team

Hospital-based palliative care teams should consider joint out-patient clinics as part of their development in acute general hospitals. Joint clinics allow the specialist palliative care team to become involved in patient care at an early stage in the disease process. There is also scope to develop combined rounds, particularly involving specialist palliative care teams, oncology (medical and radiation), surgical oncology and pain/anaesthetic services. More recently, developments in interventional radiology have contributed enormously to the range of palliative treatments on offer. One such example is the use of imaging in the performance of pleural aspiration or paracentesis. Increasingly, the use of stenting techniques to relieve obstruction of the oesophagus, colon, biliary tree or renal tract has also contributed enormously to patient care. The important principle is that palliative care patients should have ready access to all interventions and treatments offering an enhanced level of care and comfort, with a view to improving overall quality of life.

The work of the hospital-based palliative care team

Irrespective of the structure of the team, the aim is always to improve the care of patients with advanced disease. The model of hospital palliative care used throughout the country is based on that pioneered by Dunlop and Hockley in St Bartholomew's Hospital in London in the late 1980s (Dunlop and Hockley, 1998). The team does not take over the care of patients who need specialist palliative care, rather they act in an advisory and supportive capacity. The patient remains under the care of the referring team. When referred to the palliative care service, an assessment is undertaken by one of the team and on the basis of this advice is given to the referrer. The frequency of reassessment depends upon the patient's condition and the initial reason for referral. Common reasons for referral to the team are for advice on control of pain and other distressing symptoms; for providing additional support to the patient and their family; and to assist with planning the patient's discharge to home or hospice as appropriate.

Patients are referred at different stages of their disease trajectory. Some patients present with advanced disease and need specialist palliative care at time of diagnosis. Other patients with known advanced disease are admitted to hospital from home if families are unable to cope or if there is an unexpected event at home. Such patients would otherwise be admitted to the local palliative care unit when beds are available. Patients are sometimes referred while undergoing or awaiting active treatment or investigations. This usually occurs if they have distressing symptoms and the palliative care team may withdraw from their care once symptoms have resolved.

Patients with non-malignant disease

The majority of patients referred to hospital-based teams have cancer; however, most teams accept referral of patients irrespective of their diagnosis.

Patients with end stage respiratory, cardiac, renal and neurological conditions are often referred, depending on the speciality services provided by the hospital. Patients with non-malignant conditions are often referred for advice the first time when they are in the terminal phase of their disease. However, once palliative care teams become established and referring teams see the benefit of their involvement, patients may be referred earlier. The team at St Vincent's University Hospital were initially referred patients with cystic fibrosis for advice and support in the terminal phase of their illness. Gradually the pattern of referral changed to include patients with difficult symptom control problems earlier in their illness, and for some patients while awaiting heart and lung transplant (Lynch, 2000). This change in pattern of referrals is similar for cancer patients when a new team is being established (Ling, 2000).

Hospital-based palliative care team involvement in education and research

Hospital teams are often the first point of contact the patient and family have with specialist palliative care services. This can cause anxiety for the referring team who may be concerned that the introduction of palliative care will cause the patient distress. In some instances the referring team have concerns about handing over care to another team. This is especially true when they have been caring for the patient over an extended time period. This issue usually resolves as teams become established in hospitals, through constant communication between the teams and through education.

Educating hospital staff and providing the knowledge and skills to care for patients with advanced disease is the central tenet of most hospital-based teams. The rationale behind recommendations for a change in the patient's management is always explained to the staff caring for the patient. The fact that the team do not take over the care of the patient or make changes to the patient's prescription ensures that there is constant opportunity for teaching junior medical and nursing staff at ward level. In addition to informal teaching, the team are also involved in teaching at a more formal level including teaching medical students, non-consultant hospital doctors and nurse education (both pre- and post-registration). A study by Tiernan *et al.* (2001) measured the effectiveness of a teaching programme for junior hospital doctors in terms of changes in their knowledge of palliative care. Nevertheless, the impact of such teaching on the care of patients is extremely difficult to quantify.

Education in all formats includes the dissemination of research or evidence-based palliative care knowledge. It is therefore vital that all members of the palliative care team have the opportunity to participate in continuing education and professional development. National and international palliative care seminars and conferences provide a useful means of keeping up to date with current knowledge. However, the increasing availability of research-based material on the World-Wide-Web and access to computerized palliative care databases has made it easier for all members of the team to keep up to date with best international practice.

In addition to disseminating palliative care research, the hospital-based team has a role in conducting research. Many teams are still in their infancy and conducting research is thus part of their future plans rather than a current reality. However, the increasing number of nurse specialists participating in education to masters' level and the structured training for specialist registrars, means that more hospital-based research is likely to be undertaken in the future. Conducting research in the hospital setting lends itself well to multi-centre research because of the similarities between hospital teams throughout the country. It also provides a useful means of building close working relationships with other teams and departments when joint research can be undertaken.

The current emphasis on quality assurance and value for money in health care means that there is an increased need for hospital-based teams to demonstrate their effectiveness in improving the care of palliative care patients in hospitals. It is, however, very difficult to measure effectiveness, when the team is advising that an intervention or change in management takes place rather than making the change itself. Also it is often the case that more than one team is involved in the patient's care. Some teams try to demonstrate their effectiveness by auditing the management of a particular symptom or prescribing practice in the hospital. Examples of such audits include an evaluation of the management of constipation in cancer patients (Ling, 2000) or a one-day snapshot of control of cancer pain (Bogan and Cunningham, 2003). There are a number of validated audit tools available which aim to measure the effectiveness of the hospital-based teams and are described in detail elsewhere (Higginson *et al.*, 2002, 2003).

Conclusion

Like all aspects of specialist palliative care in Ireland at the moment, hospital-based palliative care is in a state of rapid change. Implementation of the recommendations of the *Report of the National Advisory Committee on Palliative Care* has been slower in some health board areas than in others. When the recommendations are fully implemented, a multi-disciplinary palliative care service will be available to all hospital patients irrespective of geographical location.

References

Addington-Hall, J. and McCarthy, M. (1995) Dying from cancer: results of a national population-based investigation, *Palliative Medicine*, 9(4):295–305.

Bogan, K. and Cunningham, J. (2003) *An Audit of Cancer Pain Management in an Acute Hospital*. Poster Presentation at the Research & Education Seminar of the Irish Association of Palliative Care, Dublin.

Central Statistics Office (2003) *Vital Statistics* Annual Report, www.cso.ie/publications/northsouth/health

Department of Health and Children (2001) *Report of the National Advisory Committee on Palliative Care*. Dublin: Stationery Office.

Dunlop, R. and Hockley, J. (1998) *Hospital-Based Palliative Care Teams. The Hospital-Hospice Interface*. Oxford: Oxford Medical Publications.

Higginson, I., Finlay, I., Goodwin, D., *et al.* (2002) Do hospital-based palliative care teams improve care for patients or families at the end of life?, *Journal of Pain and Symptom Management*, 23(2):96–106.

Higginson, I., Finlay, I., Goodwin, D., *et al.* (2003) Is there evidence that palliative care teams alter end of life experiences of patients and their caregivers?, *Journal of Pain and Symptom Management*, 25(2):150–68.

Keegan, O., McGee, H., Brady, T., *et al.* (1999) *Care for the Dying – Experiences and Challenges. A study of quality of health service care during the last year of life of patients at St. James' Hospital Dublin, from their relatives' perspective*. Royal College of Surgeons in Ireland, Health Services Research Centre.

Ling, J. (2000) The incidence and management of constipation in a cancer hospital. Poster presentation – Seventh congress of the European Association of Palliative Care, Palermo, Sicily.

Ling, J. (2000) Audit in practice: the referral of dying patients to palliative care, *International Journal of Palliative Nursing*, 6(8):375–9.

Lynch, A. M. (2000) The role of the specialist palliative care team in the care of patients with cystic fibrosis, presentation at the First International Conference on Palliative Care, 'Bas Solais – death with illumination', Dublin.

National Cancer Registry (2003) *Cancer in Ireland 1994–2002, Incidence, Mortality, Treatment and Survival*. Cork.

Tiernan, E., Kearney, M., Lynch, A. M., *et al.* (2001) Effectiveness of a teaching programme in pain and symptom management for junior house officers, *Supportive Care in Cancer*, 9:606–10.

8 Palliative care for children in the Irish Republic

Maeve O'Reilly

Introduction

In the Republic of Ireland every year over six hundred young people on average die before they reach the age of eighteen. Accidents remain the leading cause of death; however, between 1996 and 2001 an average of 525 children died each year as a result of a life-limiting illness. A considerably larger and as yet unquantified number of children are living with such diseases. These illnesses range from the immediately life-threatening, such as major organ failure, to conditions such as severe cerebral palsy, where the underlying condition is non-progressive but where premature death is likely although unpredictable.

Children with such illnesses have ongoing complex needs, which place a considerable burden, practically, financially and emotionally on their families and carers. Care of these children and their families also puts significant pressure on what are often quite limited community resources. There has been much published on the specific and often overlooked needs of children with life-limiting illness and several needs assessments have been conducted in the UK.

In Ireland it is generally felt that services for these children are inadequate in many areas. The *Report of the National Advisory Committee on Palliative Care* (Department of Health and Children, 2001) identified these children as a specific group who warranted a separate study. As a result, a national paediatric palliative care needs assessment commenced in 2002, co-funded by the Department of Health and Children and the Irish Hospice Foundation. The results of this assessment are due to be released in late 2004 and are expected to inform future planning of services.

Definitions

The sub-specialty of paediatric palliative care has emerged in recent years in response to the awareness of the distinct needs of this particular group of patients. Paediatric palliative care is defined as 'an active and total approach to care, embracing physical, emotional, social and spiritual elements. It focuses on enhancement of quality of life for the child and support for the family and includes the management of distressing symptoms, provision of respite and care through death and bereavement' (World Health Organization, 1990). It is provided for children for whom curative treatment is no longer the main focus of care. Unlike palliative care required by the majority of adults paediatric palliative care may extend over many years.

The Association for Children with Life-threatening or Terminal Conditions and their Families (ACT) and The Royal College of Paediatrics and Child Health (RCPCH) (2003) in the United Kingdom have identified four groups of children who are likely to have palliative care needs at some point in their illness (see Table 8.1).

Table 8.1 Categories of life-limiting conditions

Group 1	Life-threatening conditions for which curative treatments may be feasible but can fail. Where access to palliative care services may be necessary when treatment fails, e.g. cancer, irreversible organ failure
Group 2	Conditions where premature death is inevitable, where there may be long periods of intensive treatment aimed at prolonging life and allowing participation in normal activities, e.g. cystic fibrosis
Group 3	Progressive conditions without curative treatment options, where treatment is exclusively palliative and may commonly extend over many years, e.g. Batten disease, muscular dystrophy
Group 4	Irreversible but non-progressive conditions causing severe disability leading to susceptibility to health complications and likelihood of premature death, e.g. severe cerebral palsy, spinal cord insult

The identification of these four groups of children serves as a useful guide in identifying which children may have palliative care needs at different points of their illness. Clearly not all children will need active palliative care throughout their entire illness trajectory. It is suggested, however, that the above categorization is useful for service planning and needs assessment.

In the Republic of Ireland there are three tertiary referral paediatric hospitals. Care of children with serious illness is often shared with regional hospitals nationwide. Unlike the United Kingdom (UK) there are only a limited number of community paediatricians and community paediatric nurses in Ireland. Most of the day-to-day care of children in the community is the responsibility of the primary care team with support from voluntary bodies and in some cases from adult palliative care services.

The child with cancer

Over the past three decades there have been significant scientific and techno-logical advances in the treatment of childhood cancer. These have resulted in an improvement in overall survival rates from 10 per cent to 75–80 per cent. Cancer remains, however, the leading cause of non-accidental death in childhood and unfortunately now one in four children suffering from cancer will eventually die from their disease. In the Republic of Ireland each year approximately 170 children are diagnosed with a malignancy and each year approximately 30 children die with cancer. Unlike many other countries the vast majority of these children die at home in keeping with the wishes of their families.

The main centre for treatment of childhood cancer in the Irish Republic is Our Lady's Hospital, Dublin (known locally as 'Crumlin') where children are cared for during their illness by a team who share care with local paediatric units and primary care teams. Unfortunately for some of these children a point is reached where their disease is found to be incurable. Following discussion with the parents, and where appropriate, the child care is transferred to local palliative care services. Usually at the point of transition a multi-disciplinary team meeting is organized by the child's oncology liaison nurse. This is attended by all involved in the child's future care and includes GP, public health nurse, local adult palliative care team, social worker, teacher and others. A care plan is developed for each child according to their individual need and circumstances. Most decisions regarding treatment from this point on are the responsibility of the GP and the local palliative care team with the hospital-based team adopting an advisory role as necessary.

While the majority of children die at home, some die in hospital. On rare occasions neither is felt to be an option and some in-patient palliative care units in the country will offer to admit children, despite being adult services. When the child dies, bereavement support is offered by the local palliative care teams and parents are also invited to bereavement days held in the paediatric hospital.

The child with non-malignant disease

Children with non-malignant disease comprise a diverse group of illnesses (Table 8.2). These diseases result in a limited prognosis with very few children surviving past the age of eighteen years.

Children with life-limiting disease are not seen as a distinct group and as such there is no database currently in existence for collecting information. Currently, care of these children poses a significant burden on carers in the family and on health care professionals in the community. There are,

Table 8.2 Life-limiting conditions affecting children

- Metabolic conditions (e.g. mucopolysaccharidoses)
- Diseases of the blood and blood-forming organs (e.g. thalassaemia major)
- Diseases of the nervous system (e.g. severe cerebral palsy, spinal muscular atrophy)
- Diseases of the cardiovascular system (e.g. inoperable congenital anomalies of the heart)
- Diseases of the respiratory system (e.g. cystic fibrosis)
- Diseases of the digestive system (e.g. chronic liver failure)
- Diseases of the genitourinary system (e.g. chronic renal failure)
- Congenital anomalies
- Chromosomal disorders
- Malignant disease
- Non-malignant brain tumours
- Diseases of the immune system e.g. HIV

however, many voluntary organizations in existence in this country pro-viding various forms of support to families. Some examples are listed in Table 8.3.

The type of support offered by these organizations varies from counselling and support and financial assistance to practical nursing help. Some centres such as Sunshine Home will offer respite to certain categories of children as well as long-term residential care. The Jack and Jill Foundation provide support from specialist nurses and financial support in order to provide carers, giving respite to parents. All of these organizations are invaluable in enabling parents to care for their child in the community.

Table 8.3 Voluntary organizations providing support for children with life-limiting conditions

- A Nurse for Daniel
- Barnardos
- Barretstown Gang Camp
- CanTeen Ireland
- Central Remedial Clinic
- Down Syndrome Ireland
- Irish Cancer Society
- Irish Hospice Foundation
- Irish Society for Inherited Metabolic Disorders
- Irish Stillbirth and Neonatal Death Society
- Sunshine Home
- Suzanne House
- The Jack and Jill Foundation

Needs of children and families

Research has been conducted in the UK regarding the special needs of families caring for seriously ill children and the difficulties they experience. The needs have been described in the ACT document (2003) and can be broadly summarized as follows:

1. A need to have a community-based team to provide care according to an individual care plan. This would involve the identification of a key worker whose responsibility would be to co-ordinate the plan and modify according to the child's changing needs.
2. Effective symptom control at all times to maximize the child's quality of life. This includes attention to psychological and spiritual distress.
3. Psychological, social and spiritual support for the family. One of the main burdens for families is psychological distress often associated with social isolation and there is a great need for support and guidance.
4. Assistance with practical and financial concerns is essential given the extra cost involved in caring for children with significant illness.
5. Short-term breaks are essential for parents when the care continues over many months or years. Chronic tiredness greatly affects parents' health, relationships, family life and general ability to cope.
6. Care at the time of death and into bereavement.

The needs of every child and family are different and likely to change over time. It is generally felt that to best address these needs a spectrum of services is required. This would involve the creation of a co-ordinated, locally-based children's palliative care service led by a paediatrician or children's hospice doctor or senior professional with a special interest. The team should be multi-disciplinary to cover all needs (medical, nursing, physiotherapy, occupational therapy, dieticians, psychology, etc.) and should also have access to respite care. Twenty-four-hour nursing care should be available to families in the terminal phase of the illness regardless of diagnosis. Bereavement support should also be provided as necessary.

Current challenges for paediatric palliative care

Many challenges lie ahead for the development of paediatric palliative care services in the Republic of Ireland. These will be addressed by the forthcoming Irish needs assessment. One difficulty is that children in the terminal phase of their illness are often, out of necessity, cared for by doctors and nurses trained in adult care. To date there is no paediatrician in the country who is trained in palliative medicine. Currently there is only one adult palliative care physician who has been assigned specific paediatric sessions. Many of the principles that underpin good adult palliative care are common to both adults and children, in particular the emphasis on symptom control, good communication and family support. Children are, however, not just 'mini-adults' and adult-trained caregivers may lack the expertise to deal with the unique medical and psycho-social needs of children.

Another difficulty is insufficient support for children with non-malignant disease, particularly in the terminal phase of their illness. There is heavy reliance upon voluntary organizations in this setting for the provision of much needed support. Children with non-malignant disease often don't have the same access to adult palliative care services as children with cancer. There are inadequate respite facilities available to parents. Respite care availability often depends on diagnosis and where the child lives. Training in the whole area of paediatric palliative care is underdeveloped although this is improving. Finally there is no mechanism for the collation of data on such children, such as a database, which would greatly facilitate service planning and delivery.

Conclusion: Summary of paediatric palliative care

The death of a child remains one of the greatest tragedies to affect a family. Many of our hopes and expectations are linked to the health and the normal development of our children. For parents to hear that this is not possible is a devastating blow. Parents need constant support from the point of diagnosis through their child's protracted illness, death and ultimately into bereavement.

There is a need for more co-ordinated community-based services to facilitate parents in their desire to keep their child at home. It is hoped that the forthcoming needs assessment will help in identifying where the greatest need lies and guide the development of a quality, national, co-ordinated equitable service for children with life-limiting conditions and for their families.

References

Association for Children with Life-threatening or terminal conditions and their families and The Royal College of Paediatrics and Child Care (ACT and RCPCH) (2003) *A Guide to the Development of Children's Palliative Care Services*. Bristol (2nd edn).

Department of Health and Children (2001) *Report of the National Advisory Committee on Palliative Care*. Dublin: Stationery Office.

World Health Organization (1990) Cancer pain relief and palliative care: Report of a WHO Expert Committee. Geneva.

9 Day hospice as an integrated model of care

Jacqueline Holmes and Geraldine Tracey

Introduction

The National Advisory Committee on Palliative Care (Department of Health and Children, 2001) recognized the importance of providing palliative day care to patients. The development of palliative day care promotes the provision of community care, responding to patients and relatives choice for care at home and 'forming a vital link between primary and secondary care' (Spencer and Daniels, 1998).

The function of specialist palliative day care as defined by the National Council for Hospice and Specialist Palliative Care Services (1999) is to enhance the 'independence and quality of life of patients through rehabilitation, occupational therapy and physiotherapy, the management and monitoring of symptoms and the provision of psychological support. It is set in the context of social interaction, mutual support and friendship and may provide some physical care and respite to home carers.'

In Ireland, different models have evolved from social day care to more therapy based day hospice. This chapter will present data on the existing services and will examine in detail how one service has evolved from a social model into a more therapeutic model. The implications of extending this therapeutic model with an expanded health care team, to patients in their own homes, will also be examined.

The development of palliative day care

Myers and Hearn (2001) have suggested that hospice and palliative day care provision are the most rapidly expanding components of palliative care in the United Kingdom. In 1980, St Christopher's Hospice Information Service recorded eleven day care services and by 2004, 294 day care services were recorded on the website directory (Hospice Information, 2004).

The first purpose-built palliative day care centre was opened at St Luke's Hospice in Sheffield in England in 1975 (Myers and Hearn, 2001a). The general principle behind the establishment of the day care service at St Luke's Hospice was to provide a day out for the terminally ill patient and a day off for their carer. The specific aims of the service were to maintain contact with and provide support for patients discharged from in-patient units. The service also aimed to build up relationships with new patients and support them throughout the progression of their disease and to help them to feel at ease if and when they came to be admitted to an in-patient unit (Cockburn, 1982).

Palliative day care services in the Republic of Ireland

Our Lady's Hospice, Dublin, set up the first palliative day care service in the Republic of Ireland in 1993, and by 2001 five such services, all attached to in-patient units were recorded in the directory of the Irish Association for Palliative Care (IAPC, 2001).

The five services cater for between eight and sixteen patients from two to five days per week. The model of care differs in each unit (unstructured, holistic, social/medical, therapeutic). While all these services are managed by a registered nurse, access to other members of the multi-disciplinary team members in these services varies. Some units do not offer the services of a physiotherapist, occupational therapist, social worker, or complementary therapist, nor do some have access to a secretary. The availability of the various disciplines, including medical cover, is also variable, ranging from a few hours per week to full-time. Chaplaincy support and volunteers are available in all units.

Development of palliative day care service at
Our Lady's Hospice

The first palliative day care team consisted of two nurses, two care assistants, an aromatherapist, physiotherapist, occupational therapist and a secretary and had the services of a medical doctor, social worker, a chaplain and volunteers. The service operated a social model of care with some therapeutic input.

Between 1996 and 1998, the service expanded from one to three days per week and by 1998, a medical out-patient service had been established (O'Síoráin, 1998). In September 2000 a new multi-disciplinary out-patient

Day-care Attendance	1997	1998	1999	2000	2001	2002
	2 d/w	*3 d/w*	*3 d/w*	*3 d/w*	*3 d/w*	*3 d/w*
Number of patients on weekly attendance list	34	40	33	42	42	42
Total number of referrals	96	100	87	89	130	127
Number of patients who attended (ex-register)	59	49	59	50	63	74
Total attendances	1092	1389	1309	1371	1404	1356
Out-patient attendances	851	1102	1080	1211	1288	1211

Figure 9.1 Number of patients attending day care (1997–2002)

service was set up (Kearney, 2000). This comprised of physiotherapy, occupational therapy and complementary and creative arts therapies.

A review of all referral and admission data to Our Lady's Hospice at the start of 2000, showed both an increase in demand and a change in the patient population throughout all the services within the palliative care unit. Larger numbers of patients were being referred to palliative care services. These were often patients with complex symptom control and psycho-social problems, being referred at an earlier stage of illness, and patients who would benefit from increased rehabilitation (O'Síoráin, 2003). These changes were not unique to Our Lady's Hospice and were experienced by other providers of palliative care services, reflecting both national and global changes in cancer and palliative care.

In 2001, a comprehensive review of day care services was undertaken at Our Lady's Hospice. The review was to assess 'the structure of day care, the process of care and any outcome measures available' (O'Reilly, 2002). The service was looked at under five general headings; fairness of access, timeliness, effectiveness, patient and carer experience, and communication between professionals. This report was presented to senior management in 2002. A small multi-disciplinary working group representing all health care professionals within the palliative care unit undertook the implementation of the recommendations of the report throughout 2003.

A therapeutic rehabilitation model of care was chosen to meet the needs of the patients in an equitable, patient-centred manner, with an emphasis on quality and accountability. The aim of this model of palliative day care is to:

- be part of a fully integrated, comprehensive palliative care service which incorporates community palliative care and in-patient services and which is easily accessed by health care professionals from both community and acute sectors (Myers and Hearn, 2001a);
- support patients, aiming to normalize their life (Neale, 1992);

- support patients so as to allow them to focus on ways of improving their well-being and to achieve the confidence to regain a role in society (National Council for Hospice and Specialist Palliative Care Services, 1995).

The service at Our Lady's Hospice has operated with this model of care since the end of 2003. The service is available for patients with advanced malignant disease who are living at home and are well enough to attend for at least part of the day. Patients with non-malignant disease are considered on a case-by-case basis. It is a specialist palliative care service provided by a multi-disciplinary team of health professionals skilled in palliative care. The day hospice team works closely with the primary care team, which continues to have all primary nursing and medical responsibility for the patient.

This change in the palliative day care service at Our Lady's Hospice has promoted individualized patient care, based on patient need and has also enabled more patients to access the service at any one time. The service is offered to patients currently under the care of the home care team. By attending day care, not only the patient and family benefit but the efficiency of the home care service is maximized enabling them to visit a different patient on that day. Day care is also sometimes offered to patients referred for home care who are not yet appropriate for this service but who require palliative care at a different level. Patients discharged from the in-patient unit may also avail of day care.

All this implies that the service should be a more cost-effective and efficient service. The challenge for the day hospice team now is to prove this through appropriate research studies.

Implications of extending this therapeutic model with an expanded health care team

Fisher and McDaid (1996) described palliative day care services as the hub of community palliative care, bridging the interface between home care services and specialist in-patient units so that patients can be referred smoothly from one to the other, as they require. There are many positive implications of the expansion and integration of therapeutic palliative day care services with an expanded health care team, and some potential negative implications that must be considered and managed.

The outcome of individualized, needs-based, care for patients is that they experience benefit from the therapeutic effect, thus gaining a more positive view of palliative care. Palliative day care services offer a safe introduction into the 'hospice' as the patient returns home the same day. The therapeutic model of care facilitates the discharge of patients on achievement of their goals. Two benefits of this are the promotion of a sense of achievement for the patient and an increased access to the service for a greater number of patients.

The *Report of the National Advisory Committee on Palliative Care* (Department of Health and Children, 2001) highlights the expectation that the number of people dying from cancer and the number of patients living with cancer will rise in future years. This is due to the ageing population, earlier diagnosis, improved treatment and longer survival. Palliative day care services can provide supportive care to complement cancer treatments and can facilitate earlier access to palliative care services.

In recent years, the number of non-cancer patients availing themselves of specialist palliative care services has increased and the spectrum of disease for which patients receive palliative care has broadened (Department of Health and Children, 2001). A review of the evidence for extending palliative care to all found that patients dying from non-malignant disease need improved care, and that their needs lie within the remit of specialist palliative care (Field and Addington-Hall, 1999). Palliative day care services may be one way of extending specialist palliative care to patients with non-malignant disease.

In *Primary Care: A New Direction* (Department of Health and Children, 2001a) the current deficiencies of community services in the Republic of Ireland are recognized. However, in order to facilitate patient preference regarding place of care for the dying, greater resources need to be made available to support community health and social services to provide care at home (Tiernan *et al.*, 2002). The therapeutic model of care will not exclude social needs but acknowledges psycho-social needs of the patient alongside the physical needs.

The change in service at Our Lady's Hospice appears to have had a positive impact on the home care services, but a degree of caution is warranted. The integration of palliative day care services into community palliative care services must not result in inappropriately late referrals to the home care. What is required is effective communication and co-operation between the services, along with an appreciation of where the patient is on their cancer journey. Patients should be able to flow between all aspects of the specialist palliative care service – day care, home care, in-patient care and hospital care, accessing one or more as is required.

Future challenges

The National Advisory Committee on Palliative Care (Department of Health and Children, 2001) highlights that specialist palliative care services should be available for all patients in need whatever their disease. Palliative day care services may promote the movement towards palliative care for all if developed as part of a national strategy that has adequate planning and funding.

With the recent rapid growth of palliative care services in the Republic of Ireland, palliative day care services is an area of increased interest. In response to this and in the current climate of North/South co-operation, a Day Hospice Special Interest Group is being formed under the auspices of the Irish Association of Palliative Care. O'Keefe (2001) advises that in developing a palliative day care service there are issues and problems that will arise and that will be at once similar to and different from those faced by older or more established services. Documenting and publishing these experiences will ensure that others can learn from the process.

The biggest challenge for all providers of palliative day care services is to be able to demonstrate the quality, efficiency and cost-effectiveness of their service. There is overwhelming anecdotal evidence for the benefits of palliative day care services for both patients and their families, but this is in stark contrast to the lack of proven evidence on the effectiveness and evaluation of service delivery in comparison with other formats of care.

Myers (2001) has identified some key questions for research including:

- What are the benefits of palliative day care?
- Which group of patients and carers benefit most and under what circumstances?
- Are there particular components of palliative day care services that bring about greater benefits than others?
- Are there groups that are excluded from current palliative day care services and why?
- To what extent does palliative day care substitute, supplement or duplicate other health and social services that patients might receive?

Conclusion

Palliative day care is a complex service (Myers and Hearn, 2001). The evolution to a therapeutic and rehabilitative model of care is how one service is rising to the challenge of meeting the increasingly wide-ranging, changing and complex needs of its patients. It is hoped that the continued development of this model will offer greater flexibility, use of services, access, and equitability to the growing and different groups of patients.

Palliative day care continues to be an area of much interest and growth throughout the Republic of Ireland, with many new services being developed. The potential for palliative day care services to be integrated within our expanding health care service is evident. To realize this potential successfully it will be necessary for services to maintain the philosophy of palliative care and the principle of multi-disciplinary teamworking in order to respond appropriately and effectively to patients' needs, develop in partnership with other health care services and prove the benefits of the services provided.

References

Cockburn, M. (1982) A different kind of day unit, *Nursing Times*, 18:1410–11.

Department of Health and Children (2001) *Report of the National Advisory Committee on Palliative Care*. Dublin: Stationery Office.

Department of Health and Children (2001a) *Primary Care: A New Direction*. Dublin: Stationery Office.

Field, D. and Addington-Hall, J. (1999) Extending palliative care to all?, *Social Science and Medicine*, 48:1271–80.

Fisher, R. A. and McDaid, P. (1996) *Palliative Day Care*. London: Arnold.

Hospice Information (2004) Hospice and Palliative Care Services in the United Kingdom and Republic of Ireland. www.hospiceinformation.info/findahospice/directory.asp. Available on 19/04/2004.

Irish Association for Palliative Care (2001) *Directory of Palliative Care Services in Ireland*.

Kearney, M. (2000) *Report of the Medical Director, Palliative Care Services. Annual Report, Our Lady's Hospice Harold's Cross*. Dublin: Our Lady's Hospice.

Myers, K. (2001) Future perspectives for day care, in J. Hearn and K. Myers, *Palliative Day Care in Practice*. Oxford: Oxford University Press.

Myers, K. and Hearn, J. (2001) Preface, in J. Hearn and K. Myers, *Palliative Day Care in Practice*. Oxford: Oxford University Press.

Myers, K. and Hearn, J. (2001a) An introduction to palliative day care: past and present, in J. Hearn and K. Myers, *Palliative Day Care in Practice*. Oxford: Oxford University Press.

National Council for Hospice and Specialist Palliative Care Services (1995) *Specialist Palliative Care: A Statement of Definitions*. London: National Council for Hospice and Specialist Palliative Care Services.

National Council for Hospice and Specialist Palliative Care Services (1999) *Palliative Care 2000: Commissioning through Partnership*. London: National Council for Hospice and Specialist Palliative Care Services.

Neale, B. (1992) *Palliative care in the community: the development of a rural hospice service in High Peak, North Derbyshire, 1988–1992*. Occasional Paper no. 7. Sheffield: Trent Palliative Care Centre.

O'Keefe, K. (2001) Establishing day care, in J. Hearn and K. Myers, *Palliative Day Care in Practice*. Oxford: Oxford University Press.

O'Reilly, M. (2002) Day Care Review. Unpublished Document. Dublin: Our Lady's Hospice.

O'Síoráin, L. (1998) *Report of the Medical Director, Palliative Care Services. Annual Report, Our Lady's Hospice Harold's Cross*. Dublin: Our Lady's Hospice.

O'Síoráin, L. (2003) Day Care Review 2002–2003. Unpublished Document. Dublin: Our Lady's Hospice.

Spencer, D. J. and Daniels, L. E. (1998) Day hospice care – a review of the literature, *Palliative Medicine*, 12(4):219–99.

Tiernan, E., O'Connor, M., O'Síoráin, L. and Kearney, M. (2002) A prospective study of preferred versus actual place of death among patients referred to a palliative care home-care service, *Irish Medical Journal*, 95(8):232–5.

10 Palliative care teamwork in the Republic of Ireland – the key to physical and psychological function

Deirdre Rowe, Ann Keating and Eithne Walsh

Introduction

The multi-disciplinary team is integral to the concept of palliative care. This chapter specifically describes the philosophy of teamworking practised at Ireland's oldest and largest palliative care unit, Our Lady's Hospice, Dublin.

A holistic approach is central to the ethos of specialist palliative care. A collaborative model of teamworking should be promoted among health care professionals, regardless of the size, location or composition of the service. The family unit (which includes the patient) is seen as an integral part of the multi-professional team, working in partnership to achieve best outcomes.

Historical perspective

In 1989, Michael Kearney was appointed as the first palliative care consultant in the Republic of Ireland in a joint appointment to Our Lady's Hospice and St Vincent's University Hospital, Dublin. He joined the existing team of doctors, nurses and chaplaincy. This appointment was a catalyst in broadening the in-patient multi-professional team to include access to occupational therapy and physiotherapy in order to optimize the functional independence and physical comfort of patients. In recognition of the special psycho-social needs of patients and families, the first 'dedicated' hospice-based social worker joined this team in 1990. Further expansion occurred in 1993 and 1996 respectively with the appointment of a 'dedicated' occupational therapist and physiotherapist, employed exclusively for the palliative care service. The first department of complementary and creative arts therapies was established in 1998, to provide additional emotional and psycho-spiritual support and included touch therapies, and sessional music and art therapy. All the above appointments were the first of their kind in the Republic of Ireland.

In the 1980s, palliative care was provided primarily by doctors and nurses working in the community or in-patient units, liaising closely with community GPs, public health nurses and other community care professionals. Their work was goal-focused and essentially a collaborative model of care. As the team expanded, a continuing care model of multi-professional teamwork emerged at intra-agency level. This encouraged liaison across multi-professional boundaries promoting the seamless delivery of patient and family care. The emphasis was primarily on terminal care and end-of-life issues, as the majority of patients were seen later in their disease trajectory. A co-ordinated inter-agency model was also developed which included monthly team meetings, with oncologists, radiologists, nurses, palliative care consultants and social workers.

This original palliative care teamwork model of the 1980s and early 1990s, whether in the community, or the in-patient unit, was synonymous with terminal care. Over the intervening years there has been a paradigm shift in palliative care teamworking with a broadening of emphasis from 'end of life' to 'quality of life' issues. This has created the cultural climate from which a rehabilitation approach to palliative care in the Irish context has emerged. External factors that influenced this evolution include:

1. Successive World Health Organization policies on cancer and palliative care during the 1990s;
2. A cultural change towards consumerism and individual 'rights';
3. The health strategy *Shaping a Healthier Future* (Department of Health, 1994), with an emphasis on improvement in health status and quality of life;
4. The cancer strategy *Cancer Services in Ireland – A National Strategy* (Department of Health, 1996), which identified rehabilitation as being of benefit to cancer patients;
5. Medical advances bringing with it changes in the disease trajectory;
6. Increasing numbers of patients with non-malignant conditions being referred to palliative care;
7. Expansion and development of the multi-professional team.

The first specialist in-patient palliative care unit was developed at Our Lady's Hospice, on a site shared with an existing specialist in-patient rheumatology rehabilitation service and a continuing care facility mainly caring for the elderly. The philosophy of care practised in these units was to enhance the quality of life no matter how short or long the prognosis. This cross-fertilization of clinical expertise and practice influenced the evolution of a palliative rehabilitation approach. As multi-professional teams have expanded in other sites around the country this approach has been modified and adapted to meet local needs. It is one of the models underpinning multi-professional teamwork practice, in specialist in-patient and day hospice settings.

Recent literature refers to a rehabilitative approach in palliative care (Tookman *et al.*, 2004; Bray and Cooper, 2004; Doyle *et al.*, 2004). This may appear to be a contradiction in terms, however, upon further reflection the concept of rehabilitation does fit well within the principles of palliative care, with its emphasis on quality of life. The palliative rehabilitation approach differs in concept from traditional mainstream rehabilitation which may require readjustment and a shift in perception for some team members. Sensitivity to patient choice and wishes remain paramount, and should dictate realistic goal setting and collaborative teamworking. This approach accommodates the changing and fluctuating needs of the palliative care patient from diagnosis to pre-terminal care. The key elements of a palliative care approach are described comprehensively by Tookman *et al.*, (2004). As the patient's condition deteriorates the emphasis progresses from rehabilitation to end-of-life care – which extends into bereavement support.

The key elements of a rehabilitative approach include:

- Support
- An interdisciplinary approach to care
- Enabling maximization of comfort and minimization of dependence
- Enabling adaptation to current situation, coming to terms with illness and changed circumstances
- Enabling the facing of uncertainty and loss
- Realistic approaches to patient goals
- Rapid response of the team to changing need
- Anticipation by the team of potential deterioration, allowing time to address relevant issues with the patient and/or family and carers
- Effective co-ordination and liaison across care boundaries to promote seamless care
- Education and commitment of all staff to enable consistency of approach

Team composition

It is a fundamental principle of palliative care that no one individual or discipline possesses the range of skills necessary to comprehensively meet and address the varied needs of patients and their families. A good palliative care team should be composed of members of multiple disciplines representing a variety of areas of expertise.

(Department of Health and Children, 2001)

Currently, there is considerable variation in the composition of multi-professional palliative care teams throughout Ireland. Contributing factors to this have been the relative recent emergence of the specialty itself; lack of a blueprint until recently, for developing palliative care services; shortage of skilled professionals and the financial resources required to provide this specialist care. The composition of the team is further influenced by the type of care setting and the level of ascending specialization being provided – palliative care approach, general or specialist palliative care.

The roles of the medical and nursing professions are well defined and acknowledged on the core clinical team. Social workers are also well established team members. Since the early 1990s, the specialist contribution they make to the psycho-social component of patient and family care has been well integrated at core team level, irrespective of team size or palliative care setting. The role expands into bereavement support. To date, there are over 25 palliative care social-worker posts throughout the country, with some newer positions still vacant.

At present, there are fewer than ten occupational therapists employed exclusively in specialist palliative care services around the Republic of Ireland. In palliative care, occupational therapists have a unique role to play in optimizing functional independence in daily living skills that are purposeful and meaningful to the patient. They are a vital link in facilitating patients' wishes should they choose to visit, return or remain within their home environment. For many years in the Republic of Ireland community occupational therapists, employed by the Health Boards, have provided a service to palliative care patients living in the community as part of a general and large caseload. There is close inter-agency co-operation and liaison between the specialist palliative care occupational therapist and their hospital or community colleagues. In some services occupational therapists working in specialist palliative care have developed short-term equipment loan-banks to facilitate speed of discharge and to alleviate pressure on patients who require equipment immediately.

There are less than ten physiotherapists working specifically in specialist palliative care in the Republic of Ireland. Physiotherapists treat patients throughout all stages of their illness into end-of-life care and play a valuable role in maintaining the independence and mobility of the palliative care patient for as long as possible. Short- or longer-term negotiated goals focus the physiotherapists' attention on quality of life. Their specialist skills, in particular in respiratory care, are well recognized as a vital component of palliative care. The role of the community physiotherapist in palliative care is developing.

The *Report of the National Advisory Committee on Palliative Care* (Department of Health and Children, 2001) recognized the needs of patients and their families in both in-patient and community settings. They recommended that occupational therapists, physiotherapists and social workers based in specialist palliative care units should extend services to the community in order to provide a seamless and integrated care package for patients. This recommendation is currently being implemented. When recommended staffing levels are achieved it is hoped that both community and specialist palliative care services will develop new models of integrative working, being both a resource and support to each other in the delivery of total patient care. In response to staff shortages, particularly in occupational therapy and physiotherapy, the government have opened new schools providing additional training places. Among the allied health professions in the Republic of Ireland there is growing interest in the speciality of palliative care. This is being enhanced by the development of special interest groups which provide opportunity for support and networking, and increased undergraduate and postgraduate clinical training opportunities. The challenge for the future is to build on these initiatives in order to meet the projected requirements for palliative care service delivery.

Complementary and creative art therapies are described as those approaches to patient care that complement existing interventions, in order to improve the quality of living which may for that particular individual be a unique way of offering emotional and spiritual support. This definition describes a holistic attitude and approach to caring, recognizing that body, mind, emotions, soul and spirit are integrated aspects of the whole person. The belief, therefore, is that complementary and creative arts therapies within an integrated model of care can offer another choice to the patient in their healing. They are classified as touch therapies such as massage, aromatherapy, reflexology and therapeutic touch, and the creative psycho-dynamic therapies such as art and music therapy. These therapies are increasingly being offered as part of hospice care and also being independently sought by people with cancer (Maher *et al.*, 1994).

Essence of teamwork in palliative care and challenges to practice

Effective teamwork does not just *happen*. In palliative care, as in other settings, it requires a positive attitude, commitment and action by all team members. Hull *et al.* (1989) suggest that part of the function of a palliative care team is to optimize the collective skills of all its members together with a willingness to enlist additional skills and expertise when required. In return, the genuine support that team members can provide for each other is a powerful motivator and an essential part of effective teamwork in palliative care.

Specialist palliative care multi-professional teamwork functions best in the presence of:

- An agreed philosophy of care and model of teamwork practice;
- A leadership ethos that promotes and facilitates the team process;

- A common purpose, identified and understood by all team members;
- Mutual respect, trust and understanding of each team members' role, skills and capabilities;
- Flexibility to respond rapidly to changing circumstances;
- Clear and open communication;
- Co-operation and collaboration between team members;
- Co-ordination of patient care at both inter-disciplinary and inter-agency level;
- An organizational culture that values and underpins the principles of teamworking.

An awareness of the teamwork model underpinning practice is essential. Palliative care practice has moved from its pioneering phase to greater integration in the broader Irish health care system. It has been suggested by Garner and Orelove (1994) that conflict and frustrations occurring within teams may not be due to differences in values, style and philosophy but rather to incompatible expectations by team members regarding the role and function of the team itself. In different palliative care settings such as hospices, acute general hospitals and community care, various models of teamwork may be operating or overlapping, with subsequent variations in the expectation and interaction of team members. The subtle difference in practice and expectation needs to be appreciated in order to avoid misunderstanding and conflict. In this respect, the role of the team leader or co-ordinator is very influential in guiding the overall team process.

In palliative care, due to the fluctuating nature of patients' conditions, their health status can change rapidly, necessitating speed of response and effective decision-making. At the outset, the principles of decision-making as well as the parameters of each person's authority should be clarified at team level. This will reduce the potential for communication difficulties and tensions in situations where decisions have to be made quickly and where it is unrealistic to consult with all team members.

Challenges to the team also arise from the role-ambiguity and blurring of boundaries demanded by a holistic approach. This is a particularly important issue in palliative care where aspects of the service can be offered by a variety of professionals whose roles frequently overlap (Hill, 1998). The interdependence of team members on each other for information, assistance and co-operation can promote either co-operative or competitive inter-disciplinary relationships (Mystakidou and Tsilika, 2000). As different health professionals join existing teams there is a potential for territorial behaviour and interprofessional competition which if not addressed at the outset becomes a major barrier to effective teamwork. Non-disclosure and withholding of information between team members due to perceived inexperience or hierarchical attitudes can put pressure on new members who feel they have to prove their worth and commitment in environments where excellence inpatient and family care becomes an overriding priority for the team.

Speck (1996) and Tookman *et al.* (2004) refer to these 'unconscious processes' which can take place in palliative care. 'Chronic niceness' is a phenomenon alluded to by Speck (1996) where both staff and the organization collude unconsciously to split off the negative aspects of caring daily for this complex client group. Dealing with emotional pain, physical distress and a pressure, whether realistic or unrealistic, to 'get things right' for the patient, often results in the unconscious external projection of negative feelings and can place enormous strain on the individual, the team and the patient (Speck, 1996). Identification and awareness of these complex teamwork issues is essential for continuing team effectiveness. Both team development and patient care will be enhanced by addressing these 'unconscious processes' in an open and sensitive manner. Comprehensive induction programmes together with ongoing team-building and staff support should be provided for all palliative care teams.

Conclusion

The principle of a holistic approach to patient care together with the challenging multi-factorial requirements of patients and their families underpins the need for collaborative multi-professional teamworking in palliative care. It is the key to physical and psychological function. The outcome of such teamwork has a positive impact on the quality of patient and family care and is both rewarding and enriching for team members.

Acknowledgement

Our thanks to Sr Anne O'Halloran, Co-ordinator of Complementary & Creative Arts Therapies, Our Lady's Hospice, Harold's Cross, for her contribution to the section on team composition.

References

Bray, J. and Cooper, J. (2004) The contribution of occupational therapy to palliative medicine. In The contribution to palliative medicine of allied health professions. Doyle, D., Hanks, G., Cherny, N. and Calman, K. (eds), *Oxford Textbook of Palliative Medicine* 3rd edn. Oxford: Oxford University Press.

Department of Health (1994) *Shaping a Healthier Future – A Strategy for Effective Healthcare in the 1990s.* Dublin: Stationery Office.

Department of Health (1996) *Cancer Services in Ireland – A National Strategy*. Dublin: Stationery Office.

Department of Health and Children (2001) *Report of the National Advisory Committee on Palliative Care*. Dublin: Stationery Office.

Doyle, L., McClure, J. and Fisher, S. (2004) The contribution of physiotherapy to palliative medicine. In D. Doyle, G. Hanks, N. Cherny and K. Calman (eds.) (2004). *Oxford Textbook of Palliative Medicine*. 3rd edn. Oxford: Oxford University Press.

Garner, H. and Orelove, F. (1994) *Teamwork in Human Services Models*. London: Butterworth Heinemann.

Hill, A. (1998) Multi-professional teamwork in hospital palliative care teams, *International Journal of Palliative Nursing*, 4(5):214–21.

Hull, R., Ellis, M. and Sargent, J. (1989) *Teamwork in Palliative Care*. Oxford: Radcliffe Medical Press.

Maher, E. J, Young, T. and Feigel, I. (1994) Complementary therapies used by patients with cancer, *BMJ*, 309(6955):671–2.

Mystakidou, K. and Tsilika, E. (2000) Team dynamics and the difficult patient, *European Journal of Palliative Care*, 7(2):56–9.

Speck, P. (1996) Unconscious communications (editorial), *Palliative Medicine*, 10:273–4.

Tookman, A. J., Hopkins, K. and Scharpen-von-Heussen, K. (2004) Rehabilitation in palliative medicine. *Oxford Textbook of Palliative Medicine* 3rd edn (ed. Doyle, D., Hanks, G., Cherny, N., Calman, K.) Oxford: Oxford University Press.

Part III

Beliefs and bereavement

11 The bereavement journey: the Irish experience

Matthew Farrelly

Introduction

Supporting bereaved people is an integral part of hospice care in Ireland. Initially the Irish Hospice Foundation pioneered work in this area, training professionals and volunteers to work with the bereaved. This was followed by the development of multi-disciplinary teams. It is now usual to find comprehensive bereavement support services in the different hospices around the country, usually provided by the social work department. While the type of bereavement services offered varies from hospice to hospice, almost all provide some sort of support. Most rely on a combination of professional social workers and trained bereavement volunteers to carry out this work.

The starting point of bereavement care can be considered to be the referral of the patient to the hospice team and the first meeting between hospice staff, the patient and their family. In general, ongoing assessment, care planning and psycho-social support continue throughout the duration of an individual's illness. Part of this psycho-social care will be the consideration of the possible impact of the death on both individuals and the family group. Hospice staff will provide information regarding the nature of bereavement and tell families about bereavement services offered by the hospice team. In addition, if particular individuals are considered vulnerable and at risk of abnormal grief reactions, it is likely that specific efforts will be made to offer appropriate support.

In different hospice settings around the country these bereavement services may include large-scale services of remembrance, bereavement information lectures, bereavement groups, or individual bereavement support sessions and counselling.

Narrative therapy and bereavement

Having worked with bereaved individuals and families over many years, I am aware of a personal struggle to make sense of the fit between the personal stories of loss and bereavement which unfold in front of me and the theoretical models which have been developed to explain these life experiences. My initial training taught me about models describing stages or phases of grief through which individuals apparently moved in order to complete the process of grieving. I was introduced to the work of Elisabeth Kübler-Ross (1969) and her model of different stages of the grieving process. I worked with some people who were familiar with the concept of the different stages: denial; anger; bargaining; depression; and the final goal of acceptance, as a necessary point towards which people are to be moved. This model, while helpful, was increasingly challenged and refined.

Perhaps the most significant development in the theoretical understanding of bereavement came with William Worden's (2003) model identifying four basic tasks of mourning which were necessary for the bereaved to achieve in order to complete the process of adaptation after a death. These were:

Task I: To accept the reality of the loss
Task II: To work through the pain of grief
Task III: To adjust to an environment in which the deceased is missing
Task IV: To withdraw emotional energy from the deceased and to reinvest it in another relationship

In subsequent editions of his book the fourth task was refined to take account of newer understandings of the process of bereavement. It now reads:

Task IV: To emotionally relocate the deceased and move on with life

This radical change to the fourth task of Worden's model reflected the growing awareness that the bereaved do not in fact 'move away' from the dead but rather maintain an ongoing relationship with the deceased. The relationship is obviously a different kind to that which existed when the person was alive but it is nonetheless significant and influential. This newer understanding of the process of mourning reflects the 'continuing bonds' theory based on the work of Klass, Silverman and Nickman (1996). This theory suggests that the bereaved person remains connected to the person who has died and that this emotional relationship endures over time.

This shift in the understanding of the grief process sat more comfortably with my professional experience as I listened to bereaved people. My experience certainly endorsed Worden's view when he wrote,

> I suggest that the fourth task of mourning is to find a place for the deceased that will enable the mourner to be connected with the

deceased but in a way that will not preclude him or her from going on with life. We need to find ways to memorialise, that is, to remember the dead loved one – keeping them with us but still going on with life.

(Worden, 2003, p. 35)

This mirrored more appropriately the experience of the bereaved people we met on a daily basis. Furthermore, this concept of a 'continuing bond' with the deceased seemed to be easily accessible to many Irish people brought up within the tradition of Irish Catholicism, praying to saints and dead relatives for continued help in their daily lives.

Drawing on the narrative tradition, particularly the work of Michael White (1998) and Hedtke and Winslade (2004) it has been possible to develop counselling practices that are most appropriate to the Irish experience of bereavement. I will illustrate these practices by reference to my work with John, a 44-year-old man, whose mother died in the hospice recently.

Central to this approach is what White has referred to as 'Saying Hullo Again: The incorporation of the lost relationship in the resolution of grief' (White, 1998, p. 17). Rather than encouraging the 'letting go' or movement away from the lost relationship, it is an approach that prefers to honour the relationship with the person who has died and to acknowledge the influence of the 'continuing bond'. Furthermore, this approach elicits aspects of John's life story, which may otherwise remain untold. His narrative becomes richly described rather than being destined to remain a 'thin description' of pathologized grief.

Hedtke (2003) also describes this approach used in her work as follows:

When I am speaking with a person who is living with grief, I assume that keeping a precious connection alive is more sustaining than encouraging a person to 'move on' from their loved one who has died. This practice can be a resource for strength, resiliency, love and hope for those still living.

(Hedtke, 2003, p. 58)

John's story: reconnecting with mother

During his first counselling session John described how he perceived he was having difficulty coping with his bereavement. Both of his parents had died in the last two years, most recently his mother approximately six months ago from lung cancer. His father had died suddenly at home two years ago from a heart attack. Around this time his mother was diagnosed with lung cancer and while grieving the death of her husband, began the process of treatment and hospital care which would eventually lead to referral to the hospice. John related how, since the death of his mother, Josephine, he had initially experienced a period of intense grief with overriding feelings of sadness and loneliness. As in the case of his father's death, he had found the funeral to be a supportive experience when the local community gathered to offer support and relatives travelled from England and the USA to be with him. These included his brother and sister who came home for that time, but since their return to their families he has been finding it difficult to adjust to life alone. Over the years he had a small number of close relationships with girlfriends but was not seeing anybody at the present. My strongest recollection of our first meeting was that John repeated several times that he needed to 'get over this and let go of his mother'. While he described a good relationship with his father, he believed that his major difficulty was his inability to let go of the relationship with his mother and to move on with his life. John works in the financial sector and he enjoys his work. He was being told that he was failing in his efforts to grieve his parents. Supportive friends and colleagues were telling him that he had to let go of the relationships which were so significant. He was being invited to say goodbye and abandon two of the most significant people in his life. This was being described as the natural and necessary grief work which was required of him before he could complete the necessary tasks to allow him to live a more healthy life. However, this was not happening for John and it did not appear to fit with his preferred way of living. It appeared much more natural for John to maintain an ongoing relationship of influence with both his parents. While this was his natural inclination, it was proving quite difficult to do. When he attempted to include the influence of these relationships when dealing with other people, he was being told that he was experiencing abnormal grief and needed therapy!

We were faced with a choice. We could continue to meet together engaging in a process whereby I joined everybody else in the unsuccessful mission of forcing John to suppress the reality of his ongoing relationship with his dead parents, or I could invite him to 'say hello' to them again and to assist him in the process of living in a new way with these relationships of memory as an ongoing influence in his life.

When we discussed the choice we faced, John was quite puzzled but curious. I asked John if it might be helpful to consider how his life might have been if his mother had not died and if we might 'say hello' again to her in a new way. I was able to explore what qualities John could appreciate in himself if he were viewing himself through his mother's eyes. I asked him questions which brought forward information about his mother's loving opinion of her son. John described how his mother saw him as a strong and reliable person who cared deeply for others. I asked him how she might know these things about him and he described different experiences of interpersonal relationships where he had demonstrated care for others and received reciprocal love. He began to reminisce about his childhood and tell stories about family holidays with his siblings. He spoke about how he would sit with his mother late into the evening reminiscing about her own family history and how her relationship with his father had developed.

John smiled as he told different parts of the story and I asked him what difference it would make to his relationships with others if he kept alive the positive and enjoyable things which his mother and father knew about him.

During a later session, having reviewed this rediscovered information about himself and the qualities he possessed I invited John to consider how he could let others know about this aspect of his life and the reconnection of relationship with his mother. At this point John surprised me by informing me that he planned to visit his brother in the USA for the first time. He also had plans to visit some of his mother's relatives in England from whom he had recently received a letter. Arrangements were made to meet after these visits in about six weeks' time.

At this next session John eagerly described how he had spent time talking to his sister-in-law about his relationship with his mother and the impact of his ongoing reflections about their relationship. She had only met his mother on a couple of occasions and he was able to introduce his mother to her in a new way which his sister-in-law greatly appreciated. While aware that his mother was physically dead he described the joy of being able to introduce the story of her life and values to his sister-in-law in this way. In turn his sister-in-law provided an audience to the ongoing connection he had with his mother.

His recent visit to relatives in England had also helped him considerably. In this case he had met cousins of his mother who were interested to hear about the story of her life since their separation from her in early adulthood. While John described the relationship between himself, his parents and siblings to them, he also received information regarding the story of his mother's life prior to his own birth. He heard about her early childhood experience in poverty and how she was described as both 'caring' and 'humorous'.

Clearly these experiences had impacted on John and I asked him how focusing on the experiences of his relationship with his mother and hearing other people describe her in her youth had affected him. He replied that he enjoyed hearing stories about his mother's life from her relatives and also introducing her in a new way to his sister-in-law. Sometimes it made him sad to focus on his mother's feelings about him but at the same time it gave him strength to know how much she loved him and admired particular personal qualities which he had. I asked him whether it was okay to talk like this and he said that he thought it really helped him. He said 'it brings her really close to me and now I know I haven't lost her forever'.

These statements that John makes and his struggle with his experience of feeling a failure in 'letting go' of his parents, replicate the experience of many of the bereaved people I work with in the hospice. Worden describes the need to 'memorialise' the dead person and I believe John achieves that task well.

The work described above is influenced by Myerhoff's (1978, 1980, 1982) concepts of 're-membering' and 'membership'. Hedtke (2003) describes how these metaphors stress the importance of the role of 'relationship' in the construction of meaning and identity in our lives. She also draws on the work of Michael White (1998) who introduced these ideas into narrative therapy. White states:

> The image of membered lives brings into play the metaphor of a 'club' – a 'club' of life is evoked. This metaphor opens up options for the exploration of how a person's club of life is membered – of how this club of life is constituted through its membership and how the membership of this club is arranged in terms of rank or status.
>
> (White, 1998, p. 22)

The focus on the importance of relationship in the construction of meaning and identity is a significant shift from the ideas of traditional psychology which viewed the construction of identity as an essentially individual journey. Postmodern thinkers claim that identity is co-constructed through our experience of relationships in our 'membership clubs'. These 'membership clubs' also continue after somebody dies and influence the relationships which contribute to meaning and identity of others.

The process of memorializing which Worden refers to obviously contains an aspect of reciprocity in its operation. This is clearly demonstrated by John's experience when he says 'goodbye' to the physical presence of his mother in death but 'hello' again in a new way. This is described well by Wyndgard and Lester (2001) as follows:

> Finding ways to bring people with us, those who are no longer living, can make a big difference in people's lives. When we re-connect with those we have lost, and the memories we have forgotten, then we become stronger. When we see ourselves through the loving eyes of those who have cared for us our lives are easier to live.
>
> (Wyndgard and Lester, 2001, p. 43)

The work described with John and the process of reconnection with his mother represents a significant shift in our understanding of working with bereaved people. Those working to offer support to the bereaved are now inviting people to share stories which enrich the ongoing connection with the dead person. The trained volunteers who also carry out this work often bear witness to these stories of changed but continuing relationships as new meaning and identity is constructed for the bereaved.

Voluntary bereavement support services

As I listen to the stories of relationship between the bereaved and those who have died I am aware that I am often affected by this experience. With the telling of the relational story, I am introduced to people whom I have never met before. These people may have lived so-called 'ordinary' lives but I am bearing witness to the remarkable impact of the relationships which they built and lived through. In the context of describing this work I know that I am certainly not unique in this experience.

As I described at the beginning of the chapter, it is common for hospice services to include volunteer bereavement support services. As a social worker supervising this work I meet with many volunteers whose experiences 'companioning' the bereaved are similar to my own. Volunteer services are made up of trained and experienced volunteers who provide a non-directive listening service to bereaved people, usually on an individual basis. It is in this context that the bereavement volunteer is a 'companion' to the bereaved person as they travel the journey of bereavement. Many of the people who participate in this work have experienced bereavement themselves. This personal experience has often played a part in their later decision to apply to become bereavement volunteers.

Alan Wolfelt developed this model of 'companioning' and describes the nature of the bereavement support relationship required as follows:

- Companioning is about honouring the spirit; it is not about focusing on the intellect.
- Companioning is about curiosity; it is not about expertise.
- Companioning is about learning from others; it is not about teaching them.
- Companioning is about walking alongside; it is not about leading.
- Companioning is about being still; it is not about frantic movement forward.
- Companioning is about discovering the gifts of sacred silence; it is not about filling every painful moment with words.
- Companioning is about listening with the heart; it is not about analysing with the head.
- Companioning is about bearing witness to the struggles of others; it is not about directing those struggles.
- Companioning is about being present to another person's pain; it is not about taking away the pain.
- Companioning is about respecting disorder and confusion; it is not about imposing order and logic.
- Companioning is about going to the wilderness of the soul with another human being; it is not about thinking you are responsible for finding the way out.

It is these guiding principles that reflect a framework for the work of the bereavement volunteers. In listening to the story of the bereaved, volunteer and professional workers alike become an audience to the telling of relationship stories. I consider these stories invite reconnection of the bereaved with the lives of those they are grieving for.

It is important to acknowledge that in bearing witness to these stories, it is common for the listener to be touched and inspired by what they hear. They join with the bereaved person in the experience of 'saying hello again' to the person who died. The listener is exposed to the potential influence of the deep flowing waters of memory which the bereaved person taps into. Almost all of us who work with the bereaved are able to recall inspirational moments of particular stories that have enriched or inspired us. There is no position of neutrality in the audience.

Again, as Hedtke (2003) states: 'As audience members, we become inextricably bound to the storyteller, as they are to us. As outsider-witnesses, we share in the re-membering. We are touched and reinvigorated by the stories of the deceased person's life' (Hedtke, 2003, p. 62). In addition I would suggest that we are often reinvigorated not only by the stories of the deceased person's life but also the stories of the unfolding narrative of the bereaved person's journey of reconnection.

Closure versus integration

My conversations with bereaved people suggest that a further challenge to consider is whether the journey through bereavement brings one to a point where it can be said to be finished. Over recent years the language of bereavement has included the concept of 'closure'. This suggests that certain actions by the bereaved can bring about a state of mind, or emotional status, whereby they can be said to have 'dealt with' their grief. This description suggests an ending, or finality, to the process of grieving which is not one I observe from my work with bereaved people.

Talking to Mary, whose husband died ten years ago, she relates her recent invitation to a dinner party, where she knows she will be introduced to a male friend of her work colleague. This colleague has wanted to introduce her to this man for some time, suggesting that she would be likely to get on well with him and that he is a potential partner. Mary described how she enjoyed the evening and meeting this person. In particular, she described how before leaving the house she had spoken to her dead husband, Michael, asking him to help her. She asked, that if she was to form a new relationship, could he help her to meet somebody appropriate?

It might be suggested that Mary's conversation with her dead husband before she went out to meet a potential suitor was indicative of 'unfinished business' or was maybe reflecting the fact that she was not coping well with

Michael's death. Exploration of Mary's aspirations suggest otherwise. She states clearly that she feels she would like to meet somebody else with whom to develop a new relationship. One of her children is in college and her second son is likely to leave home next year. She is aware of the family's life-cycle change and feels that her parenting role will continue to change in the coming years. Rather than believing that her request to her dead husband is restricting in any way, she describes it as supportive and healthy. She acknowledges her connection to Michael and the ongoing influence of her relationship with him. She says she is now at the point where she is open to a second relationship but she does not believe that she has to deny the ongoing connection with Michael. Mary states: 'Of course I still talk to him and ask him to help me. I said "Michael, if it's meant to be then please help me in any way that you can. Help me choose wisely and meet somebody I can be happy spending time with in the future."'

When asked her views about the concept of 'closure', she describes how she understands the concept as involving the ending of the bereavement process and one that suggests finality. She says this does not fit with her experience of her own loss and adaptation over the past ten years. She has experienced the natural process of maintaining the relationship between her children and their dead father and has also found the ongoing connection between herself and her husband to be positive. As she spoke about this ongoing relationship, she became tearful saying that while she is now undoubtedly open to the possibility of a new relationship, she is aware that she will always be able to touch into the sadness of what happened to her when her husband died of a brain tumour. She spoke about how this impacted on her as a mother of two young sons, how she had thrown herself into doing the best she could to parent them while also taking up part-time work to earn additional money to pay school fees. Mary said that she believed she would always get upset when she reflected on the loss of her husband, the reality of his diagnosis, the period spent caring for him and his eventual death. She said:

> I think that's natural for anybody whose husband dies and is left with two young children. If I was to meet somebody I don't think I would forget Michael. It doesn't mean you can't love somebody else, but you don't have to deny the love for the person who died to enable you to love again. The experience of Michael dying is a part of me. It is part of who I am and always will be.

This description of Mary's experience challenges the concept of 'closure' which has been imported over recent years. It would be more consistent with the concept of 'integration' as an aspect of the bereavement process. Mary describes how, from time to time, she is affected by the experience of the death of her husband, some ten years after the event. She understands that the bereavement process does not have a specific ending but is rather one whose influence is ongoing. At the same time, it is not one that has immobilized her, or prevented her from considering new possibilities for the future. Mary reflects on the changes in her family as her boys enter a new phase of their life. In the context of a conversation which is hopeful and open to potential change in her own life, she describes how she will bring the influence of her past experience into her future life. Mary is most certainly 're-engaged in living' and has 'integrated' the loss experience, namely, the death of her husband, Michael, into her daily life. This is consistent with Worden's fourth task of grieving, which described how one has to find a place to 'memorialise' the dead person within one's emotional life and to bring forward this experience into the future.

I have often been struck by the power of the descriptions that bereaved people relate regarding the ongoing relationship with the dead person. Undoubtedly the rich flowing rivers of memory continue to influence people many years after the death. My work often involves helping people acknowledge that ongoing influence, to give permission for that influence to be given voice and to find language that describes it. When I ask bereaved people whether they still talk to the dead person, it is common that, initially, they sheepishly acknowledge that they do, but they don't tell too many people! This illustrates the double message which many bereaved people receive at present. On the one hand they are told that they must 'let go' of the lost relationship and get on with life, while on the other hand, their personal experience indicates that such a request is a tall order. Their personal experience of grief does not seem to work like that.

I remember giving a talk at an annual memorial service describing this very concept. Afterwards a woman approached me, and said that for the first time she had heard somebody describe why, each morning while she watched the children going off to school, she remembered her child who had died over twenty years ago. She described how, when watching the children each morning, she remembered her daughter as she was as a child but also wondered what kind of adult she would have become and what she would be doing now. This practice of daily honouring the relationship with her dead daughter did not prevent her living a healthy and full life in any way. This is another example of the influence of the 'rich flowing rivers of memory' which are an integral part of the bereavement journey.

Maintaining the lost relationship

Contemporary Irish society has seen increased urbanization and demographic change. Until very recently emigration among young people was at a very high level. It was common for large numbers of young people to emigrate to England, Australia and the USA. However, one aspect of the bereavement experience still commonly encountered is that of the family member living abroad who returns home to spend time with a dying relative before death and during the period of the funeral. They then return to a social network that often has no knowledge of the person who has died. Talking to some of these people, they describe an experience that contrasts sharply with that of the bereaved family members who live at home. Social support is recognized as one of the most important factors in facilitating the bereavement process. This process is often enhanced if you can talk and grieve with people who knew the person who has died. A difficulty for somebody who is only able to come home for a funeral and spend a few days participating in the important rituals and grieving, is that they can often then return to a social group which does not easily accommodate their needs to grieve. Those family members living in Ireland often describe a level of concern for a family member who has returned to their immediate family in Australia or the USA because that person experiences 'dissociation' from the grieving family and circle of friends who are offering support during the bereavement. For this reason, when rituals such as memorial services are being organized by the hospice, it is common to contact family members living overseas, in order to allow them time to travel back to attend these ceremonies. The written invitation can also reassure the person that their relative or friend is being remembered and included in the rituals that the hospice organizes. On occasion people have decided to travel long distances to attend these hospice events and reconnect with family and friends. Sometimes people have travelled back from New York and regularly return from England for memorial masses and ceremonies of remembrance.

Bereavement care into the future

The *Report of the National Advisory Committee on Palliative Care* (Department of Health and Children, 2001) suggests that three levels of bereavement support should be developed in Ireland. The report suggests a first level of general support provided by well trained palliative care staff and bereavement volunteers. A second level is proposed in the form of bereavement counselling provided by trained counsellors. The third level suggested takes the form of intensive psychotherapy provided by specialist health professionals. These proposals are accompanied by a recommendation on the use of risk assessment to determine which type of support is appropriate for an individual or family.

Most hospice and palliative care services attempt to provide different levels of bereavement support. For example, at St Francis Hospice, Dublin, the first level referred to in the report takes the form of a number of bereavement information nights throughout the year. Families are invited to attend these events which take the form of a lecture describing the grieving process and giving general information about bereavement. This first level of support also includes monthly bereavement ceremonies, in which the families of those who have died in the hospice in-patient unit are invited back to a memorial service which includes a candle-lighting ceremony of remembrance, a Mass or liturgical service and a brief talk about bereavement. From these events individuals may request an appointment with a member of the Hospice Volunteer Bereavement Support Team, made up of trained volunteers working under the supervision of the social work team.

The second layer of support takes the form of bereavement counselling which is provided by the professional social work staff who have specialist skills and competence in this area. One of the social workers is a trained family therapist and the service also has sessional access to a psychologist who is a member of the Irish Hospice Foundation staff.

While these different layers of service provision may represent the model that most Irish hospices and palliative care services would seek to provide, there is still a significant variation in the level of service provision throughout the country.

Where services exist, bereaved individuals usually decide whether they will seek support themselves, rather than undertaking any formal risk assessment. It is important to note that the recommendation of the *Report of the National Advisory Committee on Palliative Care* stating that assessments of needs for bereavement support should be routine in all specialist palliative care services is problematic. There has been no agreement regarding an appropriate risk assessment tool to be applied on a systematic basis. Furthermore, while it is acknowledged that the issue of risk assessment is a more complex process than the completion of a short questionnaire during a bereavement follow-up visit or phone call by a member of hospice staff, there is no general forum considering this issue at present. The need for such a forum, which would bring together the growing number of palliative care services providing bereavement support, is evident.

Historically, HEBER (Hospice and Allied Bereavement Services of Ireland) a group set up by Thérèse Brady of the Irish Hospice Foundation, was intended to meet this need. However, following Thérèse's death and without a constitution and sufficient resources the organization closed down. In the absence of this or a similar organization, the Hospice and Palliative Care Social Workers Group is presently the only forum likely to maintain an interest in this area. This forum contains most of the professional social work services that provide the bereavement support in the country. Whether this group is the appropriate one to address issues relating to national policy and standards in the area of bereavement support is another question. Until an appropriate organization is constituted which will take responsibility for the accreditation and regulation of bereavement services the lack of standardization among different services will persist.

One model of psycho-social care which is receiving critical acclaim is 'family focused grief therapy' (Kissane and Bloch, 2002). This model shifts the focus of care very much on to the family system and uses a family therapy approach to work with families dealing with terminal illness and bereavement. While Kissane and Bloch present evidence of successful outcomes for families experiencing family focused grief therapy, it is important to note that the duration of therapeutic contact in their study was generally between nine and eighteen months. This included family sessions before death as well as during bereavement. It would be most unusual for a hospice or palliative care service in Ireland to offer a family professional counselling or therapy for such a prolonged period. To adopt this model would require a major increase in resources. However, I believe the shift in focus from the individual to the family system is invaluable. Increasingly, those working with bereaved individuals are aware of the influence of the family system. I would suggest that there would be much to be gained by increasing the level of training in family therapy skills among all disciplines working in palliative care. This would be particularly helpful for those working with bereaved families. While family focused grief therapy stresses the 'integration of psycho-social and bereavement care into one seamless process' (Kissane and Bloch, 2002), it is unlikely that such a comprehensive model of service delivery will be incorporated into an Irish setting in the immediate future. It is more likely that this model may inform practice in Ireland. A systemic frame may be used to support a distinct short-term piece of work within the longer-term process of family adaptation.

The focus of psycho-social care within the hospice setting in Ireland to date has very much been on offering one-off family meetings or relatively short-term individual work to assist families in the pre-death and immediate post-bereavement period. The advent of family focused grief therapy may be an invitation to reconsider that approach.

Conclusion

This chapter has attempted to present the experience of bereavement in an Irish context. From my work in the hospice setting it is evident that there is a changing understanding of the grieving process. At present many bereaved people hear conflicting messages regarding how they should respond when someone close dies. It is the struggle to reconcile the perceived goal of 'letting go' against the actual experience of 'continued connection and influence' that is the challenge. A powerful influence in my own search for new understandings of the grieving process was the daily experience of listening to bereaved people's stories which contained aspects of ongoing relationship with people who had died. In many cases they were describing historical influences of people from generations before them. Children had been told stories about grandparents whom they had never met yet they felt had some influence on them as individuals and as families. This reality has been described by William Worden as 'memorializing the dead person'. I have attempted to outline the 're-membering practices' and conversations which are used in inviting bereaved individuals to maintain the 'ongoing relationships of influence' with those who have died.

References

Department of Health and Children (2001) *Report of the National Advisory Committee on Palliative Care*. Dublin: Stationery Office.

Hedtke, L. (2003) The origami of remembering, *International Journal of Narrative Therapy and Community Work*, 4:58.

Hedtke, L. and Winslade, J. (2004) *Re-membering Lives: Conversations with the Dying and the Bereaved*. Amityville, N.Y.: Baywood Publishers.

Kissane, D. W. and Bloch, S. (2002) *Family Focused Grief Therapy. A Model of Family-centred Care during Palliative Care and Bereavement*. Philadelphia: Open University.

Klass, D., Silverman, P. and Nickman, S. (eds.) (1996) *Continuing Bonds: New Understanding of Grief*. Washington, D.C.: Taylor and Francis.

Kübler-Ross, E. (1969) *On death and dying*. London: Tavistock Press.

Myerhoff, B. (1978) *Number our Days*. New York: Simon & Schuster.

Myerhoff, B. (1980) Telling One's Story, *Center*, 8(2):22–40.

Myerhoff, B. (1982) Life History Among the Elderly: Performance visibility and re-membering, in J. Ruby (ed.), *A Crack in the Mirror: Reflexive Perspectives in Anthropology*. Philadelphia: University of Pennsylvania Press.

White, M. (1998) Saying hullo again: The incorporation of the lost relationship in the resolution of grief, in C. White, D. Denborough, *Narrative Therapy: A Collection of Practice-Based Writings*. Adelaide: Dulwich Centre Publications.

Wolfelt, A. *Principles of companioning the bereaved*. www.centreforloss.com

Worden, J. W. (2003) *Grief Counselling and Grief Therapy: A Handbook for the Mental Health Practitioner*. London: Brunner-Routledge.

Wyndgard, B. and Lester, J. (2001) *Telling our Stories in Ways that Make us Stronger*. Adelaide: Dulwich Centre Publications.

12 Religion, faith and spirituality: 'a difficult journey'

Christy Kenneally

Introduction

The Republic of Ireland is a predominantly Catholic country. Its religion and history are inextricably entwined and the preservation of the Catholic faith and the Irish language during centuries of English rule have left deep impressions on the Irish psyche. Religion, for many people, has been hugely important in their lives and the Catholic church has had an enormous influence on many aspects of peoples' lives.

What were the roots of Irish spirituality? Many would refer to the time of the great monastic settlements in the eighth and ninth centuries which spread throughout Europe. Of course, the monastic story is a glorious chapter in Irish spirituality. When Europe lay under the pall of the Dark Ages, monks made their way to the threshold of Europe; to Inishmurray, Skellig Mhichil and other places. They carted earth in leather boats from the mainland to create tiny, pocket-handkerchief fields and fertilized them with kelp harvested from the sea. When they were assured of shelter, warmth and food and of course, peace, they turned their attention to make the beautiful things that reflected the glories of their faith. They could live a life of prayer where the environment was not extraneous to their spirituality but an integral part of it. Theirs was indeed a glorious chapter in the story of Irish spirituality but it wasn't the first chapter.

Thousands of years before Pope Celestine sent Palladius or before Patrick, the former slave, followed his dream to Ireland in the fifth century AD, there were men and women who had a highly developed theology and spirituality. Even Julius Caesar, a committed enemy, took time out from campaigning, to refer to their society and allude to their religious beliefs. The Celts believed in Gods who were the creators of all things. They believed in the immortality of the soul and established the druids as a priesthood to intercede with their God and to defend them against demonic forces. These druid/priests doubled as judges and teachers in the community. There is little evidence of persecution against early Christians in Ireland and it appears that the Celts who already worshipped hundreds of gods had little difficulty absorbing one more. By the eight century, Christianity had become the predominant religion and the druids were no longer pre-eminent. The success of Christianity was partly due to the existing spiritual awareness of the people and the Church assimilated many of the so-called pagan festivals into its own calendar in recognition of this, for example, Samhain which became Halloween.

The early Church was organized into dioceses which were governed by bishops appointed by the pope in Rome. This structure still exists in Ireland and bishops continue the traditions of the early Church in ordaining clergy, blessing churches and providing visible leadership for Irish Catholics.

The Normans arrived in 1169 but England struggled to establish control over Ireland for almost 400 years. Their main sphere of influence was 'The Pale' an area on the eastern seaboard encompassing most of Dublin, Kildare and Wicklow. With the advent of Henry VIII to the throne and his subsequent conversion to Protestantism, a period of rapid change followed. Henry's scheme of surrender and regrant allowed that any rebellious Irish lord could have his lands confiscated and subsequently sold or rented to reliable, usually Protestant, settlers. Thus began the plantations of the fifteenth and sixteenth centuries. The old-established Irish families were provoked into rebellion and defeated by the English and their lands were planted with English tenants or Irish tenants who were perceived as loyal to the Crown.

By 1641 the old Irish families had regrouped and this led to a full-scale rebellion. The still Catholic descendants of the Normans known as the 'Old English' joined the rebellion. They had been allowed to keep their religion but faced an extreme Protestant Parliament which wanted all Catholics dispossessed of their lands. The Civil War in England between King Charles I and Parliament provided an opportunity for the rebellion but there was little co-ordination among rebel armies and at the end of the Civil War a victorious Parliament sent a large battle-hardened army under Cromwell to Ireland.

Cromwell is remembered for massacring entire garrisons who refused to surrender in Drogheda and Wexford. By 1652 the last Irish resistance had collapsed. Cromwell's campaign in Ireland had been intended to revenge the earlier murder of Protestant settlers in 1641 but the English Parliament also wanted to dispossess Catholic landowners and to repay its Protestant backers who had helped to fund the war effort. In passing the Act of Settlement in 1652 all lands belonging to the rebels were confiscated and Catholic landowners were ordered to move to the west of Ireland to the province of Connaught. The transportation of Catholics coincided with an attempt to rid Ireland of Catholicism. Priests were hunted down and executed and Catholics forced to attend Protestant services. These attempts were unsuccessful, partly because most Protestant clergy could not speak Irish.

By the early eighteenth century, 90 per cent of Ireland was owned by Protestants of English or Scottish origin. The new Protestant Ascendancy established control through a series of penal laws barring Catholics from political activity, access to education and from owning land or firearms. The Irish language also suffered and with it the Irish culture preserved in language-related activities including poetry, storytelling, music and folklore. It would be another 150 years before Catholic emancipation.

The Catholic Church in Irish life

The Catholic Church which emerged after Catholic emancipation in the early nineteenth century was a phenomenal agent for change. After centuries of repression the Church exploded into activity and many of the religious orders, including the Sisters of Charity, were founded during these times.

Education and health care were the two areas of enormous need and broadly Irish Catholic religious orders concentrated on one or the other. Not content with just working within Ireland, many of these orders had a missionary branch leading to a wave of Irish Catholic religious emigrating to countries all over the world. In the chapter on multiculturalism, mention was made of the importance to an Irish family, of having a priest or a religious sister. In many ways the last century was a golden age for the Catholic Church in Ireland. Times have changed for the Church with falling vocations, a more educated and multicultural society and scandals from within.

Many of those educated by religious would qualify and then contest the jobs of their teachers, rendering the *raison d'être* of teaching orders obsolete. Many would eschew the ideal of religious life as the primary vocation and opt to live out their commitment to the Gospel in marriage and service to the community. Even more tellingly, this educated class, who would excel in the arts, sciences and all areas of intellectual achievement, would turn their analytical skills on the theology they had been taught and the spirituality they had been encouraged to practise and find it wanting – not because of the flawed nature of that theology but because the teaching of it terminated in their adolescence and it would not withstand the intellectual rigour of their adulthood.

For many Irish Catholics, religion started with Rome. Lucky enough to be born into the one, true Church which had the bulk of history for backup and the definitive answer to all the important questions available on request, we had the security of being the new chosen people. What kind of spirituality flowed from that perception? It was largely a hierarchical model, with God as Creator/Judge at its head, Jesus who had brought us from damnation through his blood on one side, and Mary, a model of motherhood and virginity, on the other. For most of us, the Holy Spirit was as ethereal and incomprehensible as the name suggests.

In descending order of power, there existed a vast array of saints who were held up as models for our spiritual lives and practice, always ready to intercede for us if they were petitioned to do so. These were models we could never emulate, because of our human (read fallen) nature. The best we might hope for was purgatory and our eventual release, after a suitable period of chastisement designed to purge us of all imperfection, into the bliss of heaven!

Spirituality in practice, for example prayer life, is always a natural outflow from perception. Prayer then, was, at one level, an acknowledgement of God's perfection, justice and mercy and, at the same time, our own worthlessness, and our desire that justice would be tempered by mercy. We would pray therefore for what we wanted, for Divine intervention to secure a job, pass an exam, or deliverance from all the misfortunes we were heir to as sons and daughters of Adam and Eve. Or, we would assail the saints with prayers, offerings and promises if they would only stay God's wrath or sway God's favour. For some Irish people religion is a fundamental coping mechanism. For all their lives during times of crisis they have turned to their religious faith to comfort and help. This framework can also sustain them through life's last great crisis: death.

There was also a sense of the presence of God in the world around us, in the loves we experienced in parent, spouse, friend and child. Buried in there was the precious nugget of Scripture underlining the importance of the horizontal dimension of our spirituality. 'How can you say you love God whom you have not seen when you don't love your brother and sister whom you can see.' This particular text, put into the mouth of Jesus, was our clearest indication that it would be in our ordinary and everyday dealings with others that we would encounter God, not as some all-powerful and distant entity, but as someone who loves us and who reveals himself through our human encounters in the here and now.

The idea that our humanity might have been affirmed and validated by the Incarnation, seems to have been outweighed by the idea that we were, by our nature, unlovable and inherently sinful, and could only be saved by a blood sacrifice. How did this affect our self-image?

We learned early and often to speak ill of ourselves. Praise was an embarrassment or suspect, protestations of inability the norm. Had modesty been an Olympic sport we could have walked away with gold every four years, but we'd be much too modest to attend the ceremony. This denial of giftedness was endemic in our culture.

Small wonder then that so much spirituality was centred almost obsessively on the sacrament of penance and so much practice revolved around regular recourse to the confessional. We began to see our humanity as an excuse for weakness (I'm only human) rather than as a privilege affirmed by the Incarnation. The net result was the desertion of gifts coupled with an implicit denial of the God who was their source. The ultimate sadness is that many of our people hung on 'like grim death' to a faith which in its essence promised a full life here and the fullness of it hereafter.

It is understandable that people who lived in hard times, when infant mortality was high, life expectancy short, and material comforts few, would espouse a belief system that promised all would be well in the hereafter. It could hardly be worse than what they had here. A faith that exhorted people to be 'in the world, but not of it', was simple enough for those who had little by way of material things to seduce their hearts from the right way. A theology of death as a release from the burdens of want, hard work and ill health, held out a welcome relief in the form of 'eternal rest'. If someone understands and experiences God as a punishing and wrathful being and that attaining heaven or paradise is extraordinarily difficult, they may experience 'religious pain' (Satterly, 2001), rooted in guilt and shame for not having lived up to the expectations of a selfless and blameless life. Consequently their dying may be a difficult journey ending with a meeting with a judgemental Maker. If however one embraces a God-image that assures one of Divine love and caring intercession one may look forward to eternal rewards and be in a hurry to get the journey over with.

The agony of present

There is a passage in the book of Ezra, which, I contend, sums up the tensions and pain at the heart of Irish Catholicism today. The writer is describing the laying of the foundation of the New Temple in Jerusalem, which replaced the wreckage of what stood there before. There are, he tells us, two groups present at the ceremony of dedication: those older people who remember the glories of the first temple and weep at the memory, and those who rejoice at the potential of the new temple. He concludes, 'One could not distinguish between the sound of laughing and the sound of weeping.'

We have in the Irish Catholic Church an older population who remember the Church of pomp and ceremony; who remember the familiarity of daily Mass and Sunday Mass as the spiritual and social high-point of their week. Theirs was a spirituality buttressed by, and given expression to, first Fridays, Lent, sodalities, confraternities, novenas, benediction and devotions. Theirs was a spirituality made sacramental in scapulars, medals and the holy pictures that hung in their homes. Theirs was a perception that the priest was a man of God, to be respected for his devotion to his calling and the succour he could bring to 'the poor of heart', especially the dying. We could say that their belief in the message was almost inextricably linked to their belief in the minister. It is all too easy to imagine their sense of disillusionment in the face of scandal. As it is all too easy to state that those who are disillusioned had to have clung to an illusion in the first place, namely, that these ministers were somehow immune to the frailties that beset ordinary mortals. The fact remains that there is a sadness and sense of grief, coupled with an anxiety in the face of the flux and flow that is their Church today.

The exposure of institutional abuse, while not restricted just to Ireland, seems to have had a deeper impact here perhaps because priests and nuns were so revered and respected. It will take the next generation of thinkers, historians, sociologists, theologians and writers to render a balanced account of the impact of these events. Those who endure a holocaust rarely write objectively about it. There is the danger of losing sight of the men and women who gave lives of devotion without agendas; men and women who wholeheartedly nurtured the young and cared tenderly for the elderly, sick and dying. Those men and women are scarred and tarred by the wrongdoings of a minority. Much of modern-day anger at these crimes is directed at the institutional Church whose primary impulse was the protection of the system against scandal, rather than admitting to the vicissitudes of the institution and the degree to which its own selection, training and the emotional and moral development of those in ministry, contributed to the problem.

For younger people sadly, many seem to have been intellectually embarrassed by the belief system of a previous generation and have either totally abandoned it or pay lip service to it when the communion, confirmation or wedding service of their own children hoves into view – ignoring the admonition of Ghandi that before disobeying any law we must first live it to the full and find it wanting.

Many Irish people of this generation protest that they are not religious but that they are spiritual. The rise of interest in New Age, Christian sects, Zen and Buddhism attest to this search for spiritual meaning. We are faced, particularly in the case of those who come to die, with a multi-faceted challenge. In a time of great uncertainty, how do we create an environment conducive to that quality of life where people's spiritual nature is not only catered for but enhanced? There is surely more to this than bringing in the priest, rabbi, immam, monk, shaman or guru, as appropriate. Like all challenges involving the care of another, it is a two-edged sword that hacks back at ourselves. It calls for a frank and perhaps frightening questioning of what we believe, how we express our spirituality and how that is reflected in our caring.

The hospice in a multicultured Ireland

As Irish society becomes multicultural it presents us with a wonderful opportunity to expand our hearts, minds and spirits, not so much to assimilate and 'Irish' these cultural influences, but to learn from them not only intellectually but culturally and spiritually. We have much to learn from a people whose spirituality is expressed in prayer five times a day, or from those whose sense of being 'chosen' imbues them with such a sense of justice that they have produced the greatest champions of social justice in the world and earned themselves the title, 'the conscience of the world'. I refer to the Muslims and the Jews. But, what of the Hindus and Buddhists? Consider the awareness of the Hindu that life is the gift of Brahmin, the great breath, and should be lived in giftedness and harmony with all creation. Consider the Buddhist exhortation to free ourselves of ego, the desire for advancement and prestige that is called Tanha, and be liberated to the enlightenment of knowing ourselves and our true position in the universe.

Traditionally, hospices in the Irish Republic have been Catholic institutions, geared to the spiritual well-being of those who profess that faith. In former times, this spiritual well-being was catered for by chaplains, the celebration of the sacraments and various spiritual excercises such as the recitation of the rosary. It was essentially a 'top-down' approach. The assumption was that because the institution was Catholic, all of the above were appropriate to those admitted of that faith. In practice, some who came to such institutions did not give total credence to that belief or obedience to the dogmas of that Church and, did not find the spirituality of that institution conducive to the development of their own. A basic tenet of hospice is to 'encounter people where they are at', and to provide an environment and service that is conducive to their own sense of well-being. To do otherwise is to run the risk, so tartly expressed by a certain Jesuit theologian when asked about the apparent failure of the Christian mission to Japan: 'We provided a massive scratch', he said, 'for an itch that wasn't there.'

The challenge to today's hospice is surely to meet people of our faith, all faiths and none, and do everything in our power to create an environment that values 'where they're at', in their own spiritual journey, and to facilitate its growth and the expression of it in symbols, rites and spiritual exercises that are appropriate. Genuine attempts have been made to accommodate those of other faiths and those of none. Representatives of other faiths should be an integral part of the pastoral team, no longer just coming for the spiritual needs of their own particular people but enriching the spirituality of the hospice as a whole. This I believe is part of the greater challenge to the hospice.

We have, I believe, moved beyond a 'one true Church', model of faith that regarded all others as the 'poor relations'. We are moving beyond the sectarianism of them and us, that split the people of God and scandalized the non-Christian world. We are moving toward a concept of faith that perceives the particular pathway of any individual, not only as not perverse, but as a totally valid path for them within their tradition and as an enrichment of our own.

Patients may not bring preformed religious world-views to their experience with serious illness but rather develop their own spiritual frameworks from their life experience. This duality of religion and spirituality is explored by Penson *et al.* (2001) who describes religion as a formal system of values, beliefs and practice, and spirituality as a life principle that influences a person's entire being; emotional, moral, volitional, ethical, physical and intellectual, generating a capacity for transcendent values. The old certainties of organized religion with history and tradition to the fore are being challenged. Klass (1999) captures these changing times: 'our grandparents, for the most part, were born into one religion. Our children are born into a world in which all religions have a voice.'

The significance of faith

In some ways, faith, belief, religion and spirituality are words and concepts that conjure up distinctions rather than attempts at expressing something fundamental held in common. All spirituality starts in seeing ourselves and other human beings as worthy of respect and love, not for who they might be to some deity, and who they might become through the ministrations of some religion, but for who they are in themselves. The wholeness of hospice should not just be patient and family-focused but people-focused, and that includes all of us.

Spirituality will always be a difficult thing to define. We could say it is a way, a medium or path, or perhaps a set of values we develop from our awareness of God which guide our steps as we attempt to live fully in relationship with that God and one another. Spirituality, at its core, seems to be an awareness of a dimension beyond the physical reality we inhabit. But, perhaps it means more than that. It is also the difference that awareness makes to the people we are and the lives we lead.

The particular faith, professed by most of us, is surely an accident of birth and geography. Were we born in another country, culture and time, is it not likely we would hold the faith dominant under those circumstances? Surely each person weaves his or her spiritual awareness out of the history, culture and period through which they live, creating a world-wide tapestry of kaleidoscopic and wondrous difference. That difference is the dynamic tension that should keep us either from smugness or xenophobia.

Strength of religious belief can vary over a life course (Ingersoll-Dayton, 2002). Some people identify events such as child rearing and adverse life events with increasing religiosity while disillusionment with the Church is identified as a factor in decreasing religiosity.

Although religion is usually portrayed as a source of comfort, individuals may also experience strain in their religious lives. A study by Exline *et al.* (2000) conducted on college students in the United States examining associations between religious variables and psychological distress, found that religious strain was associated with greater depression and suicidal tendencies. This is an important study, which if extrapolated to the patient at end of life, raises questions as to whether religious patients who have unresolved religious guilt may be at risk of harmful psychological distress.

Primitive peoples believed the death of the human being did not leave a gap in the world spirit as the human spirit would be replaced by the birth of another, or, indeed, find another dimension of existence beyond and yet within the world they knew. Isn't it ironic that we regard the times we live in as modern? We think of and define that word as meaning that we are an advanced people, civilization and culture. Our modern eyes look back to the form of what our ancestors did, and see barbarity and superstition. We miss the essential 'why' of it all. We miss the essence that precedes the action. We miss the fact that these people addressed God, or the spiritual world through the perception and using the available linguistic and ritualistic tools of their times. It suggests we have lost contact with the real world, developing an insulation between ourselves and close intimate contact with the living world about us. The word 'insulation', has, as its root, the Latin word for 'island'. So, we are adrift from the mainland. What has interposed itself between the foot and the floor, the island and the mainland? It is too simple to answer the 'shoe' or the 'strait'; too simple as well to say 'materialism'; usually interpreted as focusing on the things of the world and becoming blind to their source and purpose.

Would it startle us moderns to consider that we set time aside to 'do' nature, or 'do' prayer, or 'do' family, as in 'quality time'? Would it startle us further to consider that we work longer hours than our ancestors did, spend less time than they did with our partners, children, friends and neighbours, or even time considering the world we live in and the position we inhabit within that world? Surely, talk of taking 'time out' for spiritual things begs the question: why is spirituality seen as something outside the norm, the ordinary and everyday?

Here is a story of Irish duality. Two friends 'happen' upon a bale of goods, conveniently shed by a passing lorry. Never ones to examine 'gift horses' too closely, they sell the goods and drink the proceeds. The morning brings remorse and they go to confession. The first penitent has hardly made knee to kneeler contact when he is back in the pew. His companion emerges a good hour later suitably chastened and somewhat chagrined at his friend.

'What took you so long?' his friend asked. 'What did you tell him?'

'I told him about selling the goods of course.'

'Ah, man dear', his friend says, shaking his head in amazement, 'You told him all your business, why didn't you tell him your sins?'

Is is possible that we have made a distinction between real life and spirituality and that 'prayer' is something we do rather than are?

Prayer at the end of life

As a hospice chaplain, I was often asked to pray with the dying. The request usually came from the staff; after all, what was the chaplain for? The request was also accompanied by a small black booklet of prayers. They were largely from the 'save us from the devouring demon and the jaws of Hell' genre. I dreaded it and discarded it. Left up to my own devices, I took comfort in my store of 'learned prayers'. 'O Jesus, who for love of me, didst bear thy cross to Calvary. In thy sweet mercy grant to me, to suffer and to die with thee.'

This proved popular and regular in my repertoire until a particular patient pointed out gently but firmly that nobody in his right mind prays to suffer. Tentatively, I began to solicit favourite prayers from the patient or relative as circumstances dictated. Gradually, I found myself taking baby steps into the uncharted waters of silent presence; of solidarity with another spirit. In the beginning, it was a frightening situation. I had been trained 'to do' and this didn't seem like doing anything. Now, I consider that silence was probably the first step in a genuinely spiritual relationship.

If words are appropriate to prayer, they should be drawn from the vocabulary of the patient's life experience; things as mundane as bed, ward, a fellow patient, a glimpse of garden through the window. Anything the patient sees, hears, and feels would dictate the prayer form.

The interesting thing about any ritual such as prayer, is that it flows naturally out of the experiences, perceptions, cultures and the desires of a particular person or people in a particular time and place. The maddening thing is, that as the generations replace one another, a ritual that made perfect sense to the first generation must be explained to the second and can be totally incomprehensible and even embarrassing to their children. Unhappily, rites, like commandments set in stone, can end up as rote. Prayer, once pressed between the pages of a book, can dry up with repetition. The challenge to every generation is not to repeat the 'what' of a former generation but to rediscover the 'why' and parse it into a spirituality that is appropriate to their time and place.

Spirituality is like music humming from a chord held in tension by our perception of the reality around us and our awareness of another dimension or other. That is the tune, common to all generations back to our first ancestors. The challenge to every individual is to compose a lyric for the tune that is of their time, place and culture.

A holy death

How does all of this impact on our caring when we come to the time of death? Historically an assumption has developed in the literature that when faced with a terminal illness people search for meaning and thereby are more predisposed to embrace religion. Handzo (1996) suggests that a life-threatening illness evokes a patient's ultimate existential and spiritual concerns. Many questions are posed by such assumptions: How do individuals without a traditional religious belief deal with dying? Are people facing their deaths more likely to turn towards religion? Do individuals, religious or otherwise, think about an afterlife? Are people who are religious always spiritual? McGrath (2003) sheds some light on this. In her study of cancer patients with advanced disease, the majority did not seek religious comfort or conversion as a response to the challenge of a terminal illness even when this was seen as desirable. Some patients did turn towards religion but this was expressed as a strengthening of previous beliefs rather than the embracing of new ideas. Research carried out by Braun *et al.* (2001) examined the potential roles of faith communities in end-of-life care. The clear implication was that as a member of a faith one should expect that 'church' and faith community to support the dying person and their family. Cancer patients with religious faith have also been shown (McIllmurray *et al.*, 2003) to have less reliance on health professionals, less need for information and less need for help with feelings of guilt. They also had fewer unmet needs overall when compared with patients expressing no faith.

We live in a time and in a country where much of the basics for decent living are attainable or provided. How does that situation impact on care? When all the basics are catered for, what more is there? It was, in some ways, a lot easier to 'bind up their wounds' and prepare them for death than it is to facilitate their moving beyond pain control to a quality of life that is enhanced. When the pain has been alleviated and assurance given of life-long medical commitment, to the physical comfort of a patient, he or she may validly ask, 'Is that all there is?' 'How can my dying be "the time of my life"? How can I attain a new quality of living with myself, family, friends, God? How can I grow through death so that the quality of my life is "changed not ended" and an ascending graph of living to the fullest within the parameters of my illness rather than a spiralling down to die?'

We have a long history in our religious tradition of the 'holy death'. Definitions may differ, but generally it meant 'getting' the last sacraments of the Church, becoming reconciled through the sacrament of penance and maintaining that pure state unsullied until we met the purity of God. Real life doesn't work that way – I wonder sometimes if people weren't pressured into someone else's version of the holy death. What does it mean? If 'holy' is related to 'whole', then it means to embrace dying as an act of life; to live as fully as we can do within the parameters of our final illness so that the quality of life 'is changed not ended' by death. That can hardly come about if the patient considers they should become somebody else.

What is right for one person may be considered irreverent or irreligious for others. Lighting candles, Cross-kissing and the liberal sprinkling of holy water may be entirely appropriate for someone to whom these are meaningful and comforting. By the same token, they may be incongruous and intrusive for others.

Conclusions

If the hospice is truly a home from home; a place where the spiritual, physical, mental and emotional needs of the person terminally ill are enhanced to ensure the fullest quality of life, then the spiritual needs of that person, even if they differ from our own in terms of belief and expression, cannot be left to the ministrations of those who share their view. They are a challenge to the entire hospice community.

Much of what is written here is patient-focused and, in that, I am guilty myself of divisiveness. Is a hospice divided, as Eliza Doolittle declares darkly in another context, into 'them what does and them what's done to?' What of the spirituality of the staff? Let it be said immediately, that a staff member's beliefs and spirituality, or lack of them, is his or her own business and should have no bearing on recruitment, conditions or advancement. In that sense the rights of any individual staff member are identical to those of every individual patient. Having said that, it seems reasonable to assert that someone who opts to 'buy into' employment in a hospice would do so aware of the rights of the patient to hold diverse beliefs and to express them diversely and be commited to facilitating this in every possible way.

The traditional Christian view of God as unchanging and impassive has been challenged by theologians reflecting on the meaning of God's love for the world in the light of contemporary understanding of what it means to be human. Saunders (1981) emphasized the revelation of God in suffering when she expressed the view that 'God uses the losses of our lives and our deaths to give us himself. He travels with us in his redeeming strength because he has suffered and died and did so with no more than the equipment of a man. And he rose again.'

This view of suffering is shared with Frankl (1963) in *Man's Search for Meaning* where he proposes that suffering and evil may in some way be transformed and that hopelessness may be replaced by a sense of meaning and purpose. Underpinning this is the idea that God walks with us and is not a separate reality dwelling apart from the world, the implication being that God suffers alongside the sufferer. As a co-sufferer of each person in pain, his fairness and justice cannot be challenged and God's involvement within human suffering becomes a way of affirming the meaningfulness of suffering and the sustaining of hope.

This is surely a time to move beyond the noise of our own certainties so that we can listen repectfully and reverently to the vision of others. In so doing, the quality of life and the breadth of vision we all aspire to may be achieved.

References

Braun, K. L. and Zir, A. (2001) Roles for the church in improving end-of-life care: perceptions of Christian clergy and laity, *Death Studies*, 25(8):685–704.

Exline, J. J., Yali, A. M. and Sanderson, W. C. (2000) Guilt, discord, and alienation: the role of religious strain in depression and suicidality, *Journal of Clinical Psychology*, 56(12):1481–96.

Frankl, V. (1963) *Man's Search for Meaning*. London: Hodder & Stoughton.

Handzo, R. (1996) Chaplaincy: A continuum of caring, *Oncology*, 10(9):45–7.

Ingersoll-Dayton, B., Krause, N. and Morgan, D. (2002) Religious trajectories and transitions over the life course, *International Journal of Ageing and Clinical Development*, 35(1):51–70.

Klass, D. (1999) *The Spiritual Lives of Deceased Parents*. Philadelphia: Brunner/ Mazel.

McGrath, P. (2003) Religosity and the challenge of terminal illness, *Death Studies*, 27(10):881–99.

McIllmurray, M. B., Francis, B., Harman, J. C., Morris, S. M., Soothill, K. and Thomas, C. (2003) Psychological needs in cancer patients related to religious belief, *Palliative Medicine*, 17(1):49–54.

Penson, R. T., Rushdia, Z. Y., Bruce, A. (2001) Losing God, *The Oncologist*, 6:286–97.

Satterly, L. (2001) Guilt, shame and religious and spiritual pain, *Holistic Nursing Practice*, 15(2):30–9.

Saunders, C. (1981) in Summer, D. and Teller, N. (eds) (1981) *Hospice: The Living Idea*. London: Edward Arnold.

13 | Whole person care: the Irish dimension

Michael Kearney

Introduction

In this chapter I discuss whole person care as it applies to palliative care in an Irish setting. 'Whole person care' is an approach to patients and their families that recognizes and responds to persons as body, mind, and spirit. The term was first used by Professor Balfour Mount and colleagues (1999), who drew on the World Health Organization's definition of palliative care as: 'The active total care of patients . . . control of pain, of other symptoms, and of psychological, social and spiritual problems, is paramount' (World Health Organization, 1990). By definition, therefore, palliative care is whole person care in the setting of advanced and terminal illness.

At the outset I set the context with some introductory remarks. I then reflect on some of the foundational ideas of palliative care, and discuss how these are the core ideas of whole person care. I also look at some more recent ideas in whole person care, and examine the relevance of these ideas to health care education. I conclude by looking at some of the implications of the ideas of whole person care for palliative care in Ireland.

There is an Irish cultural predisposition towards whole person care. When one speaks of whole person care to an Irish palliative care audience, for example, people immediately understand what you are talking about. The collective Irish cosmology is one that recognizes the spiritual dimension, conceptualized traditionally as 'the otherworld', which is thought of as being separated by just a thin veil from the everyday material world that we euphemistically call 'the real world'. One does not have to argue long to persuade an Irish person that we humans are 'body, mind and spirit'; except that he or she is likely to add 'and what about the heart and soul?' This familiarity to the point of kinship with the otherworld, allied to a strong sense of the importance of nature, place and family, is seen in Celtic spirituality, a healthy mix of paganism and Christianity.

This 'natural predisposition' to ideas of whole person care may also explain why hospice care had some of its earliest beginnings in Ireland, especially in the work of Mother Mary Aikenhead and the Irish Sisters of Charity. One sees this reflected in the stated core values of this religious Order: human dignity, justice, advocacy, quality and compassion (Our Lady's Hospice, 2003). Their holistic model of health care is also evident in the Mission Statement of Our Lady's Hospice, in Dublin, which states that their goal is: 'Through a team approach and in an atmosphere of loving care to promote wholeness of body, mind, and spirit.'

Working within this philosophical atmosphere in the early stages of her career, Dame Cicely Saunders planned the opening of St Christopher's Hospice in London. She frequently acknowledges the formative influence the Irish Sisters of Charity had on her at this time. The words spoken by her patient, David Tasma, 'I only want what is in your mind and in your heart' (Du Boulay, 1984), which became her guiding metaphor in pioneering the modern palliative care movement, echoed the holism she had encountered at St Joseph's Hospice in Hackney.

My own encounter with the natural holism of Irish health care was a variant of the 'first there is a mountain; then there is no mountain; then there is' experience. While I was a medical student and junior doctor in Ireland, I lived and breathed in this atmosphere but did not really appreciate or see it for what it was. During my ten years of working in palliative care in the United Kingdom, I experienced something different when I spoke to patients about the deeper aspects of their suffering, although I could not have said what it was. Looking back, I remember how it felt as if we had to work extra hard on what we called 'spiritual issues' in an English setting. In Ireland when I asked a patient, 'and how are you in yourself?' I could take for granted that he or she would understand that I was asking about his or her 'whole' experience. With an English patient I had to spell out exactly what I meant. While this greater precision with language was a useful discipline in many ways, it also had its limitations as I found it was impossible to put the intuitive underpinning of language into clear and discrete concepts. As I thought more on this, I wondered if it may reflect more of a disconnection, more of a body–mind split within an English cultural setting. It seemed to me that the patients I met there were either very secular or very religious. My impression was that the middle ground of native spirituality that I had previously encountered was missing.

On my subsequent return to working in Ireland, I recall immediately experiencing a sense of relief in my encounters with patients. Was it simply that I was 'home again', Irish among Irish? Was it just because we shared the same metaphors as well as the same vocabulary, and lived from many similar cultural assumptions? Undoubtedly this was partly the case, but I suspect there was something more to it. Once again, when I asked a patient 'how are you in yourself?', he or she talked without prompting about what really mattered; about what was in his or her heart as well as what was on his or her mind. I realized then that there is an endemic valuing of the imaginative, the intuitive, the creative and the spiritual, of what has been called 'the indigenous mind', within Irish culture and that this works synergistically with the concepts of whole person care.

Even if one allows that there are factors in the Irish psyche and culture that make it fertile soil for a philosophy of whole person care, Irish palliative care is still vulnerable to the same sorts of pressures as elsewhere. Chief among these are economic issues and questions of the status of the specialty. The need to justify expenditure on the basis of quantifiable outcome measures, and the need to be seen and accepted as a 'serious' specialty, can mean that we compromise on the invisible, intangible essentials that embody the essence of the whole person care that is palliative care. There is a danger that as we become more effective as time managers and symptomatologists, we may develop a more fragmented and compartmentalized view of our patients. There is, in other words, within Irish palliative care as in palliative care elsewhere, a danger of selling the soul of the specialty in a need to succeed and belong.

Whole person care: the key constructs

But what exactly is in danger of being lost? Or, put more positively, what are the key constructs that comprise whole person care? Some of these are the core ideas of palliative care; others have been articulated more recently.

Total pain: Team response

Cicely Saunders used the phrase 'total pain' (Saunders, 1996) as a metaphor to describe the nature of human suffering. According to Saunders, total pain comprised physical, mental, social and spiritual components, with an overlapping of boundaries and a dynamic interplay between these different aspects of experience. Among the assumptions in this way of describing human suffering are that human experience is multi-dimensional and interconnected, and that human beings are inherently relational. This implies that pain in one aspect of the human experience can impact on another, and that the experience of suffering is worsened by social and spiritual alienation. The idea of total pain assumes, in other words, that human beings are whole persons and that the most appropriate and effective response this demands is one of attention and care to all aspects of that person's experience, including his or her relationships.

In many ways, the construct of total pain is the most influential of Saunders's ideas, and it has determined the shape and priorities of the evolving specialty of palliative care. It demands that each health care discipline reflect on the implications of total pain for its own approach to patients, its education of its students, and the sort of research questions it considers. It necessitates a multi-disciplinary and an inter-disciplinary approach because no single discipline, no matter how inclusive its philosophy and practice, can possibly respond single-handedly to all aspects of a patient's suffering. By fostering teamwork, and by calling on the humanity of individual caregivers, the construct of total pain shapes a model of care that is sensitively attuned to the varied needs of patients and families living with advanced and terminal illness. Working from this construct means that patients and their families are more likely to be appropriately managed. It also means that caregivers are more likely to find satisfaction in their work and be less likely to suffer the burnout that can result from trying to respond to unrealistic expectations.

Palliative care and healing

At an international palliative care conference some years back, American psychiatrist, Sam Klagsbrun, challenged the audience with the following question: 'Symptom control – *for what?*' (Klagsbrun, 1989). Even though symptom control is the cornerstone of palliative care, it is not *just* an end in itself. It is also in the service of something more. Palliative care is about doing what is possible to reduce suffering for the sake of promoting the optimal 'quality of life' (QoL) of patients and families living with advanced and terminal illness.

A further articulation of the goals of palliative care has come from the collaborative work of recent years between Our Lady's Hospice, Dublin, and Professor Balfour Mount and his team at the McGill Programs for Integrated Whole Person Care in Montreal. Within this conceptualization, palliative care is seen as being concerned with promoting a patient's *healing*, even in the face of the impossibility of cure. 'Healing' as used here describes a relational process involving movement towards an experience of integrity and wholeness, which may be facilitated by a caregiver's interventions but is dependent on an innate potential within the patient (Faculty Working Group on Healing, see below, p. 129). It is not dependent on the presence of, or the capacity for, physical well-being (Kagawa Singer, 1993) and, indeed, as Mount reminds us, 'it is possible to die healed' (Mount, 2003).

The implications of these ideas for palliative care are worth considering. In particular, they make a strong case for palliative care not being exclusively wed to the biomedical model. While a problem-solving approach is an appropriate and effective response to many of our patients' and families' needs, something more is needed if our aim is also to catalyse the innate healing potential of our patients.

One way to talk about this is in terms of the two original paradigms of Western health care; the Hippocratic approach, and what has been called the Asklepian approach (Kearney, 2000). The Hippocratic approach is synonymous with the biomedical model of evidence-based medicine. The Asklepian approach is a term which refers to the ritual practices associated with the Greek god of healing, Asklepios, which can be understood metaphorically as an attempt to activate the innate healing principle within the patient's *soma* and *psyche*.

A defining feature of the Hippocratic approach is that therapeutic change is initiated by the caregiver. In contrast, with the Asklepian approach the locus of control that enables healing is within the patient him- or herself. While the caregiver-healer does not heal the patient, *per se*, he or she can facilitate this process by providing a secure environment grounded in a sense of connectedness that Buber termed 'I–thou' relating (Buber, 1973). When healing occurs, there is a change in an individual's subjective experience, which may be transformative, and which corresponds with an improvement in quality of life. One patient attempting to describe this inner change commented, 'The pain is still there but I can live with it now.' Another patient said, 'It's an experience. Something inside me that comes from here [pointing to the middle of his chest]. I feel proud of myself that I have it in me.' Yet another, who was by then very close to death said, 'I know the Lord is healing me'. In the research literature, the subjective experience of healing has been described in terms of 'response shift' (Wilson, 1999), which also offers a helpful terminology for the study and discussion of these concepts.

How can we promote healing?

If healing is to take place, both the Hippocratic and Asklepian approaches must be offered as a seamless whole to patients and their families. This is what we mean by whole person care, the goal of which is to cure and alleviate suffering where possible, and to create the conditions that facilitate healing.

As illustrated in Figure 13.1, whole person care comprises a number of overlapping elements that are shared by both the Hippocratic and Asklepian approaches, as well as one element that is unique to each approach.

The Hippocratic Approach	The Asklepian Approach
Who we (caregivers and patients) are as persons	
The therapeutic relationship	
Intervening to solve problems	Working directly with the healing principle
How we do what we do	

Figure 13.1 Whole Person Care: elements of two interdependent systems

Who we are as persons

Psychiatrist Michael Balint talks about the 'Doctor [caregiver] as drug' (Balint, 2000). He suggested that who we caregivers are as persons (as opposed to our professional persona), is the most potent medicine we give our patients. Continuing with this metaphor, he suggests that we know far less about this drug – in terms of how it works, its interactions and side-effects – than we do about almost any other medication in our pharmacopoeia. Who we are as persons determines both the quality of our relationships, and the quality of the care we offer our patients, and so is the core issue in our role as healers. Ideas such as that of *The Wounded Healer* (Guggenbuhl-Craig, 1999) which suggests that our potency as healers stems, paradoxically, from a knowledge and acceptance of our own powerlessness, are valuable in understanding and promoting the inner dynamics of healing. To paraphrase Hindu teacher Sri Madhava Ashish: ' "[Caregiver] heal thyself" would appear to be the axiom . . . [For] when you want to help a person towards healing you must, in some way, retreat into yourself to the level from which the healing flows' (Ashish, 1992).

The 'we' that is primarily intended in the phrase, 'who we are as persons' are caregivers. However, this idea also applies to the patient. A patient's ability to be in and let go to the experience of the present moment, or putting it another way, the degree of his or her inner/subjective openness to the healing principle, is also relevant to the process of healing.

The therapeutic relationship

The relationship that is formed between caregiver and patient is the factor common to both approaches. It forms the therapeutic container in which healing occurs; it is a channel for empathy, compassion and reassurance; and by modelling an egalitarian, meaningful connectedness that is respectful of difference, it promotes subjective integration and wholeness.

Intervening to solve problems

A defining characteristic of the Hippocratic approach is what we do to and for our patients. Our knowledge and skills as caregivers determine our clinical effectiveness. Through the curative and palliative interventions we perform for our patients, through the psycho-social interventions we offer them and their families, and through competently planning and organizing their care, we lessen fear, give comfort and build trust. By expertly treating problems, Hippocratic interventions create the preconditions in which healing may happen.

Working directly with the healing principle

Just as the healing principle is visible in its physical expression as the granu-lation tissue that grows across a wound, so it is psychologically manifest in the process of dreaming. Its language is that of image, music, touch, movement, and silence. This idea calls for a re-visioning of a variety of therapeutic approaches that were previously seen as 'diversional therapies', which at best temporarily distract patients from the awfulness of their situation. Approaches that work directly with the patient's innate healing potential are outlined in Figure 13.2.

The challenge for the caregiver is not necessarily to be skilled in these ways of working, but to appreciate their potential value, and to make it possible and easy for patients to access one or more of these approaches if and when necessary and appropriate.

How we do what we do

Our identity as healers is primarily shaped by our attitudes and perception, and the quality of the care we offer, rather than by our proficiency with a demanding new knowledge base and skills set. As Saunders observes, '*The way care is given* can reach the most hidden places and give space for

Non-rational therapies	Body therapies	Religious practice
Dream-work	Massage	Prayer
Music therapy	Yoga	Ritual
Art therapy		Spiritual practice
Reminiscence therapy		Meditation

Figure 13.2 Therapeutic approaches

unexpected development' (Saunders, 1996). That healing is about doing what we are already doing for our patients with a new attitude, rather than doing new or different things (which we have yet to learn), is a reassuring thought to those who wish to deepen their role as caregivers.

Whole person care: an experiment in medical education

In June 2001, the Dean of Medicine at McGill Medical School, Montreal established the 'Healing and Healthcare' initiative (Mount and Kearney, 2003). One aspect of the initiative was the establishment of the McGill Faculty Working Group on Healing and Healthcare, who were asked to consider three questions: What is healing? Is healing part of the health care mandate? And, if so, what are the implications of this for clinical practice, education and research? The working group was also asked to undertake a detailed review of undergraduate medical curriculum content to assess current approaches to teaching about healing, and to make recommendations as to how best to develop this aspect of the curriculum.

Part way through the working group's meetings, one participant offered the diagram in Figure 13.3 as a representation of medical students' understanding of healing.

From discussions with first-year medical students in small group sessions held shortly after entry to medical school, it was clear that they already had an understanding of the nature of healing from their own life experience, and their predominant view was that healing was indeed part of their

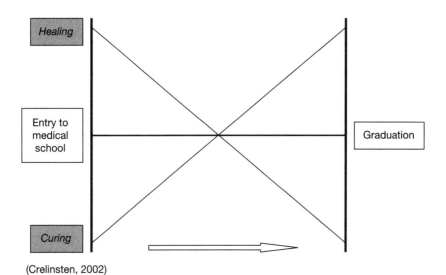

(Crelinsten, 2002)

Figure 13.3 Medical students' understanding of healing

mandate as caregivers. This contrasted starkly with views expressed by final-year medical students shortly before graduation. They felt that they now knew a lot more about curing than they had on admission to medical school, but added that what they had known of healing had neither been validated nor developed during their medical training, and had now receded far into the background of what seemed relevant and important. These views are encapsulated in the following comments of a female medical student who was speaking in a small group session on the theme of 'Being a Healer': 'This is why I came into medicine . . . but I have been turned into such a cold person. I don't want to be with patients anymore . . . I am thinking of leaving medicine.'

These remarks, and others like them, challenged the working group to reflect on what could be done to prevent the medical students' understanding of healing being buried beneath a mountain of biomedical knowledge, skills and values. Put more positively, how might it be possible to build on the students' own wisdom, while simultaneously helping them to achieve academic excellence in the science of medicine? Influenced by Balint's idea that in regards to healing 'we are the medicine', the working group concluded that the most effective way of promoting healing in medicine would be to enhance the opportunity for integration of the subjective, inner-life experience of the students during their undergraduate education. To this end, it was proposed that students keep a journal/portfolio documenting their emotional reactions, insights and questions relating to their evolving clinical experience, in the manner described by Charon (2003). In addition, regular small-group discussions, with the same attendees and mentor, would run throughout their undergraduate years, offering students the opportunity to discuss their insights and experiences in a confidential forum. In this way the gap between the students' personal and professional experience could be bridged. Such integration, it was argued, would promote healing in both student and patient. This proposal is currently being piloted with undergraduate medical students at McGill.

Whole person care: the implications for Irish palliative care

In addition to Our Lady's Hospice's collaborative involvement with the McGill Programs in Integrated Whole Person Care, there are a variety of other clinical, educational and research projects on whole person care within Irish palliative care. Examples of these are the palliative care services throughout the country that offer a range of creative and supportive therapies of the kind discussed above; there are also palliative care education programmes that offer training in the theory and practice of healing in health care and research on quality of life, using subjective measures

(Waldron *et al.*, 1999). Another example is a recent initiative to bring the philosophy and practice of whole person care to an acute hospital setting. This is the Lios Aoibhinn Cancer Support Centre, recently established at St Vincent's University Hospital, Dublin. The director of the centre, Anne Hayes, says of its name: '*Lios* can mean the enclosed area of a Ring Fort (Inner) and *Aoibhinn* is Beauty/Delight. Therefore, *Lios Aoibhinn* is a metaphor for the space, where people who are affected by cancer can find calm, support and healing for body, mind and spirit . . . a place apart.'

While acknowledging these and other positive developments, it is fair to say that palliative care in Ireland is at a crossroads in its development as a health care specialty. Financial expediency, a materialist mind-set that values problem-solving and tangible results above all else, and peer pressure on a medical consultant-led service to conform to the *status quo* of the supremacy of the biomedical model, could push Irish palliative care down the road of becoming 'just another specialty' (Kearney, 1992). Indeed, some might argue that this has already occurred, or is certainly well on its way in that direction. If this were true, it would be unfortunate, if not tragic, as palliative care has the potential to be more than this. This is relevant because the founding vision of the pioneers of hospice and palliative care was that a concern for whole person care should be the central priority. It also matters because this is what our patients and their families want, need and expect from us as caregivers. Whole person care, which combines the best of medical science with the art of healing, which treats problems while simultaneously promoting integration and wholeness, is the most appropriate and effective response to persons living with advanced and terminal illness.

Irish palliative care is uniquely positioned to be a world leader in the field of whole person care. In addition to the reasons just discussed, there is a similarity here to the argument often made for Ireland's potential to be a leader in ecological and environmental concerns: that there are already natural resources in place that lead in this direction. The indigenous Irish mind is one that is already attuned by default to values of soul and spirit. There is already a long tradition of valuing caring and connectedness, the imaginative, the creative and the intuitive. But this is not something that will happen without conscious and deliberate choice and action. The cultural pressures that pull in other directions must not be underestimated. Unless we positively discriminate for the values of whole person care in decisions about clinical practice, education and research, palliative care will settle for less than it could be; we will have squandered a very real opportunity; we will have betrayed the founding vision of our specialty; and we will have failed our patients and their families.

Conclusion

Palliative care has already succeeded in achieving the status of an established specialty within Irish health care. This is a significant achievement in itself and one to be proud of and grateful for. Nonetheless, the issues highlighted by whole person care mean that once again we are confronted with important choices about the core values of palliative care. The choices we make will affect how we allocate resources, how we organize services, what content we include in health care curricula, and the sort of research we support. I believe the poet Rilke offers a signpost to Irish palliative care at the beginning of the twenty-first century when he writes:

Work of the eyes is done;
Now, go and do heart work.

References

Ashish, Sri Madhava (1992) Personal communication.
Balint, M. (2000) *The Doctor, His Patient and the Illness*. Edinburgh: Churchill Livingstone.
Buber, M. (1973) *I and Thou*, Trans. R. G. Smith, Edinburgh: T & T Clark.
Charon, R. (2003) Narrative Medicine: teaching empathy and clinical courage. Presented at McGill Medical Education Rounds, 30 January, 2003 (publication pending).
Crelinsten, G. (2002) Personal Communication.
Du Boulay, S. (1984) *Cicely Saunders*. London: Hodder & Stoughton.
Guggenbuhl-Craig, A. (1999) *Power in the Helping Professions*. Woodstock, CT: Spring Publications.
Kagawa Singer, M. (1993) Redefining health: living with cancer, *Social Science and Medicine*, 37:295–304.
Kearney, M. (1992) Palliative Medicine – Just Another Specialty? *Palliative Medicine*, 6:39–46.
Kearney, M. (2000) *A Place of Healing: Working with Suffering in Living and Dying*. Oxford: Oxford University Press.
Klagsbrun, S. (1989) St. Christopher's Hospice, International Conference, London, July.
Mount, B. (2003) Spirituality and Health: Developing a Shared Vocabulary. *Annals RCPSC* 35:305.
Mount, B., Boston, P. and Cohen, R. (1999) *A Proposal for the Development and Implementation of Education and Research Programs in Integrated Whole Person Care*, Gerald Bronfman Centre, McGill University, 546 Pine Avenue West, Montreal, Quebec, Canada, H2W 1S6, p.15.
Mount, B. and Kearney, M. (2003) Healing and Palliative Care: Charting our Way Forward (Editorial), *Palliative Medicine*, 17:657–8.
Our Lady's Hospice (2003) *Core Values of Irish Sisters of Charity*, Annual Report. Dublin.

Rilke, R. M. 'Turning Point' (extract), *The Selected Poetry of Rainer Maria Rilke*, ed. and trans. S. Mitchell, New York: Vintage International.

Saunders, C. (1996) Foreword, in Kearney, M. *Mortally Wounded: Stories of Soul Pain, Death and Healing.* New York: Scribner, 1996.

Saunders, C. *The Management of Terminal Malignant Disease.* London: Edward Arnold.

Waldron, D., O'Boyle, C. A., Kearney, M., Moriarty, M. and Carney, D. (1999) Quality of Life Measurement in Advanced Cancer: Assessing the Individual, *Journal of Clinical Oncology*, 17(11):3603–11.

Wilson, I. (1999) Clinical understanding and clinical implications of response shift, *Social Science and Medicine*, 48:1577–88.

World Health Organization (1990) *Cancer Pain Relief and Palliative Care.* Technical Report Series 804. Geneva.

14 Irish Travellers and specialist palliative care services

Onja Van Doorslaer and Regina McQuillan

Introduction

Ethnic and cultural diversity within most societies is a demographic reality and there is a growing realization that this diversity cannot be ignored by hospice and palliative care services (McNamara *et al.*, 1997). Travellers are a distinct ethnic grouping within Irish society. Many Traveller families also have links to extended families in the United Kingdom. According to the most recent national census in 2002, there are 23,681 Travellers living in Ireland. In Dublin, Wicklow and Kildare (the area covered by the Eastern Regional Health Authority) there are 6,676 Travellers (Central Statistics Office, 2004). There are a number of active Traveller organizations in this region (for example, Pavee Point, The Irish Travellers Movement, and The Parish of the Travelling People) as well as a Traveller Health Unit funded by government. The Traveller population in Ireland is notable in having a poorer health status and a lower life expectancy than the rest of the Irish population (Barry *et al.*, 1987; Pavee Point, 2001).

Travellers' health issues have recently been the focus of much attention with the Traveller Health Strategy (Department of Health and Children, 2002) highlighting many of the problems facing Travellers with regard to their health and use of health services. This strategy does not refer to palliative care services nor does the recent *Report of the National Advisory Committee on Palliative Care* (Department of Health and Children, 2001) refer to the needs of Travellers for specialist palliative care services.

Anecdotal evidence points towards Travellers having little or no interaction with hospice services. Pavee Point[1] note that: 'Travellers inhabit two worlds – the Settled world and the Traveller world' (Pavee Point, 2001a). Irish health services, from primary through to tertiary care, are modelled on the settled community's world. There is a lack of current information or research on Travellers' use of health services including specialist palliative care services (Pavee Point, 2001; Van Doorslaer *et al.*, 2002). The 'Traveller Health Strategy' goes some way towards identifying areas for action.

This chapter summarizes a research project carried out in 2002 to explore the context within which Irish Travellers use palliative care services and their views and experiences of service provision. The study focused on Travellers' knowledge about hospice and palliative care in the Eastern Regional Health Authority (ERHA) encompassing Dublin, North Wicklow and East Kildare. The attitudes of these Travellers to cancer, serious illness, death and dying and hospice and/or palliative care services were explored. In addition, specialist palliative care staff's personal experiences of caring for Travellers in this region were surveyed.

The methodology chosen was both qualitative, involving focus groups and interviews, and quantitative through a questionnaire to specialist palliative care professionals working in the region. Data from the focus groups and interviews were analysed using the computer-based analytical software 'Nudist' and the survey data were analysed using 'Datadesk' software.

Collaboration with existing Travellers' organizations was critical in gaining access to allow focus group discussions. In total, 32 Travellers took part in five separate group discussions. Sixteen specialist palliative care professionals from a number of disciplines (for example, doctors, nurses, social workers) took part in interviews or group discussions to explore staff's experience of caring for members of the Travelling community.

A questionnaire was designed based on these interviews and on pre-existing questionnaires (O'Donovan *et al.*, 1995). The aim was to survey all palliative care staff in the Eastern Regional Health Authority (approximately 230). The questionnaire enquired about the number of Travellers referred; recording of ethnic group, whether 'Traveller' is recorded as a separate group; specific provision for Travellers including staff training; personal experiences with caring for Travellers and identified needs. A total of 215 questionnaires were distributed to eight different organizations that provide specialist palliative care services. Eighty-one completed questionnaires were returned, giving an overall response rate of 38 per cent.

The number of Travellers utilizing palliative care services appears to be low. Over the previous 12-month period, 86 per cent of respondents had not cared for any members of the Travelling community. During the previous five-year period over 50 per cent of all respondents had not cared for any Travellers. Training and education opportunities for staff regarding Travellers also appear to be very limited. Over 88 per cent of respondents indicated there were no such training facilities in their work-place and only 15 per cent of respondents had received any education/training about Travellers.

A number of themes emerged from both the focus groups and the questionnaire. These are outlined in the following section.

Knowledge about palliative care services

Clearly most Traveller participants have little knowledge or understanding of the philosophy of hospice and palliative care and limited knowledge of home care and hospices. Fears were expressed about dying in a hospice, which was viewed as a place of last resort despite positive comments about the friendliness of staff, its wonderful facilities and the high levels of care. Home care was seen as acceptable as a specialist team advising on pain relief but not as a provider of emotional support which was viewed as a family duty. The home care team would be seen as strangers and providing emotional support would always be done by the family.

Factors affecting use of services

The research suggests that there are many factors influencing use of palliative care services by Travellers. These include fear of cancer, reluctance to embrace institutional care, fear of prejudice and of mistreatment. Fear and denial of cancer were major themes. This was expressed in different ways including reluctance to talk about cancer. When mentioning cancer in the context of this study, many participants blessed themselves to protect themselves from its 'evilness' and some remained very uncomfortable with any discussion relating to cancer, illness or dying and death in general.

Many health services do not accommodate the needs of Travellers, such as space to accommodate large family groups. The practical barriers to accessing services include lack of information and awareness of services. Service providers noted issues such as Traveller mobility with a lack of continuity of care and lack of awareness as being central issues. Lack of knowledge of the different beliefs and culture held by Travellers, as well as prejudice against Travellers from the public and service providers, were the second and third most commonly identified barriers to effective delivery of care. Additional issues relating to large family networks (which provide important support to the ill family member, but also cause problems with overcrowding in the in-patient setting), a need for greater chaplaincy input, and the social isolation sometimes experienced by Travellers in hospital.

Identified needs of health care providers concern the lack of training/ education about the customs, culture and belief systems of Travellers. Many respondents expressed the belief that greater knowledge of these areas would improve the quality of care delivered to members of the Travelling community. This was reflected in the Travellers' assessment of the importance of service providers trying to understand their needs and in taking time to communicate clearly so that Travellers could understand them. The importance of creating an environment that allows Travellers the choice of using a service and of removing any practical or cultural barriers was highlighted.

Service providers' views

The opinions, experiences and ideas of palliative care service providers were explored. The level of experience of having cared for or treated Travellers was examined as well as the views of participants on service use, preferred place of death and some insights into the issue of cultural diversity. Many service providers had little or no experience of caring for Travellers. Certain themes were identified such as compliance, security, cultural differences, communication difficulties and illiteracy. Possible solutions for overcoming these issues or potential problems were offered. These included the need to reach out to the Travelling community, to forge links and open pathways of communication. Problems within services were also highlighted such as lack of resources and high staff turnover. Service providers indicated that the issues perceived as potential difficulties in delivering a service to the Travelling community are also encountered in caring for those in the settled community. The main issue of cultural difference is one they wish to embrace and accommodate, indicating that services are eminently flexible and that they are willing and eager to learn the ways in which they can adapt the service to meet the needs of Travellers. Participants emphasized that respect for difference and individuality is central to their approach and philosophy as palliative care service providers.

Rituals and behaviour at the time of illness, dying and death

Travellers practice a range of rituals and customs during times of illness, dying, death and during bereavement. These vary among families of Travellers in different regions of Ireland just as they do for those of the settled community (Van Doorslaer and Keegan, 2001). At times of illness, it is a Traveller tradition to visit the sick and dying in large numbers. Travellers will often seek both conventional medical advice and the help of healers and cures. In Traveller culture it is important for the family to seek blessing for the sick and dying. On occasion 'healers' may visit the dying person. Although insistent that healers are still used, many noted that they did not have as strong a faith in their abilities to heal as they once may have had.

There is a strong fatalistic belief that if you are meant to die you will. Cancer is not considered as something that can be cured by healers. Excepting some of the younger Traveller participants, most Travellers stressed the overriding importance of the priest at times of illness and imminent death. Many of the women who took part in the discussion groups talked about the role of alcohol during illness and when people are dying.

A number of traditions and rituals are practised at the time of death and during the funeral. Traditionally, there would have been strict changes to the eating and cooking practices around the time of death. Chrissie Ward (1992:56) recalls: 'You'd never get anybody cookin' or washin' vessels or doin' anything in the home. They wouldn't be interested in that.' There is also the possibility of fasting at the time of a funeral (O'Brien, 2000). Although none of the women in the focus group referred to fasting, they did refer to the lack of interest in food at this time. Some talked about how settled peoples' funerals would lay on food and that Travellers would not be interesting in eating at this time but would prefer to drink.

Traditionally Travellers would be waked before their burial as is common practice in Ireland. The definition of 'wake' can be vague, referring sometimes to a drinking session in the pub before the funeral or in other cases to the gathering for drinks after the funeral. In its original sense it referred to the ritual of food, drink, storytelling, song and games prior to the funeral in the company of the corpse (Van Doorslaer and Keegan, 2001). McCann (1992) notes how traditionally the Traveller would be waked with singing, dancing and smoking. One feature that remains associated with Traveller deaths and wakes is that of the open-air fire.

Travellers are renowned for the many wreaths and flowers that adorn the coffin and later the grave of the deceased (O'Brien, 2000). Floral wreaths are often elaborate and can take many unconventional forms. Okely (1983) notes how floral wreaths can take many forms from a miniature horse and wagon, a replica lorry, a horseshoe, a floral television set or the motif of 'the gates of heaven'. The replicas usually relate to the preferences of the deceased.

In the period after death certain rituals and traditions are also practiced by the Travelling community. One tradition is that of burning the trailers, caravans and belongings of the deceased. O'Brien (2000) writes how traditionally in Traveller culture, the trailer and the belongings would be burned to free the spirit of the dead person and to cope with the intense pain of remembering or with memories associated with the dead person (O'Brien, 2000). Some believe that burning of possessions is a sign of how much the deceased was thought of by their family (Carr, 1992; McCann, 1992; Reilly, 1992). The extent to which property is destroyed can vary from family to family and is often determined by their own situation. For some, burning all the belongings was not an option and just the clothes were burned.

Traveller women talked at length about this tradition. Many felt this custom is dying out because of practical and financial concerns. The practical implications of burning a trailer or leaving a house are fast negating the need to adhere to tradition in that many cannot afford to replace the trailer or find another home. Other traditions include: moving on from the place where the family live, the curtailing of social activities, the tradition of returning to the grave nine days later for prayers, a month's Mass, mourning cards, the blessing of the cross, and the blessing of the graves. Many of these traditions are shared with the settled community.

It was clear from this study that Travellers compared themselves and their customs and way of life to those of settled people or 'country people' as Travellers call them. When noting the differences that exist between Travellers and settled people it was largely the Travellers that stressed the differences.

Crowds

One of the recurring issues around Travellers and palliative care was the issue of crowds. Much was said about the numbers of Travellers that gather and remain in the locality when a family member was ill or dying and then at the funeral afterwards. Both Travellers and service providers noted this as being a potentially difficult issue. It was clear that the phenomenon of such large crowds, numbering up to three or four hundred, gathering for funerals is not as common in the settled community:

> With settled people say your friend was dying, you'd just go to the hospital and visit one by one and you'd go home but Travellers they don't do that, they'd sleep outside the hospital. So that they're close.
>
> (Traveller-FG3)

The importance of the extended family for Travellers means that at times of crisis, including death, large crowds gather. This was recognized by Travellers as a potential problem for health care providers, and suggestions on how to manage this included identifying key members of family or clergy to liaise with the family, providing waiting areas and avoiding the use of security staff.

Different treatment by clinical staff

The Travellers and service providers both raised the issue of prejudicial care as experienced by Travellers. This issue was also raised in relation to the barriers that may prevent Travellers from using palliative care services, but also applies to health services in general:

I had a cousin that was killed in an accident out on the road and he was brought out there and he was a week in the hospital and I remember us all, everyone was going in to see him coz he knew he wasn't going to make it. I remember us going out and they wouldn't let us in to see him. So they never wanted any crowd in, they never wanted a crowd to be there and there was no welcome for the Travellers.

(Traveller-FG1)

Comparison to settled people

Travellers remarked on the differences between themselves and settled people. Travellers felt that settled people were more educated and had greater self-confidence. They suggested that settled people are more aware of their entitlements and are more confident around clinical personnel and less likely to get embarrassed in situations around medical care and hospitals:

L: It's a way of looking at it, a settled person would know more about their rights than a Travelling person would. We mightn't have as much education as to what they have.

M2: Like if I were in the hospital now and the doctor came over to me and said to me 'please leave the hospital', I'd leave the hospital, I wouldn't say well 'why' or 'why are you not asking her to leave and you're asking me to leave' I wouldn't say that, I'd just walk out of the hospital.

L: It's embarrassment.

M2: It's embarrassment.

(Travellers-FG2)

Different ideas about hospice

The issue of leaving a family member in a hospice or home was discussed. Travellers commented that settled people seem more prepared to do this. They felt that they were too close to their families to be able to leave them in a hospice. Settled people, according to Travellers, were better at letting go:

M: I'm not being ignorant when I say this but I just find that settled people can let them go, like we wouldn't even considered me mother or father going in to it, if there was some of us to mind them, do they really want to be going there or to be putting us to anything like that ... and as K says her daddy'd be lost up there, that's the way we'd think of it and they could probably give them better care than we could ever give them but to us they'd be lost and to their ole brains God help

them they'd be lost as well, that we are leaving them, you know the
way . . .

N: I think that they die happier at home.

M: But I thinks that settled people has great willpower that they can
let that go and let them go in and it's great, you know what I mean but
we wouldn't . . .

(Travellers-FG5)

Different responses to death

Many Travellers talked about how funerals for Travellers are very different
to those of settled people. There are different ideas about what was to
be done at the funeral in terms of behaviour, practices such as cremation,
the after-funeral gathering and the tending of the grave after burial. The
idea of having food after the burial was equated to having a party
which was seen as inappropriate. Contrary to the gradual increase in
popularity among the settled community (Van Doorslaer and Keegan,
2001), Travellers reject cremation outright; 'we do not believe in it' (Okely,
1983:222).

The practice of cremation is seen as very much the domain of settled
people and Travellers will only get cremated when married to a settled person and influenced by settled ways:

K: One of my cousins, like they had big food and sandwiches, it was
like a proper do, like you know what I mean.

M: Like settled people . . .

K: Me daddy went to it but he was bewildered. It was just pure settled
peoples carry on, he was married to a settled woman. It was the same
when our K died, she was married to a settled man, she got cremated
and me daddy was bewildered . . .

M: That's one thing that Travellers won't do, even consider.

K: But she wanted to be cremated and we hadn't a clue where she was
going to go or what way they were going to do it, where the coffin
was going, we were all . . . then they had a big wake, big loads of food
and all, but that's just Travellers they wouldn't here tell of eating.

M: Now we find that, just to come back to have a big kinda . . . now
every settled person does nearly do that, to hire out a pub and have a
big kinda do, and that's just their way of kinda . . . we wouldn't have
any of that.

K: Travellers would just drink they wouldn't bother with food.

(Travellers-FG5)

Funerals

Travellers talked about funeral attendance. Most Travellers are related
or know each other well and therefore will attend most funerals that they
hear of:

> That's one thing about Travellers funerals as well, even you might not
> have known that person but you know someone belonging to them
> and there'll always be a big funeral and their might be another funeral
> with settleds and there wouldn't be quarter of the people, you know
> what I mean.

(Traveller-FG5)

Travellers attending a funeral will not be in a frame of mind to care about
their appearance and will express grief profusely in an abandoned manner,
in contrast to more restrained funerals of settled people:

> K: They [settled people] were all calm and taking it easy.
>
> M: Get up singing.
>
> K: Hair combed and makeup.
>
> M: And our hair'd be standing and we'd have no makeup.
>
> K: You wouldn't hear telling of grooming, the immediate family
> wouldn't hear telling of grooming yerself up like that, anyway and
> getting up singing in the church.
>
> M: But that's their way of doing things, just different like.
>
> M: Some women [Traveller] passes out and everything.
>
> K: Some would be roaring crying and some'd be just sitting there.
>
> M: It's not that we are any more emotional than they are it's just that
> we do things different. Sure we'd love it if we could take it that calm,
> you'd love it if you could get groomed and put makeup on but you just
> can't do it. I suppose it depends who it is, women would be very cut up
> over children.

(Travellers-FG5)

Different ideas about the grave

Ideas around tending the grave after burial were seen as being very different
between the two communities. It was seen as puzzling and upsetting to the
Travellers taking part that settled people do not tend to or even visit the
graves of their deceased in a more caring and organized manner:

> They [Travellers] just wouldn't leave the grave with nothing. I go
> down to . . . and I see some graves [of settled people] and they are there

since the 80s and they haven't even got a headstone or a little heart or nothing and you feel sad knowing the ole grave is left like that and not even kept and no one visits, you know when you go to the blessings of the graves now every year and you see graves now and there not even a sinner beside them, its like they never existed.

(Travellers-FG5)

Different ways of coping with death

Some Travellers felt that settled people had different ways of coping with death and in the eyes of Travellers have a better understanding of life and death. Travellers talked about the huge impact that death has on them and their whole community. They talked about how it is such a shocking event that no one is left untouched by a death. They also noted how detached settled people appear to be around death and how settled people can talk openly and freely about death:

> If somebody, even with a Traveller when you talk about cancer it's an awful thing to be talking about, but settled people don't find that a problem to talk about it. You often hear them talking about it. They are more free making about things, they understand life and death better I think. Especially when it comes to death, they understand how to let go. They've been learnt from a young age not to take it so badly. Whereas someone die in a Traveller family, it's the end of the world, it knocks everyone back, from the youngest to oldest, it affects them all deeply like, they take it personal but settled people don't. You'd often hear 'sure she died, she had a happy death or she suffered a lot and all' and it doesn't seem to be that big an issue.
>
> (Traveller-FG3)

Life events such as death and birth evoke a very strong reaction in Travellers and their need is to be close to the situation. They noted how settled people can sit and wait for a phone call about an impending birth whereas the Traveller is in the maternity hospital or camped outside anxiously awaiting news. Most Travellers felt that settled people are taught how to react in a calmer way and teach their children likewise whereas Traveller children learn a sense of panic from their parents:

> B: It's the same at the birth of a child, there all there. Like we slept in the van in the hospital grounds when my daughter went in to have her first baby, we slept at the door of the hospital. You'd never see settled people going to that extent, they just make a phone call, they have everything prepared but Travellers are all upside down and panicking, when is it going to happen, I can't wait, like you know.

Whereas settled people just take it in their stride 'we'll just wait now and we'll have the phone call', Travellers would be out pulling out their hair screaming.

O: The way you are saying it, it's as if settled people have a better way of doing it than Travellers.

H: They have yeah.

B: They have, they are learnt to do it better.

H: They cope better.

B: The Traveller child is growing up looking at the mother and father panicking like that . . .

M1: They are going panic.

B: It's hereditary but if they are teached from a young age that it's not a big deal and it's not a problem you're going to accept it that way too. So it has more to do with the way people are brought up, Traveller people have been brought up to be very close to each other and no body has ever tried to change it and I don't think anyone wants to change it, you know we are happy enough the way we are.

(Travellers-FG3)

Settled people were also seen as being less impulsive and more organized than Travellers:

O: So when someone's dying whether it's in hospital or at home, everyone would gather would they?

M1: Yeah

B: Some people come from England.

P: Yeah but that's the same for the settlers they do have people coming from England too.

B: Yeah they wouldn't just get up on a plane if somebody was sick, they wouldn't all go together, they'd all have it arranged, planning tickets and they'd have it all sorted.

(Travellers-FG2)

Similarities with the settled community

In the course of the interviews and focus groups with service providers it became apparent there are similarities between the communities. A lack of awareness about palliative care services was not seen as purely a Traveller issue. They were also aware of similarities with the settled community such as the use of healers, spiritual support and memorial rites.

Difference within the Travelling community

Although most talk in relation to difference focused on those that exist between the settled and Travelling communities, it was mentioned that differences naturally existed within the communities:

> Mg: There's three categories of Travellers, there's the very very down and out who drink an awful lot and sell their horses and their ole caravan and any ole thing but still in all funny enough they are happy that ole way. Then you get the middle sized Traveller she has an ole decent sized caravan and a decent car on the road and okay fair play she worked for it right, him and her, so you get that Traveller. The other Traveller then who's high and mighty gets up on her bit in the air . . .
>
> M2: Some people puts all Travellers down for one. Like if one Traveller has a fight its all Travellers. All Travellers are getting blamed for it but its not.
>
> Mg: It's not the same.
>
> L: Travellers are all different.
>
> M: Settled people are not all put down the same though.
>
> H: No, there's Traveller people married to settled people.
>
> M2: My brother's married to a settled girl.
>
> Mg: There's good and bad in all of us settled and Travellers.
>
> (Travellers-FG2)

There can be generational differences between Travellers as well as differences between those that live in the countryside and those that live in the cities:

> O: Is there a difference between the country and up here?
>
> H: You get a lot of the old ways, old-fashioned travellers.
>
> Mary: You still see some of them like that here as well.
>
> M2: Mostly a lot of old people would keep that tradition, a lot of old people would keep it. Young people nowadays wouldn't believe it.
>
> (Travellers-FG2)
>
> K: There's a lot of Travellers too, like in England there's different Travellers like when there's a wake they might cover all the tables with white sheets, even in a trailer, they do all the trailer up in white and they bring the coffin into it.
>
> A: Different everywhere.
>
> (Travellers-FG4)

Differences between Traveller men and women

Gender differences also occur within the Travelling community as they do in the settled community. Fear of a cancer diagnosis leads to late presentation especially among men who ignore symptoms. Women will attend check-ups but claim men remain reluctant to get any symptoms or pains checked out for fear of negative outcomes. Difference in attitudes and behaviour regarding health check-ups was noted as the biggest area of difference:

> M: Men won't bother at all, what ever chance women have doing the Primary Health Care [a training course] a lot of women now will go out, going to other groups and sites say and telling them about it and getting more aware . . .
>
> K: But mens won't do it.
>
> M: Ah women are more aware and they will go and . . . you will get some women that will leave themselves go, the majority of them now will go and try to talk their husbands into it as well now.
>
> (Travellers-FG5)

Naturally there will be differences between any two groups of people with their own culture and ethnic identity. In the study, some of the differences between Travellers and settled people were raised by Travellers and service providers alike. They noted how people from either community respond to illness, dying and death. In some cases there was a sense of confusion at reactions to death, such as the Traveller who couldn't understand why people would have a party when someone had died or why a grave could not be attended to or regularly visited. In most cases the differences between the communities were respectfully noted by the Traveller participants. Perhaps being the minority ethnic group difference is a challenging part of everyday life and thus to the fore when discussing how we behave in certain situations. Being aware of how Travellers note the differences between the communities offers valuable insights into how they manage their lives as a minority group within a dominant population. It also provides a rare and important opportunity for the settled population to hear how our own behaviours and customs are viewed from the outside and to alert us to the fact that what we view as normal may in fact, on occasion, be as abnormal to Travellers as can their customs and behaviours appear abnormal to us.

Conclusion

It is clear from this study that very few Travellers use palliative care and hospice services. The reasons for this, according to the Travellers and service providers, appear to be threefold: first, most felt that it is the family's responsibility and desire to keep the sick and dying at home to be cared for. Within Traveller society most families still live close together allowing for a wide level of support for the carers of the sick through the extended family. Second, a lack of knowledge or experience about the services in general fosters and maintains well-established fears of the hospice, and in some cases general hospitals. Issues around referral to these services also arose, with service providers being dependent on primary care providers and acute hospitals for referrals. Third, these services, especially the hospice, appear to be the domain of the settled person. Travellers talked about how 'their ways' do not always fit with these places. Service providers alluded to the fact that Travellers may not 'fit in' with other patients. The cultural differences present many barriers to service use. The majority of those taking part in this study, both Travellers and service providers were certain, that with some accommodation and flexibility, it would be possible to provide a service that Travellers could use, if they chose to do so.

References

Barry, J., Herity, B. and Solan, J. (1987) *The Traveller Health Status Study. Vital Statistics of Travelling People*. Dublin: The Health Research Board.

Carr, E. (1992), in Gearoid O Riain (ed.) *Traveller Ways Traveller Words*. Dublin: Pavee Point Publication.

Central Statistics Office (2004) http://www.cso.ie

Department of Health and Children (2001) *Report of the National Advisory Committee on Palliative Care*. Dublin: Stationery Office.

Department of Health and Children (2002) *Traveller Health, A National Strategy 2002–2005*. Dublin: Stationery Office.

McCann, M. (1992), in O Riain (ed.) *Traveller Ways Traveller Words*. Dublin: Pavee Point Publication.

McNamara, B., Martin, K., Waddell, C. and Yuen, K. (1997) Palliative care in a multicultural society: perceptions of health care professionals, *Palliative Medicine*, **11**:359–67.

O'Brien, A. (2000) Journey's end; Customs around death, in Erica Sheehan (ed.), *Travellers Citizens of Ireland: Our Challenge to an Intercultural Irish Society in the 21st Century*. Dublin: The Parish of the Travelling People.

O'Donovan, O., McKenna, V., Kelleher, C., McCarthy, P. and McCarthy, D. (1995) *Health Service Provision for the Travelling Community in Ireland*. Galway: Centre for Health Promotion Studies, UCG.

Okely, A. (1983) *The Traveller Gypsies*. Cambridge: Cambridge University Press.

Pavee Point Irish Travellers (2001) *Journal of Health Gain*, Spring; 5(1):3–5.

Pavee Point (2001a), *Pavee News*, February 2001, http://www.paveepoint.ie/index.htm

Reilly, L. (1992), in O Riain (ed.) *Traveller Ways Traveller Words*. Dublin: Pavee Point Publication.

Van Doorslaer, O. and Keegan, O. (2001) Contemporary Irish Attitudes towards Death, Dying and Bereavement. RCSI: HSRC (Unpublished).

Van Doorslaer, O. *et al.* (2002) Traveller Health 2002: An investigation into the provision of health services for the Travelling community and their use. Traveller Health Unit (Unpublished).

Ward, C. (1992) Chrissie Ward, in O Riain (ed.) *Traveller Ways Traveller Words.* Dublin: Pavee Point Publication.

Note

1 Pavee Point is a partnership of Irish Travellers and settled people working together to improve the lives of Irish Travellers through working towards social justice, solidarity, socio-economic development and human rights. http://www.paveepoint.ie/

15 Irish traditions on dying and death – relevance to palliative care

Sinéad Donnelly

Introduction

The idea for this chapter arises from five questions which have interested me since I began training in palliative medicine.

1. What are the traditions in Ireland on dying and death?
2. What is the core philosophy of palliative care nowadays?
3. What do people need or want now as they prepare for death?
4. What did people want in the past and what did they have in the past in order to prepare them for their death?
5. How can the traditions in the past in Ireland inform palliative care in the twenty-first century?

My training began in Ireland and then brought me to the United States and Scotland. Within these different cultural settings, indeed multicultural settings, I became curious about the core similarities among different peoples in their needs around the time of death. I was also curious about the concept of modern palliative care, wondering how care of the dying was practised in the past. Surely good care of the dying has not just started since the introduction of the modern hospice movement? Surely wisdom about death and dying and the care of those who are dying and those who are grieving must have grown over thousands of years in many cultures?

In my years of training and practice of palliative medicine I am also curious about the importance of cultural specificity in caring for those who are dying. If palliative care is about the holistic care of an individual and the family then that also involves attention to their culture, language and the philosophy which both of these express. We do not ask when admitting someone to palliative medicine; what are your cultural beliefs, how does your language express your philosophy? So how do we identify the subtle, perhaps subconscious historical and cultural beliefs of a patient in relation to illness, dying and death? Indeed you could ask whether it is relevant to be concerned about these issues. I think it is highly relevant and right in relation to Irish culture and Ireland since it is the one I know best. It is for others to speak and write about their traditions.

In the past people were as familiar with death as they were with life, of which death was regarded as a natural extension. There is knowledge to be acquired and wisdom to be gained by reflecting on the positive aspects of the care of the dying as practised by our ancestors evolving over hundreds of years. For the past six years I have studied folklore associated with dying and death in Ireland.

The Irish folklore collections in the archives of the Department of Irish Folklore, University College Dublin, Ireland were the initial source of information. A questionnaire on death customs was circulated throughout Ireland by the Department of Irish Folklore in 1976. The initial response to the questionnaire consisted of 108 replies from male (60) and female (48) respondents from throughout Ireland which refer mainly to Catholic ritual and ceremony at death. Thus information was available on the care of the dying person, the moment of death, wakes, funerals and burials.

I then undertook field work in rural West of Ireland. Using teachers and general practitioners as leaders in the community, local people were identified and asked to participate. A total of 30 interviews were recorded in the north west, west and south west of the country over a six-month period. Individuals were asked in a non-structured interview to recount their memories of care of the dying in their area. I conducted the interviews in Irish or English according to the wishes of the interviewee. This chapter focuses on the dying process, not referring at this time to the formalities of dying such as the wakes, funerals and keening.

The moment of death

The moment of death was sacred. The body was not moved and no one cried for two hours. ENM reported that

> when someone died in the house, no one cried for two hours. Did you hear of this – 'may you be dead a half day before the devil knows you're gone'. *Maistíní an oilc* are the little devils who come ready to take the soul. One does not cry for fear they will hear you. The other reason for not crying. If you cried and the soul had not left the body, the soul might want to stay and death would be delayed. So no crying for two hours and the body would not be moved.

The rosary or *coróin paidrín* was said not only as the person was dying but also at midnight after the death, as the body left the home and again at the graveside. At the *torramh* or wake there were even specific prayers as the mourners took snuff or tobacco for the pipe, each remarking as they inhaled '*Beannacht Dé le hanam na maraibh* – God's blessing on the souls of the dead.'

Prayer was an integral part of everyday life and death. Especially at the time of impending death, the rosary was prayed. The rosary, a litany of three separate prayers repeated in decades, was said daily in every family and at the bedside of the dying. It is a prayer concerned with the earthly and celestial life cycle of Christ, particularly suited to all stages of the death situation in Ireland. It is a prayer which would have been familiar to the dying person and also very suitable for community participation. The objective was to keep the mind of the sick person on goodness and away from badness as personified by *fear an oilc*, the devil, who was believed to be most active at this time.

Candles were lit at the bedside and the number used was particular to the locality. For example, on the largest of the three Aran islands off the west coast of Galway, seven candles were used, five were used on the middle island and on the smallest or most westerly island three were used. In Tourmakeady, Co. Mayo, five candles were used while farther south in Ballyferriter, Co. Kerry, 12 candles were lit and then one was formally extinguished as representing Judas, the apostle who betrayed Jesus. The words *O mo Dhia* (Oh my God) were said repeatedly into the ear of the dying person as was the Act of Contrition and 'Everybody was praying around the bed especially the rosary'.

Simultaneously, conversation was held within hearing of the sick person, praising his or her attributes and good deeds, giving them courage, a sense of worthiness and strength. At the moment of death in Tourmakeady, Co. Mayo, the window was opened while on Inis Mór, Aran Island, the curtain was opened to allow the spirit to depart freely and in the case of a widow or widower, to join with the spirit of the dead spouse.

Care of the dying

As recounted in Tourmakeady, in caring for the dying sips of 'poitín (home-made spirit) was sometimes used to numb the pain'. 'They were constantly wetting the mouth', 'using a drop of brandy', 'a little quill was used to wet the lip', 'it was important to hold the hand.' Today, as then, palliative medicine emphasizes care of the mouth. *Biseach an bháis* was well recognized – 'ramblings going back when the person became very clear in their mind'. The people of that time were very familiar with the signs of impending death such as *gliogar nó clochar in bháis* or the death rattle.

Today nurses and doctors specializing in palliative care spend considerable time preparing relatives for the signs of death, while in the past people in general were more educated as to the actual phenomena of dying and death.

The philosophy of the people towards death

As revealed through the interviews, death was highly respected and accepted by the people not just as part of life but as a very close companion in living that life. The story of the death of a child may best illustrate this philosophy, as recounted in Irish by ENM from Co. Kerry.

> I had a brother, three and a half years old who died with the red fever [probably scarlet fever]. I was two years. He was only sick a couple of days. There was snow and the doctor, who only had a saddled horse and was seven or eight miles away, could not come the first day. It was too late when he [doctor] came and he [child] died and they were always talking about him.
>
> I remember him being laid out but I thought that if I said that to my mother that was not how it was. I was married before I had the courage to say to my mother what I remembered. 'What I remember, I'm not sure if it is true, people sitting on stools.' She said, 'Yes, they were there. They spent several hours of the day there.' 'I remember being in your arms looking out at the funeral leaving the house but then I thought you would be in the funeral.' 'I wasn't' she said. 'Mothers would not go to the funerals of the first born.' 'Then' I said, 'there was a coffin and four men under the coffin.' [He was only three and a half].
>
> 'That's exactly how it was because your father had so much respect that he wanted a large coffin so that four men could carry him.' 'Out of respect, my father did that (I was only two). No, that doesn't upset me. Well really it . . . I get a catch in my throat . . .'

People were reared with, and as part of, the elements which they respected and accepted in partnership as a good and natural upbringing. It was important that the young be familiar with death and realize its naturalness. According to EB the main concern was 'that they [dying] would have no trouble with God – very important that everything be sorted, like debts forgiven – then very content to die'. When the carers understood that death was inevitable, they helped the person who was on the edge of eternity or as they said *ar bhruach na síoraíochta*. They knew that the person in dying was entering into the presence of God. The women, in particular, understood and had a natural empathy, and they were highly skilled but men also shared in the caring and vigil.

People with terminal illness were kept at home. A person in the living of life, had laboured, married, reared a family, grown old, become ill and declined, had earned respect, love and the right to dignity in dying and in death; it was only natural to the family that they would and should care for their relative at home. Having recognized the imminence of death, which was accepted as God's will, the people would sit up day and night, often for several weeks, neglecting farm work and keeping vigil on the sick relative or friend. The death was not resisted and the inevitability of it imposed an obligation on them to ease its passage.

Humour

Striking features of these interviews were the enthusiasm with which interviewees talked about what today would be considered a morbid subject, and the readily interspersed humour which might now be considered inappropriate in some quarters. ENM worked in the city as a young woman in the 1930s. Her grandmother was ill in her village which was more than a day's journey from the city, making travelling home difficult. The young lady, who could not travel until Christmas, wrote to her own mother, 'I hope Nan lives until I come home.' Her mother replied, 'If Nan lives until you come home, your aunt and I will be dead.'

Humour can also be seen in the memory of an elderly lady who was ill and knew that she was dying. As she tried to organize her wake and funeral with her customary efficiency she wearily exclaimed: 'I suppose it won't be done right unless I'm there myself.'

When EG was asked whether she had heard the banshee, a fairy voice announcing death, she remarked: 'I never hear the alarm clock never mind the banshee.' The same lady admitted that she was somewhat afraid of dying but then philosophically added: 'it doesn't matter whether I am up above or down below, I'll have plenty of friends.'

The purpose of this folklore enquiry was to gain insight into the collective wisdom of lay people who were familiar with dying and death. Several interesting features emerged. People were eager to tell their stories and the interviewer was welcomed openly and warmly. Both humour and pathos illuminate the stories told, recalled from memory of their senior relatives or their own experiences.

While the same themes recurred involving rituals and prayers, there were some intriguing local differences as exemplified by differences in the number of candles around the bed.

The moment of death was sacred. As O'Donoghue (1997) writes in *Anam Cara*: 'When you are present at the sacrament of someone's death, you should be very mindful of their situation.' The dead body was treated with great respect and it was stressed how important it was to do so and for the young to learn and accept this, and to realize the natural place of death in the time and fullness of life; its time and inevitability should not be resisted. At the same time, courage and fortitude were enhanced by the touching of the hands and face, and in the spoken words of solace and encouragement to the dying person.

The closeness to nature, expressed in the attitude to dying, reflected the life and living of these rural people and their antecedents for thousands of years. Quoting from an interview in Co. Donegal, people had a 'simple, strong, rock-like faith. It was so strong nothing could destroy it. No fear of death in those people. It was only a slight movement from one form (of existence) to another.' I believe that the word *nádúr* (an Irish word which directly translated is 'nature') summarizes the complex philosophy underlying the attitude of the people in Ireland towards life and death. The stories in this chapter from the past and present reveal traditions, ritual, philosophy and empathy which together explain this complex word *nádúr*.

The words *nádúr* (nature) and *nádúrtha* (natural) were often mentioned in explaining the attitude to life and death. ENM said 'we were reared very close to nature.' EG said that 'they understood death, the naturalness of death. They did not go against it. That was that.' EB said that 'young people do not understand. It is not talked about. The nature is being lost gradually. The nature of death was all there; that it would be done well and naturally.' EG remarked that 'it [the wake] is not light hearted here, but it is natural.' The direct translation of *nádúr* and *nádúrtha* to nature and natural probably does not capture the depth of the Irish meaning which embraces communion, empathy and balance with the Creator and creation.

This study is unique in that the interviews were conducted by a medical doctor experienced in the practice of palliative medicine and who has worked with the dying in different cultures. As professionals caring for the dying, we have much to learn from our ancestors' skills and attitudes. By our very expertise and professionalism we may be disempowering the dying person and their natural carers who as unpractised amateurs we could sideline, forgetting that the foundation of this amateurism is love, not just in its etymological sense. By listening to the descriptions of care in the community in the past, professionals may learn to trust the natural wisdom of the dying and their caring family. Certainly, modern palliative medicine has advanced the care of the dying greatly. Reflecting on the relevant past may, however, challenge the modern direction.

The modern direction

Having determined the attitude of people in the past through their traditions and rituals in the West of Ireland, my interest evolved in determining what people use as ritual and support nowadays to prepare and comfort them in approaching death and at the moment of death. Palliative care programmes continue to demonstrate that enlightened and dedicated care can reduce markedly the suffering of patients with advanced cancer and that of their families. The vast experience required over the recent past, however, has not yet been translated into a vision of the moment of death, that moment or the final breath become increasingly marginalized.

We undertook a qualitative study looking at the moment of death and how it is perceived and remembered one-week after the death. People spoke of presence, prayer, dignity and community as important. These words form parts of the overriding construct of *nádúr*. People recounted how in the past *bhí an nádúr uile ann* – 'all the nature was there' – and today in the mid-west of Ireland *tá an nádúr fós ann* – 'the nature is still there.'

A wife and sister describe how a 50-year-old man was dying:

> It (breathing) was going slower and slower . . . and kindly enough both of us heard it, the gentle rattle . . . lovely gentle rattle . . . real gentle . . . he just went out like the candle that was flickering . . . oh he didn't rebuke, he didn't . . . He was so gentle, like a baby.

> Frank . . . just gave two gasps and he was gone. Frank . . . just went out, softly, it was beautiful.

> His hand was under his chin, actually just the same as a baby . . . that was about eight fifteen . . . he was gone half ten.

The words 'gentle', 'lovely', 'like a candle', 'like a baby' are mentioned by several interviewees – the gentleness of moving from one world to the next is reiterated.

The involvement of children reveals an attitude towards death as natural and gentle with an understanding of a spirit world. A 39-year-old man is dying and his parents describe how he talks to his daughters eight and five years of age:

> So we left the three of them inside together on the ward. There was a little square glass in the door and (we) used to look in and there he was in floods of tears . . . the three of them were crying. I never saw him crying (before). Oh my God, 'twas very emotional . . . he was crying . . . and he never used to cry now . . . and when they come out Sara came out first and I said 'what's wrong with you' and (she said) 'Daddy's after telling us that he won't be home anymore, that he's going to heaven.' He put it that way to them; he put it nicely to them.

The image of grandparents peering through a small glass square into the hospice room of their son as he explains the inexplicable to his children is stark and dignified.

In the following account, a young mother Rose received a phone call that her sister Anne has just died in the hospice. She tells no one and is getting ready to go to the hospice when her four-year-old asks where she is going. Rose replied that she is going into the hospice. To her utter surprise the little one replies 'But Anne has gone home ... and when she gets to heaven she won't be coming back.'

Anne's six-year-old son was carried over to say goodbye to his dying 36-year-old mother. He leaned over to kiss her and then proceeded to bless her by making the sign of the cross over her and saying 'Glory be to the Father and to the Son and to the Holy Spirit, Amen.' Rose was amazed at this gesture; how a child knew such a prayer.

These descriptions from interviews in 2001 echo the sentiments and understanding of death in an Ireland of eighty years ago.

Moment of death

The moment of death is still sacred and respected by relatives, friends and professional carers in the mid-west of Ireland. Stories are told of deaths in the palliative care unit linking prayer and ritual respectfully, maintaining community traditions. Prayer, rosary, candles are of major significance to the community and by extension to members of that community dying within the unit. These traditions are understood and respected by the professional carers who come from the same neighbourhoods and local areas. They are of the people, which is an invaluable asset to the quality of care provided to those who are dying.

> Maj. H: They were all there, it was lovely and the candle and the prayers and those two lovely nurses ... she (nurse) said the prayers for the dying. A lovely little prayer beside the candle lighting. It was beautiful. I thought there was a beautiful ambience in the room.

> Mrs. M: I leaned in and took his hand and we reassured him and we were saying the rosary and we got to the third decade and then he just ... and he took one more breath and I think that was it and we continued the rosary.

In the present-day care of those who are dying, relatives identify prayer symbols as integral to the care, similar to the past, with nurses appreciated for their role in saying prayers, in lighting, holding candles, in being present. The crucifix is obviously a source of comfort although such symbolism and humble reverence would seem contrary to perceived modern thought.

> CC: There was three nurses there and the nun went in before I went, she was in several times during the evening and said prayers. We said the rosary before I came home ... and I said to May ... you start the rosary and she started the rosary ... I lit the candle before I went home

and I gave her my crucifix. It was mine and I had it in her hand and I get her to kiss it . . . the nun brought in a little tray with a candle and holy water and my own crucifix.

Discussion

I have outlined remembered past practices, contrasted with those of present practices in Ireland concerning death in the mid-west of Ireland. I believe that within the 'artificial' home of the palliative care unit, practices and beliefs which are ancient are retained and respected to the benefit of patients and their families. One reason that such tradition is respectfully practised by the professional carers is that they, the professionals, are of the people; they come from the parishes of the dying, they are their neighbours. The carers are part of the community and each dying and death is their loss also.

From the qualitative enquiry into the perception of the moment of death in the mid-west of Ireland it is clear that the preparations for death of the patient and the family have a significant influence. Being given 'time', being treated with 'dignity', are phrases that emerge repeatedly as healing, soothing factors in this preparation. Humorous descriptions emerge providing light relief to their intense sadness.

The presence, words and attitude of professionals, the close presence of family members, the ritual of prayer, candles and of blessings are among those factors which combine to create an atmosphere of safety, security and tranquillity as death approaches. In the qualitative study involving patients and families ritual is requested and effectively retained. Presence was a recurrent theme and is an individual contemplative act; the presence of those who are beloved, the presence of professional carers, the pastoral presence, the presence of ritual. Above all it is the manner in which presence is enacted that is critical. To be attuned to the form of presence requires a meditative, inspired active awareness. Professional carers in this enquiry prayed with patient and family in a manner that was welcomed by them.

Fr Seán O'Duinn OSB has written (personal communication) on the rite of funerals in the Gaelic tradition. When a funeral was passing by the people on the side-line would join the funeral for a short period and this period was called *tri coiscéimeanna na trocaire*, which translated is 'the three footsteps of mercy', at which time an Irish prayer was recited. This prayerful symbolic accompaniment captures the sense of community, solidarity, mortality and spirituality of the people. From our recent study, these qualities are still clearly enunciated even in the institutional setting of palliative care and these are the qualities remembered and appreciated by relatives.

From these people, I have gained insight into the collective wisdom and customs of lay people who were familiar with dying and death. Their stories reveal a philosophy of the people in a time where daily life was a challenge simply to exist. The people I interviewed lived in a world where there was no divide between the superficial and deep but a continuum where daily life floated between the two. It is perhaps difficult to comprehend and recreate this natural rhythm of life.

The traditions of the people rooted in thousands of years of history, conscious and subconscious, may carry the equivalent of the individual dream. As the nurturing of an individual's dream may lead to healing, so the nurturing of a community's dream world or subconscious may be required for health. The language and traditions of a community encompass its evolved philosophy and express the present community subconscious; they may also be the means by which the spiritual world is made manifest.

The phrases used by interviewees concerning *nádúr* and the time of death demand a more subtle and deeper transliteration: *bhi an nádúr uile ann* – the situation was full of gentleness, kindness particularly towards relatives and family; *táimid ag cailiúint an nádúir* – we're getting hard hearted, we no longer care for our own; *bhí chuile rud go nádúrtha* – people behaved kindly, looked after their own (personal communication Fr Padraig O'Fiannachta).

For relatives in the mid-west of Ireland the moment of death seems poised in the breath of prayerful presence, within the flow of ongoing life which slows its pace in communion with the weakened body. The people present willingly enter into the breath-by-breath rhythm of the dying person. Prayer, ritual respect and dignity and the presence of the family are significant in bringing the living closer to the mysterious pace of dying.

Conclusion

The moment of death must be witnessed. Ideally it is a moment for which the dying person and their relatives prepare; as individuals creating a particular environment of atmosphere. It is preparation time for accompaniment. We acknowledge or recognize other forces which heal despite our limited understanding.

We subconsciously or consciously acknowledge the existence or presence of a soul that needs healing. Perhaps this is what the families interviewed identified as important at the time of death. The components of this soul healing by another is recognized in human terms by the presence of people, gentleness, dignity, prayer, symbolism, time and space, children's stories, the simple inspired acts of touching, speaking, the undulating rhythm from tears to laughter. All of this gentleness, dignity, prayer and presence facilitates or creates a space for God and people to be present together.

In a more recent qualitative study (2003–2004 ongoing, unpublished) into the moment of death at home, it was noticeable that family and community support are very strongly represented in the interviews. This is understandable as, in its absence, care in the home could not have taken place. This mutual care has developed over generations in the community and within the family. Neighbours are described as 'wonderful, wonderful'. A litany of names recount family, friends and neighbours who are present. The ability to give this intensive care does not arise overnight but takes years, if not generations to evolve as a mutual caring between families and neighbours.

There is an emphasis on a rota and how it works so well. The carers clearly identify that a great source of comfort to them was the fact that the dying person was at home. There are many references in this study to ritual and how the mystery of this ritual relates to the family's faith and provides a welcome support.

The process of ritual is offered by professionals to the family within a specialist palliative care unit and then instituted with the families and patient's permission. However, expression of ritual and faith appears to occur spontaneously and naturally in the home care setting. In this way, although ritual may be considered traditional and somehow a duty at the time of death, in the home setting there is a freedom around the mixing of ritual.

For example, a lady describes that as her husband was dying, the shortest prayer that they could recite together was: 'Jesus, I trust in you.' This, once again, exemplifies their spirituality and practicality. Another lady describes how the priest left his prayer book with her and had marked out the pages which would be nice to read. The lady then held her mother's hand, reading the prayers, telling her mother how much she would miss her and how much she loved her. In this we have the combination of intimacy, presence, physical contact, spirituality and reality.

Out of these qualitative studies into traditions of the past and the moment of death in the present, has arisen two documentaries. The theme of the first documentary *Anam* reflects on the nature of care traditional to Irish people, their understanding of dying and death, the naturalness of living and dying and the proximity to the spiritual world. It combines interviews with music in bilingual format, English and Irish, the latter being one of the older languages in antiquity; juxtaposing the Irish elders view of life and death with the succinct observations of visitors and professionals on the Irish way of caring. *Anam* refers to the soul of the people as a community. This soul-community reverberates in living and dying. *Anam* explores culture and folklore traditions around dying and how these are relevant to the present day.

The second documentary *Give Me Your Hands* describes graphically the importance of family and community support in time of life-threatening illness and bereavement. The three main stories bring to mind the Irish tradition of *meitheal* where neighbours relied on each other for harvesting. Now there is a 'health care *meitheal*' alive among families and communities and its presence is essential to the well-being of the entire community.

References

Donnelly, S. (1999) Traditions associated with the dying in the West of Ireland, *Palliative Medicine*, 13:57–62.

O'Donoghue, J. (1997) *Anam Cara*. London: Bantam Press.

Part IV

Future challenges and developments

16 Multicultural Ireland – weaving the fabric of diversity

Geraldine Tracey and Julie Ling

Introduction

A small island on the periphery of Europe, bordered by only the Atlantic ocean to the west: but what is it to be Irish? Guinness, red hair, Riverdance, gaelic games, forty shades of green, *ceol agus craic* . . . Ireland is changing.

The Irish Republic currently has a population of four million. In the year to April 2003 there were 50,500 immigrants to Ireland; coupled with the lowest level of emigration for centuries this has resulted in the highest population figures since 1871 (Central Statistics Office, 2003). The result is that slowly but surely multicultural Ireland is becoming a reality. If proof were needed of Ireland's new multicultural status, Dublin Bus recently announced that they have over 40 different nationalities represented throughout the company. Out of 3,300 employees, 6 per cent have a country of origin outside the European Union (EU) and a further 3 per cent are from countries within the EU. Dublin Bus has launched a poster campaign acknowledging that diversity and multiculturalism enriches both the workplace and society (Spectrum, 2003). A trip as a passenger on Dublin Bus bears this out. The increased cultural and ethnic diversity now present in Ireland has resulted in a range of challenges for the Irish health care sector and this includes those working in palliative care.

Internationally, challenges in providing culturally competent care for people of ethnic and cultural minorities groups have been identified. There can be few times when people are as vulnerable as when they are terminally ill. This is compounded when they are separated from their homeland. In Ireland palliative care professionals now have contact with people of different cultures and ethnic backgrounds, speaking different languages, belonging to different religious groups with different beliefs. As Ireland develops into a truly multicultural society, providing palliative care in a culturally sensitive fashion is paramount.

What is culture?

Culture incorporates intuitions, language, values, religious ideas, habits, ways of thinking, interpersonal relationships, artistic expression and patterns of social relationships (Oliviere *et al.*, 1998). Culture has a powerful impact on perceptions of health and illness, death and dying as well as living and life (O'Neill, 1994).

Cultural competence has gained a certain cachet in health care and refers to the clinician's knowledge of various cultures and the skills required to apply that knowledge to patient care (Mazanec and Tyler, 2003). However, there is growing concern that cultural health care needs of minority ethnic groups are not met adequately (Gerrish and Papadopoulos, 1999).

Despite being predominantly a homogenous society (MacEinri, 2002) different cultural groups have in the past integrated into Irish society. The Jewish population of the Irish Republic reached its height of almost 6,000 in the years following World War II, but by 1998 had dwindled to just over 1,000 (Margolis, 1998). Travellers imbued with distinctive cultural characteristics have been part of Irish history for centuries. Although culturally different, these groups are somewhat assimilated into Irish life with a resultant population that is predominantly white, Celtic and Catholic.

Emigration

Ireland has a long history of emigration. As a result of the potato famine up to a million people migrated to the United States and other countries around the world. During that time, the natural increase in the population was continually offset by outward migration on a scale that led to an almost continual decline in the population for more than a century (MacEinri, 2002). This pattern resulted in Ireland remaining largely a monoculture. The main reason for this emigration was economic, with several generations becoming economic migrants. Certain rural areas became depopulated as younger people sought employment in Dublin and abroad – mainly the UK and USA. Traditionally, older children left home, established a base abroad often with help from the existing Irish diaspora and then sent money home to pay for the fares of younger siblings. Some counties still have an elderly population structure mirroring decades of emigration.

Immigration

The aggregate figures for immigration between 1995 and 2000 were recorded at 7 per cent of the 1996 population (MacEinri, 2002). Figures for the Republic of Ireland include both returning Irish and non-nationals. The term 'non-national' is commonly used in Ireland to describe those from other countries and cultures. The non-national population currently consists of economic migrants, asylum seekers and programme refugees (MacEinri, 2002). Of 47,500 immigrants entering the Irish Republic in 1999, around 10,000 were refugees and asylum seekers. In 2002, Government figures estimated that as many as 340,000 immigrants were expected in the subsequent six years (National Consultative Committee on Racism and Interculturalism and Irish Health Services Management Institute, 2002).

In the United Kingdom (UK), which is often viewed as a multicultural society, 8 per cent of the population describe themselves as belonging to a minority ethnic group (Census, 2001). Non-nationals account for nearly 6 per cent of the total population of the Republic of Ireland; almost half of these are UK nationals (2.7 per cent) or nationals of other EU countries. Of immigrants, 45 per cent originate from countries outside the EU and USA, 8 per cent from central/eastern Europe and 7 per cent nationals of African countries. An unknown number of those counted in these figures are children born to Irish citizens abroad. Within the European Union (EU), the Irish Republic is relatively youthful as a nation with only 11.5 per cent of the population aged 65 or over compared with an EU average of 15 per cent. Of all immigrants to the Irish Republic, 44 per cent are aged between 25 and 44 years (Central Statistics Office, 2003).

Reasons for the increase in immigration

There have been a number of assertions put forward to explain this sudden and dramatic change in the non-national immigrant population. From early to the mid-1990s the Republic of Ireland developed as a technology hub for Europe. Many large information technology companies set up manufacturing plants, lured by tax incentives for foreign investors and the promise of a well-educated, skilled and relatively cheap labour force. The economic boom period (popularly called the 'Celtic Tiger') of the 1990s resulted in almost half a million jobs being added to the Irish economy.

In 2001, there were 36,000 work visas and permits issued to people from outside the European Economic Area (National Consultative Committee on Racism and Interculturalism, United Nations High Commission for Refugees and Know Racism, 2002). Both of these bodies suggest that the increase in immigration is less to do with the 'Celtic Tiger' and more with the increasing difficulty in applying for refugee status in other European countries. In the first six months of 2004, a total of 566 asylum seekers were recognized as refugees in the Republic of Ireland. A total of 2,118 new applications were made for refugee status and the main countries of origin of new asylum seekers were Nigeria (955) Romania (94) Democratic Republic of Congo (94) China (90) and Somalia (77) (Irish Refugee Council, 2004).

The increase in immigration to Ireland has also been attributed to Mary Robinson, who following her term as President of Ireland, where she reached out to the Irish diaspora overseas, became the United Nations High Commissioner for Human Rights (1997–2002). This is due to her high profile in conjunction with Ireland's perceived good human rights record. These facts encouraged Ireland's progress towards a more culturally diverse society. However, a recent referendum in the Irish Republic regarding citizenship may be viewed as a backward step. The catalyst for the referendum was perceived to be the influx of heavily pregnant immigrants arriving in Ireland's maternity hospitals for the purpose of seeking Irish citizenship through the birth of their child. Eighty per cent of voters were in favour of a constitutional change to ensure that birth on the island of Ireland no longer ensured Irish citizenship. This overwhelming endorsement for the changes proposed by the referendum drew praise from interested observers. The Grand Wizard of the knights of the Ku Klux Klan praised the Minister for Justice for defending Irish heritage with the passing of this referendum (Dubliner, 2004). This referendum also prompted calls for immigration to be addressed through legislation and the formation of an immigration policy for the state (Amnesty International, 2003). The Irish Refugee Council (2004) point out that while the referendum aimed to address the issue of the Irish citizenship, several well-known footballers (Houghton, Aldridge and Cascarino) have 'become' Irish and have served their new country well as other immigrants could if given the opportunity.

Immigration and nursing

In the late 1990s the Irish Republic's health services found themselves in a very unfamiliar position. Having exported countless health care staff to work in the UK, Australia, USA and other countries over the last decades, Ireland now granted visas and work permits to non-national nurses recruited to fill vacancies in Irish health care institutions. A similar pattern has emerged for non-consultant hospital doctor posts. Over the past ten years non-national doctors have filled many of the non-training service posts outside the main centres.

A total review of nursing in the Republic of Ireland (Department of Health and Children, 1998) has led to major changes in Irish nursing over the last few years. One of the recommendations of this report was a clear clinical career pathway; this led to the advent of the role of clinical nurse specialist. Nearly 10 per cent of all clinical nurse specialists in Ireland work in palliative care. This has resulted in promotion for many nurses working in palliative care and opportunities for others to fill the vacant posts.

The *Report of the National Advisory Committee on Palliative Care* (Department of Health and Children, 2001) recommended specific staffing levels. Implementing these recommendations would require increased funding and recruitment of nurses. In total, nurses from 76 different countries are currently working in the Republic of Ireland, the largest groups being Filipinos, English and Indian. Of 58,146 nurses currently registered in the Irish Republic, 2,226 nurses are from European Union countries other than Ireland and 5,297 are non-nationals from outside the European Union (An Bord Altranais, 2004). Many palliative care patients have passed through the acute hospital system where non-national nurses would have provided much of their care. However, the influx of nurses from countries other than Ireland has had little impact on current palliative care, although some care assistants and ancillary staff are non-nationals. In Ireland, palliative care is predominantly available to those with cancer and as cancer remains a disease most commonly found in old age the majority of patients seen in palliative care are older. The immigrant population are relatively young and therefore currently it is more often that palliative care teams have had contact with other cultures as fellow workers rather than as patients. The increasing populations and larger numbers of immigrants present an opportunity for those working in Irish palliative care to learn from the experiences of other countries to ensure that services will be able effectively to meet the inevitable future demand.

European Union and health care

In 1973, Ireland joined the then European Economic Community (EEC). The injection of infrastructural funding subsequently led to economic growth. In May 2004, during the Irish presidency of the European Union, 15 accession countries became member states of the European Union. As a result of this enlargement of the European Union, migration from one country to another is possible between the member states. This has implications for those working in palliative care and for patients. Health care professionals from other EU countries will be able to apply for registration in other member states and can move freely from one country to another. The old E111 has been replaced by the European Health Insurance Card (June 2004) which entitles holders to receive medical care without being charged anywhere in the European Union or Switzerland.

Health

Increased cultural and ethnic diversity has resulted in a range of challenges for the Irish health care sector. In health care it is impossible to understand a patient without first understanding their culture and ethnicity (Oliviere, 1999). The Irish health service faces challenges in relation to health policy and the provision of culturally appropriate care for people of non-national origin. In the Republic of Ireland services for this new section of society are slowly developing. Evidence from the literature identifies some of the explanations for the failure of health professionals to meet the needs of ethnic minorities in other countries. These include the lack of understanding of cultural diversity, racism, racial stereotyping, lack of knowledge, exclusiveness, and ethnocentrism (Chevannes, 2002). Currently information regarding ethnic background, county of origin and religion are not routinely collected by palliative care services in the Irish Republic. The development of a national minimum dataset was a recommendation of the *Report of the National Advisory Committee on Palliative Care* (Department of Health and Children, 2001) and would help to address the deficit.

Palliative care

Good palliative care requires that patients are viewed holistically. Beliefs about illness, health care, death and dying are often influenced by an individual's cultural background (Nyatanga, 1997). How palliative care is delivered is shaped by who we are as health care professionals and what we believe. This is a concept discussed in a paper by Larkin (1998) where the uniqueness of Irish palliative care nurses caring for dying patients is described through the Irish language and is encapsulated in five expressions *dlúchaidreamh* (closeness), *anam chara* (soul-friend), *grámhar* (loving), *áire* (caring) and *spioraid* (spirit).

Increasingly those working in Irish palliative care will be called upon to care for people of non-national origin. Issues and challenges have been highlighted in other countries where minority ethnic groups have gathered, however this is a new phenomenon for practice in the Irish Republic. Many of the facets involved in the delivery of palliative care are influenced by culture, for instance, symptom control, diet, modesty, death, burial and bereavement (Oliviere, 1999). To provide 'total care' involves treating that person within their frame of references and acknowledging their beliefs and values. Palliative care is directed towards assisting the individual to achieve the best quality of life possible. How people delineate what for them is 'quality of life' is affected by their values and beliefs. In order to assess a person holistically their culture and ethnicity must be taken into consideration to gain an understanding of what their expectations are during their death and dying. In Ireland, death, dying and grieving have tradition-ally been viewed purely from an Irish cultural perspective and palliative care delivered in a manner acceptable to Irish culture.

While Irish traditions associated with death vary from region to region, all place emphasis on the rituals surrounding the event. Many Irish Catholics would expect candles, prayers, holy pictures and rosary beads and thus when a patient dies in most health care institutions in the Republic of Ireland these items are placed in the room. The act of opening the window to 'let the spirit out' or closing blinds and curtains in the deceased person's home until after the funeral, are still widely practised. Reading about deaths in the newspaper is a national pastime. Funerals are arranged quickly and usually take place in a short time-frame, often only two or three days after the death. Attendance at removals, funerals and wakes is seen as a mark of respect for the deceased and support for the bereaved (no matter how distant the funeral-goer's link is with the person who has died). Large attendance at most funerals ensures that they are also a social occasion for meeting friends and acquaintances.

For Catholics, the 'month's mind' Mass is said for the repose of the soul of the deceased one month to the day after the death. This is for families and friends but also for those who missed the funeral (Power, 1993). The majority of Irish people still choose to be buried rather than cremated. Each diocese has a 'Cemetery Sunday' once a year in most graveyards throughout the Republic of Ireland where a bishop comes to bless the cemetery and relatives and friends of those buried in the graveyard come together to pray (Power, 1993).

Palliative philosophy

The palliative philosophy recognizes the individuality of the person by encouraging patient-led care to achieve the best possible quality of life. This holistic approach to care encompasses not only physical but also social, psychological and spiritual aspects of care. This philosophy is culturally dependant and despite including the principle of unconditional acceptance of patients who may have practices unlike our own, it finds support in individualistic societies that promote personal autonomy (Walter, 2003). Truth telling is regarded as a way to respect a patient's autonomy, which in turn is closely linked to respect of the person. Gracia (2003) argues that in Mediterranean and Latin cultures there is a tendency of 'merciful lying' rather than full disclosure.

The issue of disclosure of information to the patient is frequently referred to in palliative care literature. Fainsinger *et al.* (2003) highlighted the major differences in the perceived value of clear cognition and disclosure of information between patients and families in Madrid and Edmonton. The authors also expressed a belief that a common global culture could be expected among the more educated levels of society across the Western world, while less educated segments of the population may hold more traditional cultural attitudes. Tse *et al.* (2003) investigated breaking bad news from a Chinese perspective and recommended that although many Chinese families object to telling the patient a 'bad' diagnosis or prognosis, there are too many different views among the Chinese to justify non-disclosure of the truth to patients, if the patient wants to know. Dein and Thomas (2002) collated research findings in relation to breaking bad news. In Japan (Kashiwagi, 1999), India (Burn, 1997), Italy (Gordon and Paci, 1997) the majority of families did not wish full disclosure, instead they preferred to receive information first and filter what is given to the patient. In contrast, Firth (1997) reported that for Hindus and Sikhs a good death is a conscious and anticipated one, and that advanced knowledge is essential to allow people to prepare spiritually and practically. Truth telling in Ireland has not been subjected to the rigours of research but as in most countries levels of truth telling vary considerably.

Palliative care and non-nationals

The *Report of the National Advisory Committee on Palliative Care* (Department of Health and Children, 2001) recommends that specialist palliative care services should both recognize and facilitate cultural diversity. The challenge is to care for non-national people during the terminal phase of their life in a culturally sensitive manner. The provision of palliative care relies on an interpersonal process between the health professional and the client. This process relies on communication, trust, empathy and understanding. Communication, both verbal and non-verbal, provides the opportunity to gather information, provide support and give encouragement. Language differences can make effective communication difficult. Ireland and the UK are geographical neighbours and share a common language; however, there are huge cultural and colloquial language differences between these countries. For example 'press' in England would be to iron, in Ireland it is a cupboard. In Ireland *craic* is 'fun' rather than an illegal street drug. Discussing psycho-social and spiritual issues may be difficult with a common language but is so much more so when language and beliefs differ.

There is the challenge of recognizing how our culture shapes the care we provide. As Irish people we have beliefs and rituals that make sense to us and assist in the process of living and dying. Palliative care, and indeed all health care, is to some extent still delivered in a fashion that fits with these beliefs. The origins of Irish palliative care are firmly rooted in Roman Catholicism, which is reflected in both the ethos and physical surroundings of many palliative care units in the Republic of Ireland. However, in the UK there is a perception that because hospices have Christian roots they only cater for Christians, and this has been cited as a reason for the disproportionately low number of people from minority groups accessing palliative care services (Gatrad *et al.* 2003). Currently, the majority of patients cared for in in-patient units in the Irish Republic continue to be Catholic (reflecting the current population) and they find comfort in the familiar religious icons and pictures found in these units.

Palliative care is committed to holistic practice, which includes the need to understand the spiritual aspects of care. Terminal illness raises many questions about the meaning and nature of existence. Spirituality can be especially significant in end-of-life care, offering the patient a way to find meaning and purpose in dying as in life (Sherman, 2001). It is, however, essential that palliative care services prepare to meet the needs of patients from other religious and cultural backgrounds by putting policies in place to ensure that patients receive culturally competent care; for example, ensuring dietary needs are met and hygiene needs are catered for and by providing suitable religious reading material (for example, the Koran).

'Going home'

People live within their culture most intensively at home, where they can live as they would in their place of origin. Those who settle in a society where the dominant faith or culture is different to their own may adopt many aspects of the dominant culture, although they retain their own practices at times of birth, marriage or death. As a result of the historic absence of ethnic minorities in Ireland there are few host communities for newly arrived immigrants. When palliative care is needed not only do patients not have family living here but lack a culturally appropriate support structure (O'Neill, 2004). Patients and their families may wish to return to their place of origin, which requires much organization. In response to this, the Irish Association for Palliative Care (2002) developed practical guide-lines for health care professionals on repatriating dying patients from Ireland.

Cultural concepts of health

The literature highlights how the way in which people view health and illness has implications for the way they conceptualize illness and how they feel it should be treated (McGee, 2001). Culture is considered the 'lens' that people use to view a phenomenon (Helman, 1990). Without the awareness of cultural differences the Western values of individualism, autonomy, independence, self-reliance, and self-control may cause conflict with families of different cultures that may not hold such values (Andrews and Boyle, 1995). How the patient views cancer affects how they expect to be treated. What they believe about causation will also determine the treatment he or she will seek or accept (Grossman, 1996). These attitudes and beliefs are known to be profoundly affected by cultural beliefs and norms (Navon, 1999).

Illich (1990) claims that in every society the dominant image of death determines the prevalent concept of health. Recent literature supports the theory that Western attitudes to death and dying have changed dramatically over the second half of this century and society is adopting more holistic views (Mellor, 1993). In most non-Western societies death is not seen as a single event but as part of a process, with the deceased moving from the land of the living to the land of the dead. One such example is the practice of Orthodox Jews where the biological death is marked by rituals followed by mourning and finally rituals of social death (Sweeting and Gilhooley, 1992). There are similarities between Jewish rituals and those of the Irish as the dead are protected and the relatives are comforted in both cultures (O'Gorman, 1998).

There is a danger of reducing cultural care to a 'recipe approach' as is evident in many of the publications available on this subject. While it is important to have in-depth knowledge of different cultures, clinicians must also be aware of how closely that person identifies with that particular culture. Ultimately each person should be treated as an individual. Culture is not static, rather it is a constantly changing phenomenon.

Inequalities in access to palliative care services

The opportunity to die with dignity is a fundamental right, yet concern has been expressed about the low numbers of black and ethnic minorities cared for by specialist palliative care services in other countries (Sheldon, 1995; Smaje and Field, 1997; Kamir et al., 2000). One study showed that of the hospice and palliative care population in the UK, 97.1 per cent were white and a mere 2.9 per cent non-white (Eve and Higginson, 2000). However, the extent to which this applies to Ireland cannot be gauged as currently no data on this subject exists. In response to the widely held concern that palliative care services were not meeting the needs of black and minority ethnic groups in the UK, the Department of Health and the Cancer Relief Macmillan Fund financed a major research project (Hill and Penso, 1995). They found that there was little systematic evidence available to be able to assess the use of palliative care services by minority ethnic groups due to the lack of accurate data. The recommendations made included: recording patient's ethnicity, developing a communications plan, having policies on what is and is not acceptable and ensuring cultural specific service provision.

Interpreters and translators

The Royal College of Nursing (1998) advocates that proper translation services should be available for clients who have difficulty communicating in English. Frequently in newly arrived non-national families it is the children who have learnt to speak English first. There are particular difficulties in using patients' children to translate information in palliative care as they may wish to protect their parent and feel unable to translate objectively what is being said, or they may be too young for the interpreting role. Randhawa *et al.* (2003) recommends the provision of translators, and guidelines on the use of family members as translators.

Clinical encounters that are dependent on an interpreter may not achieve the same amount or quality of communication and can be very time consuming. It was also noted in Spruyt's (1999) study that the interpreters were deliberately selective in how they translated so as not to alarm the patient. This may cause difficulty for health care professionals working in palliative care where difficult issues frequently arise. Gender issues should also be considered as in sensitive matters relating to women's health: some women would rather go without an interpreter than have a male interpreter present (Vose and Thurecht, 1999).

There are often difficulties in locating translators in Ireland. The few interpreters available are based in the larger cities, predominantly Dublin. Although there is a higher density of non-nationals in Irish cities many also live in rural communities. In small communities the family may know the translator and this raises issues regarding confidentiality. Issues also arise around funding of translators and who is responsible for payment. There is also an art of being able to communicate through the medium of a translator and this ideally requires training for the staff involved. While planned visits can be arranged ensuring the presence of an interpreter, care or advice required 'out of hours' can be problematic as this is usually provided by telephone and there are no guarantees that an interpreter will be available.

Pain and symptom management

The influence of culture on the meaning and experience of death and dying may be applied to the fundamental domains of end-of-life care, such as pain and symptom management (Crawley *et al.*, 2002). Symptom management in cross-cultural contexts requires attention to the differences in meaning and expression of pain and suffering and to the perceptions and customs related to touching or handling the body (Bates *et al.*, 1997). Moulin (1998) elaborates on some of the social representations of pain in Western society, for example: the stoic view of pain, pain the redeemer, pain that reminds one they are alive, pain as an erotic pleasure, pain as punishment. In Taiwan, familiar concerns about reporting pain and using analgesia included: the belief that pain is an inevitable consequence of cancer and cannot be relieved; fear of addiction to analgesia or developing drug tolerance; a desire to be a 'good patient' by not complaining; concerns that increased pain signifies disease progression; and religious fatalism (Lin, 2000). In this respect there are definite similarities between Taiwan and Ireland, where patients may choose to suffer in this life in order to reap the benefits in the next and where myths surrounding the use of drugs such as morphine continue to hamper pain management. Neuberger (1999), states the palliative philosophy is to relieve pain and to allow the person to go painlessly and smoothly into death. This is one view of a 'good death' but one that is culturally specific. Providing emotional support rather than pain relief may be the respectful choice (Mazanec and Tyler, 2003). Yet, the palliative philosophy also acknowledges that individual desires should be followed.

Grief and bereavement

Grief is highly individualized and how one grieves is often dictated by socialization and membership of a cultural group. This highlights the need for professionals to address the individuals' needs and acknowledge their unique way of experiencing and expressing grief. Patients' relatives also express their emotions differently in different cultures. In Southeast Asian societies, they usually manifest self-restraint, whereas the Puerto Rican culture allows them to show their grief dramatically (Trill and Holland, 1993). For many cultures, how the surviving members cope with grief and loss of the death experience is based on their perception of whether or not the deceased had a good death (Thomas, 2001).

The Irish wake seems incomprehensible to many people from different cultures (O'Gorman, 1998). It is common practice to call to the deceased person's house to offer condolences. The body is often laid out at home surrounded by flowers and burning candles while family, friends and neighbours (including children) file past to pay their respects. Mourners may then congregate in the house to drink and talk, regaling each other with stories about the deceased for many hours, often appearing more like a party than a funeral (Power, 1993).

Lessons to be learnt

In the UK several factors have been identified that act as barriers to the uptake of palliative care facilities by minority ethnic groups (Randhawa and Owens, 2004). These include:

- The generally younger age structure of ethic minority populations;
- The history and perception of palliative care services as being only available to white middle-class patients;
- The lack of information provided to minority ethnic groups about the availability of palliative care services;
- The lack of translator facilities;
- The dietary needs of ethnic groups not being met;
- The spiritual needs of minority ethnic groups going unmet;
- Lower incidences of certain types of cancer and other chronic diseases.

In order to address these issues in Ireland and develop cultural competence in palliative care, education is needed at an institutional, regional and national level. Cultural competence should be identified as a priority in the training of all health care professionals. A further consideration is the increasing numbers of non-national health care professionals working in Ireland who also need induction and training to prepare them for the Irish culture and beliefs around death and dying.

Conclusion

Demographic changes that will magnify the importance of addressing racial/ethnic disparities in health and health care are anticipated to continue over the next decade (Betancourt *et al.*, 2003). There is awareness within the field of palliative care in other countries about issues of inequality of service provision for minority ethnic groups and the need to provide culturally sensitive care. A person's culture affects every facet of their being. End-of-life decision-making is intertwined with the level of acculturation, role of religion or spirituality, fluency of language and communication processes and as such, it affects palliative care provision.

References

Amnesty International (2003) Amnesty concerned at timing of referendum. www.amnesty.ie (accessed 19 July 2004).
An Bord Altranais (2004) Personal communication.
Andrews, M. M. and Boyle, J. S. (1995) *Transcultural Concepts in Nursing Care.* 2nd edn Philadelphia: J. B. Lippincott.

Bates, M. S., Rankin-Hill, L. and Sanchez-Ayendez, M. (1997) The effects of the cultural context of health care on the treatment of and response to chronic pain and illness, *Social Science and Medicine*, 45:1433–47.

Betancourt, J., Green, A., Carrillo, J. and Ananeh-Firempong, O. (2003) Defining cultural competence: a practice framework for addressing racial/ethnic disparities in health and health care, *Public Health Reports*, 118(4):293–302.

Burn, J. (1997) Palliative Care in India, in D. Clarke, J. Hockley and S. Ahmadzai (eds) *New Themes in Palliative Care*. Buckingham: Open University Press.

Central Statistics Office (2003) Population and migration estimates, www.cso.ie (accessed 19 July 2004).

Chevannes, M. (2002) Issues in educating health professionals to meet the diverse needs of patients and other service users from ethnic minority groups, *Journal of Advanced Nursing*, 39(3):290–98.

Crawley, L., Marshall, P., Lo, B. and Koenig, B. (2002) Strategies for Culturally Effective End-of-Life Care, *Annals of Internal Medicine*, 136(9):673–9.

Dein, S. and Thomas, K. (2002) To tell or not to tell, *European Journal of Palliative Care*, 9(5):209–12.

Department of Health and Children (1998) *Report of the Commission on Nursing. A Blueprint for the Future*. Dublin: Stationery Office.

Department of Health and Children (2001) *Report of the National Advisory Committee on Palliative Care*. Dublin: Stationery Office.

Dubliner (2004) Yes minister? www.thedubliner.ie (accessed 19 July 2004).

Eve, A. and Higginson, I. (2000) Minimum dataset activity for hospice and hospital palliative care services in the UK 1997/1998, *Palliative Medicine*, 14:395–404.

Fainsinger, R., Nunez-Olarte, J. and Demoissac, D. (2003) The Cultural Differences in Perceived Value of Disclosure and Cognition: Spain and Canada, *Journal of Palliative Care*, 19(1):43–8.

Firth, S. (1997) *Dying, Death and Bereavement in a British Hindu Community*. Leuven: Peters.

Gatrad, A., Brown, E., Notta, H. and Sheikh, A. (2003) Palliative care needs of minorities, *British Medical Journal*, 327(7408):176–7.

Gerrish, K. and Papadopoulos, I. (1999) Transcultural competence: the challenge for nurse education, *British Journal of Nursing*, 8(21):1453–7.

Gordon, D. and Paci, E. (1997) Disclosure practices and cultural narratives: understanding concealment and silence around cancer in Tuscany, Italy, *Social Science Medicine*, 44:1433–52.

Gracia, D. (2003) Are the ethics of palliative care culturally dependant? *European Journal of Palliative Care*, 10(2):32–5.

Grossman, D. (1996) Cultural Dimensions in Home Health Nursing, *American Journal of Nursing*, 96(7):33–6.

Helman, C. (1990) *Culture, Health and Illness*, 2nd edn, Oxford: Wright.

Hill, D. and Penso, D. (1995) *Opening Doors: Improving Access to Hospice and Specialist Palliative Care Services by Members of the Black and Minority Ethnic Communities*. London: National Council for Hospice and Specialist Palliative Care.

Illich, I. (1990) *Limits to Medicine*. Harmondsworth: Penguin.

Irish Association for Palliative Care (2002) *Going Home. Assisting a Palliative Care Patient to Travel Home from the Republic of Ireland*. Dublin: IAPC.

Irish Refugee Council (2004) Asylum-seeker and refugee statistics in Ireland from January to June 2004, www.irishrefugeecouncil.ie/stats.html (accessed 19 July 2004).

Kamir, K., Bailey, M. and Tunna, K. (2000) Non-white ethnicity and the provision of specialist palliative care services: factors affecting doctors' referral patterns, *Palliative Medicine*, 14:471–81.

Kashiwagi, T. (1999) 'Palliative care in Japan', in D. Doyle, G. Hanks, and N. MacDonald, (eds) *The Oxford Textbook of Palliative Medicine*, 2nd edn, Oxford: Oxford University Press, 797–8.

Larkin, P. J. (1998) The lived experience of Irish palliative care nurses, *International Journal of Palliative Nursing*, 4(3):120–26.

Lin, C. C. (2000) Barriers to the analgesic management of cancer pain: a comparison of attitudes of Taiwanese patients and their caregivers, *Pain*, 88(7):7–14.

MacEinri, P. (2002) Immigration into Ireland: Trends, Policy Responses, Outlook, Available at http://migration.ucc.ie/irelandfirstreport.htm (accessed 2 January 2003).

Margolis, P. (1998) *Ireland's Jews: A Fading Tribe on the Emerald Isle*, Jewish Heritage Report, Vol. II, Nos. 1–2, Spring-Summer. Available at: http://www.isjm.org/jhr/IInos1–2/ireland.htm (accessed 19 July 2004).

Mazanec, P. and Tyler, M. K. (2003) Cultural considerations in end-of-life care: how ethnicity, age and spirituality affect decisions when death is imminent, *American Journal of Nursing*, 103(3):50–58.

McGee, C. (2001) When the golden rule does not apply: Starting nurses on the journey towards cultural competence, *Journal for Nurses in Staff Development*, 17(3):105–12.

Mellor, P. A. (1993) Death in high modernity: the contemporary presence and absence of death, in D. Clarke (ed.) *The Sociology of Death*. Oxford: Blackwell Science, 11–30.

Moulin, P. (1998) Social representations of pain, *European Journal of Palliative Care*, 5(3):92–6.

National Consultative Committee on Racism and Interculturalism, United Nations High Commission for Refugees and Know Racism (2002) *Myths and Misinformation about Asylum Seekers*. Pamphlet.

National Consultative Committee on Racism and Interculturalism and Irish Health Services Management Institute (2002) *Cultural Diversity in the Irish Health Care Sector*. Dublin.

Navon, L. (1999) Cultural views of cancer around the world, *Cancer Nursing*, 22(1):39–45.

Neuberger, J. (1999) Judaism and palliative care, *European Journal of Palliative Care*, 6(5):166–8.

Nyatanga, B. (1997) Cultural issues in palliative care, *International Journal of Palliative Care*, 3(4):203–8.

O'Gorman, S. M. (1998) Death and dying in contemporary society: an evaluation of current and rituals associated with death and dying and their relevance to recent understandings to death and healing, *Journal of Advanced Nursing*, 27(6):1127–35.

Oliviere, D. (1999) Culture and Ethnicity, *European Journal of Palliative Care*, 6(2):53–6.

Oliviere, D., Hargreaves, R. and Monroe, B. (1998) *Good Practice in Palliative Care: A Psychotherapy Perspective*. Aldershot: Ashgate.

O'Neill, J. (1994) Ethnic minorities: neglected by palliative care providers? *Journal of Cancer Care*, 3:215–20.

O'Neill, J. (2004) Integration of refugees in Ireland: Experience with programme refugees 1994–2000. www.democraticdialogue.org/report14 (accessed 19 July 2004).

Power, R. (1993) Death in Ireland: deaths, wakes and funerals in contemporary Irish society, in D. Dickenson and M. Johnson (eds) *Death, Dying and Bereavement*. London: Open University Press in association with Sage Publications.

Randhawa, G., Owens, A., Fitches, R. and Khan, Z. (2003) Communication in the development of culturally competent palliative care services in the UK: a case study, *International Journal of Palliative Nursing*, 9(1):24–31.

Randhawa, G. and Owens, A. (2004) Palliative care for minority ethnic groups. *European Journal of Palliative Care*, 11(1):19–22.

Royal College of Nursing (1998) *The Nursing Care of Older People from Black and Minority Ethnic Communities*. London: Royal College of Nursing.

Sheldon, F. (1995) Will the doors open? Multicultural issues in palliative care, *Palliative Medicine*, 9:89–90.

Sherman, D. (2001) 'Spiritually and culturally competent palliative care', in M. Matzo and D. Sherman (eds) *Palliative Care Nursing: Quality Care to the End of Life*. New York: Springer, 3–47.

Smaje, C. and Field, D. (1997) 'Absent minorities? Ethnicity and the use of palliative care services', in D. Field, J. Hockey and N. Small (eds) *Death, Gender, and Ethnicity*. London: Routledge.

Spectrum (2003) Challenging Racism: International and European context, *Journal of the National Consultative Committee on Racism and Interculturalism*, Issue 3: August 2003.

Spruyt, O. (1999) Community-based palliative care for Bangladeshi patients in East London. Accounts of bereaved carers, *Palliative Medicine*, 13(2):119–30.

Sweeting, H. N. and Gilhooley, L. M. (1992) Doctor, am I dead? A review of social death in modern societies, *Omega – Journal of Death and Dying*, 24(4):251–69.

Thomas, N. (2001) The Importance of Culture throughout All Life and Beyond, *Holistic Nursing Practice*, 15(2):40–6.

Trill, M. D. and Holland, J. (1993) Cross-cultural differences in care of patients with cancer: a review, *General Hospital Psychiatry*, 15:21–30.

Tse, C. Y., Chong, A. and Fok, S. Y. (2003) Breaking bad news: a Chinese perspective, *Palliative Medicine*, 17:339–43.

Vose, C. and Thurecht, K. (1999) What is different when you have a baby in a new country?, in P. Rice (ed.) *Living in a New Country: Understanding Migrants' Health*, Richmond: Ausmed, 43–55.

Walter, T. (2003) Historical and cultural variants on the good death, *British Medical Journal*, 327(7408):218–20.

17 Medical education in the Republic of Ireland

Stephen Higgins

Introduction

All medical undergraduates need to be taught the basic skills and principles of palliative care. Most doctors, regardless of their area of specialization, will care for some palliative patients and so need access to appropriate post-graduate education. Those who choose to specialize in palliative care also require ongoing education. This combination will enable the provision of effective palliative care for all. This is the challenge that faces us.

Palliative care was only formally recognized as a medical speciality by the Irish Medical Council in 1995 and therefore it is not surprising that medical education remains at an early stage of development. Such, indeed is the case throughout Europe (Dowling and Broomfield, 2002; Lloyd-Williams and Carter, 2003). Irish undergraduate and postgraduate education has suffered from a lack of national and regional co-ordination. Teaching has tended to be fragmented and variable in both content and quality. Nonetheless, recent years have seen considerable progress and the continuing rapid growth of the specialty bodes well for the future.

Critically, to date in the Republic of Ireland, no medical school has an academic department of palliative medicine to add the necessary cohesion and direction to medical teaching. Formation of academic departments was one of the key recommendations of the National Advisory Committee on Palliative Care (Department of Health and Children, 2001) and progress is being made in this direction. Recently an outline agreement was reached between University College Dublin and Trinity College Dublin to jointly develop a department of palliative care incorporating a chair in palliative medicine and palliative nursing.

Undergraduate medical education

There are five medical schools in the Republic of Ireland, and all offer a similar six-year degree course with science-based years followed by clinical years. As internationally, there is a gradual movement away from didactic teaching towards a more experiential and integrated learning format with increased patient contact at an early stage. The most significant development in the next few years seems likely to be the transition of medicine to a postgraduate course. This demographic shift in the population entering medicine will lead to more mature medical students. It could be argued that this group will be more likely to have experience or an awareness of the need for palliation in our society.

The Association for Palliative Medicine of Great Britain and the Republic of Ireland produced an undergraduate palliative curriculum in 1993 but neither this nor any other formal curriculum have been used in the Republic of Ireland. This has led to great variations in what is taught, by whom, in what setting and with what outcome (Dowling and Broomfield, 2002). Palliative medicine is taught in all medical schools but the teaching is spread both temporally and departmentally throughout the students' training. Total time allotted to palliative care in each university is not known. Not surprisingly, there is minimal formal assessment of knowledge acquired from palliative teaching. Such a disparate structure inevitably leads to omissions and inconsistencies. From personal experience, newly qualified doctors seem to struggle in dealing with palliative patients. Some of this undoubtedly arises from a societal unease with death and dying but a considerable portion is simply a knowledge deficit.

Experience of a hospice – of what happens there, what patients are admitted for, what the staff do – is invaluable for any medical student and provides a good foundation for explaining the true nature and value of palliative care. Medical schools all offer students some teaching in a local hospice but this varies in duration from a mere half-day to a two-week placement. Leading the way in this area has been Our Lady's Hospice, Harold's Cross, Dublin where a medical tutor in palliative care was appointed in 1999, the first (and still the only) such appointment in the Republic of Ireland. This programme has gradually developed into a multi-disciplinary two-week course for students from two universities with placements throughout the entire academic year. It has to be emphasized that this programme was only feasible with the appointment of a full-time tutor and the lack of such posts is undoubtedly one of the major impediments to improving undergraduate education.

Without any university palliative medicine departments, it is likely that teaching will remain fragmented. The key elements of a successful undergraduate palliative care programme (Dowling and Broomfield, 2002) have been succinctly listed below. However, much remains to be done in their implementation.

- Teach effective communication, in particular, breaking bad news.
- Integrate end-of-life care into existing educational programmes.
- Emphasize symptom relief, not cure.
- Students should explore their own attitudes to death and dying.
- Emphasize team approach, multi-disciplinary setting.
- Include a broad range of clinical settings.
- Include an elective rotation in end-of-life care.
- Use role-play to practice interaction with patients, relatives and colleagues.
- Teachers should be appropriate role models for their students.
- Include an attachment to a hospice.
- Evaluate students after teaching, preferably by means other than written examination.

Postgraduate medical education

The *Report of the National Task Force on Medical Staffing* (Department of Health and Children, 2003) addressed the issue of the European Union working time directive and the subsequent reduction in junior doctors working hours. The Irish government has committed itself to fully implementing this report and this will result in a sharp increase in the number of consultants as the health service moves from being consultant-led to consultant-provided. The report pointed out that a fundamental restructuring of the postgraduate medical education system is required but remained short on details as to what this might entail. An expected outcome is a reduction in the number of 'Junior doctor' posts and a greater emphasis on training with protection from service demands. It remains to be seen whether the political conviction exists to bring this to fruition.

Hospital doctors

The amount of teaching available to doctors in general hospitals varies from hospital to hospital and from year to year. Perhaps, more than anywhere else, there is scope for improvement here. At present, what teaching there is typically comprises lunchtime lectures by the consultant, specialist registrar or clinical nurse specialist. The topic covered is almost invariably some aspect of symptom control. Attendance varies and can often be difficult for doctors working in busy posts without protected time for education. Palliative teaching must not only compete for the time of the doctors but also with other specialties equally keen to promote their field. Furthermore, such teaching tends to be confined to the large teaching hospitals with district and regional hospitals less well served. Nonetheless, even relatively modest teaching programmes have been shown to have an impact (Tiernan *et al.*, 2001).

In hospitals with palliative care teams a second and perhaps more valuable learning opportunity comes from the interaction between the team and the hospital doctors. Not surprisingly, this practical application and demonstration of palliative care can make much greater impact than didactic lectures. However, there runs in parallel with this the risk of de-skilling hospital doctors. This can arise where all palliative issues are seen to be the remit of the palliative care team and their involvement coincides with an effective withdrawal by the referring team. It is for this reason that it is important that the palliative role should remain more normally collaborative rather than exclusive.

A model not commonly seen as yet but which might offer great teaching potential would be one where junior doctors are seconded to the palliative care team for a fixed period of time. At present most doctors, after their intern year, spend two years rotating through different specialties every few months. A situation where, for example, all doctors on this scheme were encouraged to spend one week attached to the palliative care team could bring considerable benefits for doctors and their patients.

General practitioners

General practitioner trainee schemes across the Republic of Ireland all include elements of palliative care. Again, topics covered, time spent and styles of teaching are variable. Some schemes offer trainees a three-month placement in a hospice. Again, there is scope here for more leadership and, preferably, a generic curriculum.

The Irish College of General Practitioners previously offered one-day courses in palliative care. The need for these decreased as the number of day or short courses run by local palliative services grew. Since 2000 the College has instead offered a distance-learning module. This year-long course includes work on ethics, bereavement and symptom control.

Specialist registrars (SpRs)

A formalized and syllabus-based postgraduate training scheme for those wishing to become consultants in palliative care began in 1999. There were several impetuses for this: with the expansion in numbers of palliative consultants it became obvious that there would be an ongoing need for specialized palliative training to prepare doctors for these posts. Furthermore, most Irish medical specialties were at this time developing formalized teaching programmes. The introduction of the Calman training schemes in the UK had left the potential for a situation arising where the qualifications of Irish trained specialists would not be accepted in the UK or in the wider European Union area. The SpR schemes were a response to this.

The scheme lasts for four years and involves the trainee doctor rotating, usually every six to twelve months, through different palliative posts within Ireland. Experience gained includes working with in-patient, home care and hospital palliative services. The training scheme has been popular and, despite its growth from an initial four to a current eleven posts, competition for places remains intense. Applicants will typically be four to six years post-completion of their basic medical degree and will usually already have some experience in both palliative care and oncology. Entry requirements include membership of the Royal College of Physicians of Ireland, the Irish College of General Practice or equivalent qualifications. Entry requirements differ from the United Kingdom programme with a specific requirement for a longer period of acute, adult unselected take. One of the four years may be spent in supervised research. On completion of the four-year programme trainees are eligible to apply for consultant posts, although some may choose instead to work for a period in research or medical teaching. Interestingly, the gender balance is heavily female with ten of the current eleven positions occupied by women. This contrasts with consultant appointments where there are eight male consultants appointed and six female. As mentioned, the structure and syllabus are deliberately based on the UK's Calman scheme. This should ease movement of doctors to and from other EU countries and may, at some stage, allow the training scheme itself to include a period of work abroad.

General medical education

In addition to those educational activities directed specifically at doctors or medical undergraduates there are numerous multi-disciplinary one-day or short courses run by the various palliative services across the Republic of Ireland. The profusion of such events and their variety of subject matter are probably the best evidence of vibrancy in palliative education in the Republic of Ireland. They offer a chance for medical professionals from all backgrounds to sample a wide array of palliative topics and serve to encourage both teaching and research nationally.

Conclusion

Palliative medical education in the Republic of Ireland remains at an early stage of development. Nonetheless, much has been achieved and considerable progress made in recent years. It seems likely that demographic and economic factors, allied to an increasing awareness among health professionals and the general population of the value of palliative care, will ensure that this growth is sustained. There is much to look forward to.

References

Department of Health and Children (2001) *Report of the National Advisory Committee on Palliative Care.* Dublin: Stationery Office.

Department of Health and Children (2003) *Report of the National Task Force on Medical Staffing.* Dublin: Stationery Office.

Dowling, S. and Broomfield, D. (2002) Ireland, the UK and Europe: a review of medical education in palliative care, *Irish Medical Journal,* 95(7):215–16.

Lloyd-Williams, M. and Carter, Y. H. (2003) Can medical education extend palliative care? *Palliative Medicine,* 17(7):640–42.

Tiernan, E., Kearney, M., Lynch, A. M., Holland, N. and Pyne, P. (2001) Effectiveness of a teaching programme in pain and symptom management for junior house officers. *Support Care Cancer,* 9(8):606–10.

18

Palliative nurse education in the
Republic of Ireland

Philip Larkin

Introduction

End-of-life care has been a cornerstone of nursing practice in the Republic of Ireland. The roots of palliative education were firmly established in nursing and from this the principles of palliative education have developed nationwide. The historical development of Irish nursing reflects a distinguished history of Irish religious houses providing care and comfort to the poor of inner cities where social health was gaining increasing importance, stretching from the repeal of penal restrictions in the early nineteenth century through to the foundation of the Irish state and into modern health care services. Respect for the nursing component of care for the dying may also be seen in the early thoughts of Cicely Saunders as she developed her ideas about the foundation of palliative care as a twentieth-century discipline. Saunders, no doubt from her own nursing experience, clearly advocated a solid role for nursing in palliative care and offers many examples in her edited letters of where nursing has been integral to the development of palliative services (Clark, 2002).

Nursing knowledge

Nursing knowledge as an integral part of the development of the nursing profession is particularly relevant for Irish palliative nurse education where the debate between objective scientific knowledge and experientially based technical knowledge remains a critical issue in the development of the specialty. It is generally accepted that empirical or scientific knowledge is only one component of what nursing needs in order to understand practice, clearly described by Carper (1978) in her review of four domains of knowing in nursing: empirics, aesthetics, personal knowledge and ethics. Many nursing theorists have developed this framework through descriptions of intuitive practice (Benner and Tanner, 1987), subjective knowledge (Gadow, 1980) and the value of contextual knowledge (Bishop and Scudder, 1990).

The scientific, rational knowledge of medicine often fails to encompass the holistic nature of nursing. This encompasses practical knowledge, relative to tacit understanding and the recognition of conscious and unconscious complex decision-making, which describes expert professional nursing practice (Chinn and Kramer, 1991; Smith, 1998). Irish palliative nurse education reflects such ideals, attempting to provide knowledge through a balance of pure science with conceptual components such as dignity, support, care-giving and the 'emotional labour' of palliative nursing practice (Seymour, 2004). The way this knowledge is currently achieved through the Irish university system is directly related to the fundamental changes that have taken place in nursing in the Republic of Ireland.

Irish nursing in transition

The role of clinical nurse specialist was introduced in the Republic of Ireland following the publication of *Report of the Commission on Nursing* (Department of Health and Children, 1998). Key recommendations were made which have shaped the academic route of nursing through the university system which commenced as a four-year programme in 2002. At postgraduate level, the commission proposed a clinical career pathway for registered nurses as either clinical nurse specialist or advanced nurse practitioner. The introduction of the role of clinical nurse specialist initially caused confusion, as criteria for ratification of posts were not always clearly defined. A number of palliative nurses seeking accreditation at the specialist level were refused because important issues such as the number of posts required, the recognition of past educational achievement and experience in the specialty were not addressed coherently and equitably.

Development of palliative nurse education

As Sneddon (2004) suggests, education programmes should reflect the holistic and inter-professional nature of the palliative care paradigm, providing a framework for best clinical practice through attention to clinical excellence in research, management and leadership (Sheldon and Smith, 1996; Jodrell, 1998; Ford, 1998). Moreover, palliative education addresses issues of person as well as practice and enables students to meet their personal potential, as well as the needs of patients and carers (Sneddon, 2004).

The *Report of the National Advisory Committee on Palliative Care* (Department of Health and Children, 2001) consolidated this link between theory and practice by advocating a sound education system to prepare nurses to work within the specialist area. In 1987, the first dedicated palliative care education centre was opened at Our Lady's Hospice, Dublin, with the appointment of a nurse tutor to oversee the development of formal palliative education courses for both in-house staff and external applicants. Although the remit of this post encompassed a multi-disciplinary education role, notably through the annual Moving Points in Palliative Care conference, there was a clear focus towards the potential contribution of nursing to the development of palliative care in the Republic of Ireland.

A six-week course designed for nurses was extended to eight weeks and was approved nationally by An Bord Altranais – the Irish nursing board. The course was considered the gold standard for nurses wishing to pursue a career in this field of nursing and became the foundation of palliative nurse education in the Republic of Ireland. Many nurses setting up regional palliative care services were graduates of these short courses. Latterly and significantly, the eight-week course was accepted as the academic grounding which enabled nurses to be considered for clinical nurse specialist posts. Introductory programmes for nurses from other practice backgrounds who wished to learn more about palliative care were also offered and particularly attended by nurses from elderly-care and community nursing, among others.

The emphasis on clinical nursing knowledge and personal development was significant in these courses and laid a pathway for future education initiatives. The need to understand the personal impact of caring for the dying was equally important to the acquisition of skills that would be of benefit to the patient's well-being and quality of life. Courses encapsulated strong principles of adult education, valuing experiential learning and reflection on and in practice as a tool towards the attainment of global knowledge. Similar education appointments in Limerick (1987), Cork (1994) and later Raheny, Dublin (1997) laid the foundations of a more national structure for palliative nurse education and have developed into strategic departments of palliative education which provide an array of education opportunities for nurses and other health care professionals.

Academic foundations – pinnacles and pitfalls

The development of postgraduate university-based education programmes led to the need to identify links with third-level (university) centres. Both educators and practitioners saw the value of deepening nursing knowledge through more structured and formally recognized education. In 1996, the Higher Diploma in Nursing Studies (Palliative Care – later changed to

Palliative Nursing) began as a joint initiative between Our Lady's Hospice and University College Dublin. Originally designed as a two-year, day/block release programme, this was modified to offer applicants either a 'fast-track', one-year option or a longer period of three years for applicants new to academic study. The first group graduated in 1998. This course offered the opportunity for nurses who wished to work in the specialist area to consolidate their knowledge through an exploration of the wider sciences, philosophy, psychology and research methodology and an academic term exploring the specialist knowledge of palliative nursing including symptom management, communication, psychological and social issues and self-awareness. The value of practice was enhanced as candidates not only worked in clinical palliative care practice but also undertook an alternative practice placement.

Subsequently similar courses were established in Cork and Galway. These latter courses differed in content and structure from the Dublin prototype. Further changes are needed to facilitate the development of advanced clinical roles, such as advanced practice and Masters-level education for nurses. These courses serve to consolidate specialist practice in palliative care as a dynamic and innovative practice. At the time of writing, the Dublin and Galway courses remain viable and approximately 150 registered nurses have graduated and are working predominantly in specialist palliative nursing practice.

Such changes are not without problems. The Higher Diploma qualification is itself an anomaly of the Irish third-level system. Placed between a Bachelors and a Masters degree, candidates are expected to be critically articulate to Masters level by the end of the programme which in some cases is offered over a calendar year. Credit is given for clinical knowledge. However, the wisdom of expecting students to perform to this level in such a short period is questionable. The fact that the academic level of Higher Diploma is not always recognized outside the state is a further concern for educators where emigration remains a key demographic issue and nurses find that their qualification does not entitle them to access appropriate further education abroad. Equally, in recent years specialist palliative care nurses from outside the Republic of Ireland who have worked in specialist posts elsewhere find their qualifications are not recognized for registration as a clinical nurse specialist in the Republic of Ireland, leaving them no option but to undertake a Higher Diploma in order to retain or seek a similar post.

Although it is educationally sound to provide courses that are integrative and clinically linked, the way in which commensurate qualifications can be integrated into the credit system needs to be delineated more demonstrably. A particular concern has been the way in which the Higher Diploma qualification has been seen as the *sine qua non* for appointment to senior posts in clinical practice. Although it is agreed that the course provides the appropriate level of academic grounding, specialist practice is equally about clinical ability, and academic courses cannot necessarily guarantee this.

Future directions

Currently there is no chair in cancer or palliative nursing in the Republic of Ireland. The future of palliative nursing would benefit from the development of academic posts structured within an academic department of palliative care.

Another consideration for the future is the development of advanced nursing practice. In both Dublin and Galway, academic preparation is offered to enable nurses to attain Masters-level advanced nurse practitioner status. Masters-level nurse education in the Republic of Ireland is largely generic and does not focus on any nursing specialty. Nor is there an accredited post at the advanced level in palliative nursing at this time. The function of the advanced nurse practitioner needs to be appraised fully to ensure that the autonomy of practice envisaged can be adequately sustained in palliative care.

Irish palliative care nursing has reached a level of clinical and educational expertise which can be shared in a European context. Work carried out in the European Union may be far more relevant in terms of its application to the Irish context than the North-American focus currently experienced. Nurses across Europe are keen to share their knowledge and experience, although language can be a barrier. However, the Republic of Ireland has much to share in the development of palliative nurse education at a European level. The European Association for Palliative Care (EAPC) Task Force on Nurse Education (Larkin *et al.*, 2004) has recently produced consultative guidelines regarding the establishment of palliative nurse education at the basic, advanced and specialist levels, as well as suggestions for expected knowledge acquisition following training. In many ways, the achievement of this document is not so much in its content, but in the ability of palliative nurses around Europe to communicate with each other for the greater development of palliative nurse education, reflecting the EAPC view of 'One Voice-One Vision'. Irish palliative nurse education is fortunate to be at the forefront of this vision.

Conclusion

Palliative nurse education has become an integral part of the academic development of nursing in the Republic of Ireland. No doubt, there remains a challenge in putting the knowledge into the arena of clinical practice and being cognizant of roles, boundaries and above all, the patient. Most rewarding is the fact that the development of palliative nurse education in the Republic of Ireland has never forgotten the need to consider oneself as a practitioner. To some extent, this reflection on palliative nurse education comes full circle, back to the religious houses that not only provided excellent physical care but saw the need to educate their nurses. For that, modern Irish palliative care owes a debt of gratitude. Challenges remain, but palliative nurse education has exhibited innovation and tenacity in its approach which bodes well for the future development of Irish nurses in the specialty.

References

Benner, P. and Tanner, C. (1987) Clinical Judgment: How Expert nurses use intuition, *American Journal of Nursing*, 87:23–31.
Bishop, A. H. and Scudder, J. R. Jr (1990) *The Practical, Moral, and Personal Sense of Nursing: A Phenomenological Philosophy of Practice*. Albany: State University of New York Press.
Bishop, A. H. and Scudder, J. R. (2003) Gadow's contribution to our philosophical interpretation of nursing. *Nursing Philosophy*, 4(2):104–10.
Carper, B. A. (1978) Fundamental patterns of knowing in nursing. *Advances in Nursing Science*, 1(1):13–23.
Chinn, P. L. and Kramer, M. K. (1991) *Theory and nursing: A systematic approach* (3rd ed). St. Louis, MO: Mosby-Year book, U.S.
Clark, D. (2002) *Cicely Saunders: Founder of the Hospice Movement. Selected Letters 1959–1999*. Oxford University Press, U.K.
Department of Health and Children (1998) *Report of the Commission on Nursing. A Blueprint for the Future*. Dublin: Stationery Office.
Department of Health and Children (2001) *Report of the National Advisory Committee on Palliative Care*. Dublin: Stationery Office.
Ford, G. (1998) Multi-professional education, in D. Doyle, G. W. C. Hanks and N. MacDonald (eds) *Oxford Textbook of Palliative Medicine*. 2nd edn, Oxford: Oxford Medical Publications.
Gadow, S. (1980) Existential advocacy: philosophical foundation for nursing in *Nursing: Images and Ideals: Opening Dialogue with the Humanities*. S. F. Spicker and S. Gadow, New York: Springer, 79–101.
Jodrell, N. (1998) Nurse Education, in D. Doyle, G. W. C. Hanks and N. MacDonald (eds) *Oxford Textbook of Palliative Medicine*. 2nd edn, Oxford: Oxford Medical Publications.
Larkin, P., Porchet, F., De Vlieger, T. and Gorchs, N. (2004) *Palliative Nurse Education: A Vision for the Future. Report of the Taskforce on Palliative Nurse Education*. European Association for Palliative Care, Milan. (A full copy of this report can be downloaded as a PDF file through the E.A.P.C website www.eapc.org)
Seymour, J. (2004) What's in a name? A concept analysis of key terms in palliative

care nursing, in Payne, S., Seymour, J., and Ingleton, C. (2004) (eds) *Palliative Care Nursing: Principles and Evidence for Practice*. Maidenhead: Open University Press, 55–74.

Sheldon, F. and Smith, P. (1996) The life so short, the craft so hard to learn: a model for post-basic education in palliative care. *Palliative Medicine*, 10:99–104.

Smith, B. (1998) Knowing how vs. knowing that, in J. C. Nyiri and B. Smith (eds) *Practical Knowledge: Outlines of a Theory of Traditions and Skills*. London: Croom Helm, 1–16.

Sneddon, M. (2004) Specialist professional education in palliative care. How did we get here and where are we going? in S. Payne, J. Seymour and C. Ingleton (2004) (eds) *Palliative Care Nursing: Principles and Evidence for Practice*. Maidenhead: Open University Press, 636–54.

19

Reflections from abroad

Frank Brennan, Julie Ling, Peter Lawlor, Siobhán
Sheehan, Jide Afolabi and Maria Bailey

Introduction

Having finished the main task of editing, it became clear that the book did
not capture the experiences of those who have come from abroad to work in
Ireland. Who better to comment than those who had experience of working
in palliative care elsewhere? The following vignettes represent the views of a
number of different health care professionals who had worked in Ireland
and abroad and were asked to comment on the realities of working in
Ireland.

A view from 'down under'

Dr Frank Brennan
Palliative Care Consultant, Calvary Hospital, Sydney, Australia.

I am an Australian palliative care specialist. In 2003, I worked in Ireland in
two settings – Dublin and Limerick. Throughout my time, I was received with
extraordinary generosity, openness and encouragement by the palliative
care community of Ireland. As an Australian of Irish origin, dating from the
time of the Famine, it was a great privilege to be working in the land of my
forebears.

Ireland and Australia have relatively new training schemes for doctors
specializing in this discipline. In Australia, after three years of basic training
in internal medicine and a gruelling exam, there is three years of 'advanced
training' in palliative care. In Ireland the advanced training was four years.

I was very impressed by the calibre, competency and enthusiasm of the trainees.

Both countries aspire to the provision of integrated palliative care services. In Australia the tyranny of distance means that in many sections of the cities and certainly in rural and remote areas of the vast continent, palliative care is rudimentary or falls to dedicated general practitioners in collaboration with community nurses. Equally, when I was in the south-west of Ireland I was aware of the pioneering and often solo work of palliative care nurses in small hospitals: a story repeated throughout the Republic – of relatively small numbers of consultants in palliative care, general practitioners with an interest and remarkable nursing staff dedicated to the building of palliative care services with flair, imagination, humour, competency and boundless compassion. In both countries, the palliative care community is struggling to determine the extent of our role in the care of non-malignant end-stage disease.

Issues that I observed in Ireland included the resolution of charity-run/government-run services, the feminization of the specialty with most trainees being female and the inevitable ramifications this entails for consultant practice with part-time/job-sharing and, crucially, the universal issue of the maintenance of professional enthusiasm and stamina: What balance do practitioners strike between their personal and professional lives?

In terms of clinical practice there were two vital observations. The first was that there are great similarities between Ireland and Australia in therapeutics, emphasis and approach. The second was that there are great differences in communication about disease, especially the Irish phenomenon of collusion and non-disclosure. While widespread, it certainly was not universal. It was both tolerated and struggled with across all disciplines and all health professionals. Coming from an antipodean environment where openness and transparency are almost a fetish, I found this to be my greatest cultural shock. After about a month of repeated denial, obfuscation and relative-led gate-keeping I began to wonder: What is happening here? Are there truly secrets and lies being kept, or is it simply conversational etiquette that certain topics are never discussed and that everyone, including the patient, fully knows? On one extraordinary day I was met by a series of relatives, each seemingly more determined to block any discussion of the malignancy of their loved one, palliative care or end-of-life issues when I received this call from my secretary:

> Mrs W just rang. You'll be seeing her husband in the clinic today. She's asked me to tell you not to mention cancer to him. She doesn't talk about it and doesn't want it brought up. Also she said that you are not to tell him any bad news. He's not able for it. And, oh, she also said if you think you know how long he has, can you please keep it to yourself.

With time I settled. Perhaps we Australians are far too direct. Perhaps we need to learn a little of the subtlety of the doctor in Hugh Leonard's play *A Life*, when a character relates:

> I asked him if he had the results of the X-rays. He took me into his surgery ... He gave me one of those looks of his, redolent of the cemetery and said that I should buy day-returns from now on instead of season tickets.

It was a great pleasure to work in Ireland. I was consistently impressed by the qualities of all my colleagues. The combination of a high degree of professionalism, commitment to optimum care and the willingness to participate in teamwork were exemplary.

London to Dublin

Julie Ling
Nurse Advisor – Department of Health of Children

Prior to my arrival in Ireland I had trained and worked as a nurse in multi-cultural London. I had spent many weekends and holidays in Dublin and made the very misguided and somewhat naive assumption that the small strip of water known as the Irish Sea was what separated England and Ireland.

There is nothing that stokes the fires of patriotism like a major sporting event. If you are English and living in Ireland then you just have to get used to Irish people supporting any team that is playing against England. I was naively shocked to find that Argentina, France and Germany have a huge fan base in Ireland, if they are playing against England.

Irish people are very welcoming and this conviviality applies to all aspects of life. A cup of tea is always accompanied by 'will you have something with that?' Unlike England where if you decline the first offer it is retracted and not repeated, in Ireland this is just the beginning of the process which could go on for some considerable time. In short if you are offered a biscuit with your tea in Ireland just say yes, even if you don't want it. Another notable Irish trait is knowing, remembering and using peoples' names. It is commonplace for people to use your name in conversation and this applies even if there are only two of you in the room. There is something reassuring about people knowing you and who you are. However, this requires excellent memory skills in order to reciprocate. Worse still, if names are written pronouncing them is a huge challenge if you have no understanding of the Irish language (Niamh, Siobhan, O'Síoráin).

During my time living in Ireland I have had time to reflect on some of the differences between the two countries and cultures. Probably one of my first and lasting observations is that English people are often direct in their approach and tend to get straight to the point. In Ireland story-telling is part of the culture and many Irish people prefer to talk around issues. Discussions that should take place in meetings often take place in the corridor or coffee shop prior to the meeting, sometimes leaving you wondering exactly what was said or decided at the meeting itself!

Working as a nurse in Ireland is different to nursing in London. The first thing that struck me was that everyone was called by their title – doctor, matron, sister, nurse. Budgets and cost-consciousness almost endemic in the NHS did not appear to have hit Ireland. Drugs are referred to and prescribed by their trade names rather than their generic name – which took some adjusting. My nursing colleagues always seemed to 'go home' for the weekend: this usually entailed 3–5-hour journeys across country to parts of Ireland I had only heard of.

Arriving from the 'free at the point of delivery' NHS, I was surprised to find that in Ireland patients have to pay to consult with their general practitioner, and even more shocked when I had to pay cash directly to the GP myself. Irish people are usually very grateful for care and generally have huge respect for doctors and nurses. Their expectation and demands on the health service generally seem to be less obvious than in the UK system. Appropriate disclosure of information, the level of information given and the route by which this is offered differs from my experience of England, and more specifically London, in that many patients in Ireland do not ask for information.

In England, patients would often attend appointments alone or with perhaps one other. In Ireland patients bring family with them to out-patient appointments, sometimes many family members appearing at once; not always spouses or children, but aunties, cousins, uncles and in-laws. Frequently families were involved in discussions regarding a patient's treatment and prognosis before the patient themselves.

In the time that I have lived in Ireland, palliative care has changed enormously with the development of new services, which has and continues to bring with it opportunities and challenges.

Reflections on returning to palliative care in Ireland from Canada

Peter G. Lawlor, MB MMedSc CCFP
Consultant in palliative medicine at Our Lady's Hospice and
St James's Hospital, Dublin, Ireland.

I spent almost eight years in the Edmonton Palliative Care Program before returning four months ago to a consultant post in Dublin. My reflections described herein relate to the positive experiences in addition to the many trials and tribulations. They encompass a broad array of experiences ranging from socio-cultural to the more work-related, such as health care administration, clinical practice, and academic endeavours.

Recent advances in information technology, greater freedom of information and aggressive media reporting have helped to reveal and disseminate the news regarding many of the major political and socio-cultural issues of the last decade in Ireland. These issues include the following: the striking level of political corruption in Ireland, and the consequent legal tribunals and other enquiries; the Good Friday agreement and the ongoing political struggles in Northern Ireland; the level of economic growth, and the failure of infrastructural development to keep pace with this; the traffic congestion; the cost of living, especially the exorbitant house prices; the huge influx of new immigrants, and the racist discrimination that they sometimes experience; the ubiquitous use of mobile phones; and finally but not least, the ban on smoking in pubs. Most recently returned Irish medical or nursing emigrants are well aware of these prior to their return. They are also probably aware of the vast number of recently published government-commissioned health care reports. Armed with this information, one is likely to return, like me, with a varying mix of excitement and apprehension.

Nonetheless, the experience at ground level when one arrives is sometimes both shocking and depressing. The economic growth and the increasingly frenetic pace of life does not necessarily translate to increased happiness or improved quality of life for many, and the underbelly of the 'Celtic Tiger' is therefore not always a pretty sight! One might identify coping with the traffic congestion and the housing market as the most stressful experiences. The traffic congestion is further compounded, as in my case, by the clear failure of many institutions such as hospitals to ensure adequate parking facilities for their staff. The shock of the exorbitant housing market is exacerbated by the appalling hyperbole used by estate agent and auctioneering firms to describe some of the hovels that they attempt to sell. Coming from Canada, my definition of 'spacious' was also clearly at variance with that of Irish estate agents. However, if the traffic and housing market get one down, one can now retreat to the local pub, have a drink, and thanks to recent legislation, ponder over one's life decisions in at least a smoke-free environment!

My experience of health care administration both before and after my return to Ireland has been frustrating at times. It took three months for my contract to arrive in Canada following a successful interview. Although equitable patient access is an inconsistent feature of the Irish health care system, palliative care appears to perform very well in this respect, at least in the major urban centres. One cannot say the same for telephone access to hospital switchboards. I timed my marathon effort of 30 minutes on a Friday afternoon trying to access the switchboard of a major Dublin hospital.

In the clinical practice of palliative care I met many therapeutic challenges on my return to Ireland. Generic drug names are used in Edmonton, whereas trade names are used extensively in Dublin. There are differences in dose formulations of immediate release hydromorphone, in that the 1.3 mg and 2.6 mg doses are the only ones available in Ireland. This makes it difficult to administer higher doses. In Ireland, opioid treatment is frequently initiated with slow release formulations, whereas immediate release formulations are used in Edmonton to titrate to stable analgesia before switching to the slow release form. Nonsteroidal anti-inflammatory agents of both the COX-1 and COX-2 variety are used extensively as adjuvants in palliative care in Dublin, and certainly to a greater degree than in Edmonton. Small doses of benzodiazepines are used more frequently in Dublin. I suspect that the greater level of NSAID and benzodiazepine use here might also explain the lower levels of total daily opioid use in Dublin. Differences exist regarding the use of midazolam for sedation. In Edmonton, midazolam is given by a continuous subcutaneous infusion and titrated rapidly to effect. In Dublin, midazolam is added to a syringe driver and a constant dose is delivered over a 12- or 24-hour period. It is often quite difficult to estimate dose requirements, and ease of titration would appear to be more difficult as a result. I am intrigued by the insertion of 2.5 mg of midazolam in a syringe driver over 24 hours. This means that the patient receives 0.1 mg per hour, which seems like a homeopathic dose. However, no dose comparison trial evidence is available, and therefore it is difficult to comment on which is the better way to administer midazolam. I was accustomed to a computerized medication administration record in Edmonton, whereas a handwritten medication sheet is used in Dublin. The medication sheet in Dublin often contains numerous as-required orders, especially in the hospice setting. This means that the patient's registered nurse has many treatment options and great reliance is placed on her assessment. This works well when the nurse has a lot of experience in palliative care but has the potential to be disastrous if the nurse is inexperienced. This is a major concern in Dublin at the moment, given the shortage of nurses and the difficulties of recruiting.

In Dublin it is probably not commonplace for a discussion to have taken place with the patient and family on hospital or hospice admission regarding the patient's wishes for resuscitation. In Edmonton, such discussions are considered for the most part mandatory. Many patients in Canada have an advanced directive regarding proxy decision makers and honouring their wishes should they become cognitively impaired. Patients in Edmonton engage in denial but perhaps to a lesser extent than those in Dublin. Collusion and the 'conspiracy of silence' would appear to be more common in Ireland. On this topic, the words of the Irish actor, Frank Kelly, whom I heard on a recent radio interview, spring to mind. Although I am unsure as to whether the original quote can be fully attributed to him, he maintained that 'Ireland is the only country in the world where two people can have a conversation and not say what they mean, yet they both leave and know exactly what the other one meant'. Dublin has a long history of providing literary geniuses ranging from Joyce to Behan. Dubliners themselves are a particularly witty bunch and truly 'have a way with words'. There is no doubt that since my return this unique sense of humour has helped me feel more at home.

Despite all the collusion and 'conspiracy of silence' surrounding end-of-life issues, the support for hospice in Ireland is ironically very strong. In many ways, this is not surprising given the tremendous respect for the person and their family in the hospice setting – something many North American palliative care institutions could learn from. On the other hand, the limited access to radiological investigations and laboratory services is often frustrating in the hospice setting in Dublin. I have always maintained that each large hospital should ideally have a hospice structure on campus, thereby offering patients the best of medical model care in addition to the holistic and compassionate hospice approach. Unfortunately, such a hybrid structure remains elusive in the Dublin setting at the moment. I feel privileged to have access to the rehabilitative services in Our Lady's Hospice, and coupled with the new day hospice activity, there is a true sense of providing active palliative and hospice care, as opposed to the more traditional hospice care, which has tended to be predominantly terminal in focus.

The Edmonton Palliative Care Program is renowned for its academic contribution. Unfortunately, the research culture is largely only in its gestational stage in Dublin. The heavy clinical workload that is borne by palliative medicine consultants in Dublin means that precious little if any time is available for research projects. Nonetheless, moves are afoot to create a chair in palliative medicine. Although nurses in Dublin pursue higher training and qualifications in palliative care, there appears to be a shortage of ongoing training in the form of teaching rounds. Again, I suspect that this reflects the heavy clinical workload commitments.

In conclusion, through the experiences recounted herein I feel I have been on the roller-coaster since my return to Dublin four months ago. I consider this as a normal part of adjustment. My colleagues tell me that this adjustment period can last from one to two years. I am therefore prepared for a bumpy ride. What hope sustains me? The highlight of my working week is to sit down with the Dublin regional specialist registrars in palliative care for an hour-long journal club. I am greatly encouraged by their motivation and competence, and such attributes together with increasing recognition of the specialty bode well for the future of palliative care in Ireland. Now the task is to find the money to buy a house in 'dear old dirty Dublin'.

Coming home to Ireland

Siobhán Sheehan
Ward manager Our Lady's Hospice

I left Ireland in 1986 because I fell in love and married an Englishman. Oh what have I done! We moved to Orpington in Kent, which is about 20 miles from London where I lived for 15 years before returning. My early English hospital experiences were very different, particularly in the use of language. I would be looking for the press only to receive blank stares until it dawned on someone that I am looking for the cupboard! I became interested in palliative care from my experiences in district nursing and worked for Marie Curie in Caterham for a year before moving to St Christopher's in Sydenham in 1998. In 2001 I returned to Dublin following my husband's transfer here. Yes we are still in love!

I am now working in Our Lady's Hospice in Dublin. England is a very multicultural society. Once when looking after a Catholic gentleman who was approaching death I wanted to put a lit candle and crucifix beside him and when I asked to do this people were surprised as it was not the norm. Rituals around death are different in both countries, even in people of similar faiths. When someone of a Christian faith dies in St Christopher's, the body is brought down to a specially chilled room (morgue) and collected by the undertakers within three days with burial or cremation about ten days later or even longer. In Our Lady's Hospice, the patient is brought to 'Shalom', a quiet viewing room, and usually collected by the undertakers within 24–36 hours. Burial or cremation is much quicker and although cremation is becoming more frequent, most people are still buried, which contrasts with London.

The issuing of a death certificate in England is carried out by the registrar on the ward and given to the family at the day-after-death meeting. This meeting helps the family to talk about their loved one and to express their feelings. We do not have this opportunity in Dublin and it might be some weeks or months later that a family return to the ward. The death certificate is sent to Lombard House for registration and the family have to collect it there.

It is funny to be back in Ireland again listening to Irish accents after I had become used to Londoners' Cockney twang!

A Nigerian perspective

Jide Afolabi
Physiotherapist

My first impressions of working in Ireland were actually charming ones. There was an air of candid interest expressed through polite inquiries about my country of origin and approximate length of stay on the island. This was often punctuated by vague references to the number of foreigners in Ireland and the demographics of the country. This would then be followed by a direct question as to when I intended to leave.

I was first asked this question at a professional meeting in an acute care hospital. The question induced a pin-drop silence which has been re-enacted since with regularity. The profundity of the apologies that both precede and follow them, hints at the possibility of a less apparent motive. These events reinforce the notion of being different, and perhaps unwelcome, in a largely mono-ethnic society.

Working in the hospice has brought its own share of awkward moments. Here differences tend to be emphasized in much more subtle forms; easily discounted but freely reinforced by repetition. On balance though, it is a more pleasant environment and there are fewer inhibitions among staff about sending out messages about the value and importance of team members.

Furthermore, the most sincere form of acceptance I have found has been with patients in palliative care. I have often thought about the likelihood of one of the staff giving background information to the patients about what to expect before I actually happened upon them. Such has been the warmth and genuineness of appreciation and the absolute lack of the shock element that my appearance evoked in the early days.

When I am asked what it has been like working in Ireland, I often relate that it has been one of extremes. On the one hand is the challenge of being a functional and relevant member of a dynamic multi-disciplinary team. It is a fulfilling role and presents enormous opportunities for self-development. The other extreme is everywhere else and occasionally on the corridors and rooms of the work environment. It is never pleasant but, unfortunately, is a fact of life.

On reflection, working with patients in the hospice has been a positive experience. I feel now that it would have been uncharitable to come away from Ireland with only the acute care experience behind me.

The transition from England to Ireland in palliative care – a personal reflection

Maria Bailey
Nurse Tutor

The decision to return to Ireland following an absence of some 40 years was facile compared with the reality of living the dream. In England I had been employed as a home care nurse for an inner-city hospice in South Birmingham. The move back to my roots brought me to a hospice on the outskirts of a provincial city in Southern Ireland.

On reflection I see that my experiences of the transition period could broadly be described as follows: a personal bereavement process where I grieved the loss of all that was familiar to me and strived to adjust to the new; a cultural adjustment which involved adapting to different social, religious and organizational behaviours; and finally the impact of the transition on my professional life. These functions did not occur independently of each other and were frequently intertwined.

The year is 2000. I am a staff nurse in the in-patient unit of a hospice caring for a patient who is dying. The family are present. All is calm. A care assistant enters the room 'Where's the tray?' she hisses. Uncomfortable and confused I whisper back 'What tray?' 'The one with the candle – haven't you said the prayers?' comes the frustrated response. We leave the room and she runs off down the corridor returning within seconds and reverently re-enters the room bearing a silver tray complete with candle, holy water and prayer book. Lighting the candle she begins the prayers – clearly known by heart – as our patient is taking his last breaths. The relatives make no comment but join in with the prayers. Later I am told that whenever we suspect a patient is dying we must get the tray and send for a member of the pastoral care team. As the weeks go by I became familiar with the expression 'fetch the tray' which is synonymous with the imminent death of a patient. I could be described as an English Catholic if such a term exists. In my English experience of caring for the dying I am familiar with asking patients and families from many different denominations and cultures what rituals will bring comfort to them at the moment of death. I have often joined in or offered to lead families in prayer; however the candle was a new experience, its presence one of many reminders of the significant part that Catholic religious orders had in pioneering Irish hospice palliative care.

In comparison to England, community services in Ireland would appear to be considerably under-resourced. Community nursing in England is broadly divided into health visitor, community midwife, community RGN and care assistants. The public health nurses (PHN) in Ireland provide all these services for adults and children 'from the cradle to the grave'. Frameworks for supporting the PHN vary across Ireland with different health boards providing varying levels of support which may or may not include community staff nurses and care assistants.

In England, a patient receiving medication via a syringe driver will be cared for by the community registered general nurse (RGN), with advice and support as required from the home care clinical nurse specialist (CNS) and general practitioner. This arguably affords home care CNSs more flexibility in responding to the needs of palliative care patients and families. In contrast, in the Mid-Western Health Board region of Ireland syringe drivers in the community are in general set up and changed each day by the home care CNS.

Paediatric palliative care services are in their infancy. In Dublin, Ireland's first paediatric palliative medicine consultant was appointed in 2003. Access to the service is dependent on the child having previously been an in-patient at Dublin's children's hospital. In the community at present both adults and children requiring palliative care are supported by the same palliative care home care team. Palliative care for children is largely limited to those with cancer. Unlike England, as yet there is in Ireland no hospice caring exclusively for children.

Palliative Care in Ireland is a progressive and dynamic specialty. The Ireland of my childhood is fast fading into a mêlée of old familiar traditions struggling to compete with more recent social and cultural influences. At the heart of palliative care, in whatever country, lie the patient and the family. I have been privileged to witness two countries that are cultures apart yet share the uniqueness of healing in its widest sense.

20 | The future of palliative care in Ire

Liam O'Síoráin and Julie Ling

Introduction

Previous chapters of this book have described palliative care in the Republic of Ireland at the start of a new millennium. Author's styles differ, adding to the richness of the book, with some chapters having a very personal 'lived', qualitative feel, whereas others have needed to be more factual and quantitative. Therein lies one of the current debates in palliative care; how best to describe and capture the meaning of what we do. Words and language have always been important to the Irish people. Perhaps this is a reflection of our strong oral traditions. Culture, poetry, song and music were preserved for centuries, not in written form but passed by word of mouth from generation to generation. The poem 'Bás Solais' resonates with relevance and meaning when one reads how death was viewed by our ancestors as being so much part of life. 'Palliative care' and 'hospice' are words often used to describe the same thing in Ireland and yet they can have different meanings. To many, 'palliative care' defines the specialty while 'hospice' still resonates as a word with deep associations of care, kindness and holism but for some is also synonymous with death and dying. Has the movement to rename hospice been part of the death-denying culture so prevalent in our society? Are we really comfortable with the new 'palliative care' or will we in time change again to embrace 'supportive care' or some other non-threatening title.

We face challenges in Ireland to hold on to the true meaning of hospice while understanding the emergence of new names for old words, traditions and values. Perhaps Sinéad Donnelly has awakened some of this deeper awareness of heritage and culture and the importance of language, in her chapter. The meaning of hospice and palliative care in terms of who it reaches out to has also widened embracing people with earlier-stage disease

rol, psychological support and people with non-
here needs are great but prognosis is less certain.
ds us that we are still confronted with important
values of palliative care and he emphasizes the
g the holistic approach in the face of the increasing
d dying.

emands

Palliative care for older people is now receiving greater attention. This has relevance to the Republic of Ireland as the predicted demographic changes over the next few decades become a reality. The current population of Ireland is relatively young and any increase in the older population will bring increasing demands for palliative care.

The Republic of Ireland has started from a low base in terms of service provision, for example there are currently only 67 specialist palliative care beds serving the population of the greater Dublin area with a population of 1.4 million people. Some parts of Ireland, namely the midlands, the south east and the north east have no specialist palliative care in-patient beds. It is vital that, as described in the *Report of the National Advisory Committee on Palliative Care* (Department of Health and Children, 2001), these specialist palliative care units are built and staffed in a short time-frame. Without these centres of excellence to support and educate all health care staff, the ability to disseminate the principles of palliative care will be limited.

While the capital costs of building new in-patient units in every health board area occupies the minds of service planners for palliative care in Ireland, a strategic consideration must be staffing. There is a shortage of experienced palliative care staff in all professions. Currently, senior posts advertised in both nursing and medicine in palliative care attract little interest, leading to a relatively limited choice during the interview process. Therefore the development of palliative care is reliant on the infrastructures being put in place to support training and education of the staff needed to provide a countrywide, specialist palliative care service.

Staff recruitment and retention is an issue for many services. Ireland is a small country with a very limited pool of palliative care professionals and therefore the headhunting of staff that resources one service is at great cost to another. Dublin is an expensive city to live in with house prices to rival any capital city in Europe and therefore posts outside of the capital often prove tempting to those aiming to improve their own quality of life. This is creating a staffing crisis in some services but has a positive benefit also in that it encourages services to focus on education and support for existing staff to strengthen staff retention. Attracting staff from abroad has not proved very fruitful although the 'Celtic Tiger' and subsequent economic growth in recent years in the Republic of Ireland has brought some Irish health care professionals 'home' to work.

In March 2004, a national ban on smoking in the workplace in Ireland was introduced by the then Minister for Health and Children, Mr Michéal Martin. Evidence of the link between passive smoking and cancer was the catalyst for the ban. Very few institutions were exempt from this legislation and hospices were one such exemption. In the short-term, pubs are more pleasant to visit and initial reports are that cigarette sales are down, but far more important is the long-term effect that this legislation will have on the health of the nation as a whole. The inevitable impact of this legislation on palliative care will not be apparent for some years to come, however the reduction in the number of patients with smoking related malignancies will be very welcome.

The care of patients with diseases other than cancer will become the next major clinical challenge to palliative care services in the Republic of Ireland. As services are better resourced the extension of specialist palliative care will be inevitable. Currently, some services provide a limited service to patients with non-malignant disease, particularly palliative care teams in the acute hospitals. The *Report of the National Advisory Committee on Palliative Care* (Department of Health and Children, 2001) estimates that caring for patients with non-malignant disease would double the workload of specialist palliative care teams.

Future stakeholders

Who will drive hospice and palliative care in the future? The earlier pioneers have been at the coalface for 15 to 20 years in Ireland. The religious sisters are by force of numbers diminishing in their presence although not in their enthusiasm and vision. The established charities continue to support services but their role in providing funding for core clinical services will diminish as resources are made available to implement the *Report*. This should encourage the charities to concentrate more resources on education and research. A recent and exciting development is the arrival of Atlantic Philanthropies, an organization developed specifically to provide funding to a range of programmes with the specific goal of bringing about lasting changes that will improve the lives of disadvantaged and vulnerable people. They have undertaken as part of their programme on ageing to strengthen end-of-life care through expanding palliative and hospice care in the Republic of Ireland. This investment in palliative care services in Ireland will lead to further opportunities for development.

It will fall also to the professionals working in the services and their representative bodies to continue to drive development and this must be achieved in a transparent and equitable way. Services in the same health boards are already competing for limited development funding. It is important that the greater good of palliative care in a region takes precedence over local need. Similarly it is vital that the voluntary hospice movement works collaboratively with statutory bodies in the new structures described in the report to achieve the ultimate goal of best care for patients and their families.

There are several professional groups formed within the palliative care community in Ireland. The most important of these is the Irish Association for Palliative Care (IAPC), established in 1993 as an all-Ireland body that aims to promote all aspects of palliative care. The organization provides support for those working in palliative care and promotes education and research. Membership of the association is open to anyone with an interest in palliative care and thus includes health care professionals, administrative staff and volunteers. The majority of members are nurses. An elected executive committee leads the organization and a number of advisory forums and groups have been established (nursing, education and research, ethics and social work). The Irish Association for Palliative Care is seen as representative of palliative care and has thus been approached to represent palliative care opinion on national committees, for example representation from the IAPC was sought by the Department of Health and Children when both setting up the committee that went on to produce the *Report* and also for the National Cancer Forum. The Irish Palliative Care Directors of Nursing Group and the Irish Consultants in Palliative Medicine Group regularly meet to address relevant professional issues. These influential professional groups have a major influence on the shape of palliative care in the Republic of Ireland and more collaboration is needed to ensure cohesive and uniform strategic development of Irish palliative care

The Department of Health and Children is also a partner in driving the development of palliative care services. Whereas ministers will change, the civil service in the department is more of a constant and influences prioritization and policy development. The Department of Health and Children faces many challenges over the coming years. Currently, a major programme of structural reforms is underway as discussed in the chapter on managing palliative care services. The establishment of a new Health Service Executive (HSE) has significant implications for palliative care. A recent development is the announcement that palliative care is to be based in the Primary, Community and Continuing Care Directorate (PCCC) rather than the National Hospitals Office (NHO). This is an uncertain time for those working in palliative care in Ireland as traditionally community services have been underfunded when compared to hospital services. If this pattern continues then there are challenging times ahead for palliative care. If funding orientation changes and the development of community services is supported it may be that palliative care could benefit significantly. There is, however, some concern among many of those working in palliative care, in particular medical consultants, that placing palliative care in the PCCC disregards the reality of their workload, which is mainly hospital and hospice based. There is a perception that palliative medicine as a community specialty will damage it significantly and the decision to place it within the PCCC is likely to be challenged.

The Department of Health and Children also faces the challenges of ensuring equity in service provision, developing a clinical governance model and ensuring value for money. One of the current popular criticisms is that despite a significant investment in the health services over the last five years, there appears little improvement in health outcomes. The reality is that some of these improvements will take years to manifest. Palliative care can point to increased staffing levels, more hospice beds, more hospital and home care teams and an increased number of allied health care professionals. This investment primarily ensures a greater equity of access to services. The agenda of ensuring an environment to support excellence in clinical care and continuous quality improvement has not penetrated the Irish health care sector to the same extent as in the United Kingdom. Responsibility for ensuring the development of quality services is a shared one and clinicians have to embrace the need to be able to show how quality care is being delivered and that there is a value-for-money component to quality. Sometimes the cost versus quality debate is difficult to apply in palliative care settings but it is just as important for a palliative care service to have standards, outcome measures and quality measures as it is for cardiac surgery.

The public will remain a critical driver of service development. In a small democracy such as Ireland, the ability of the public to influence is manifested by the easy access to politicians. As a people we have tended in the past not to complain about services but there is now a growing realization that sometimes the only way to ensure change is to bring deficiencies in services to the attention of local politicians and to make it an issue, as demonstrated in the section relating to the development of the North West Hospice where parliamentary questions were used to make the case for funding. Health services are political because they are huge local employers and the presence or absence of a hospital/service can have repercussions beyond any immediate health effect. Because most families will have some experience of hospice services, be it direct through a family member or indirect through a friend or colleague, they comprise a large proportion of the population. As such their influence is great and their expectation of a quality service is high. Maintaining this quality in the face of greater demands and relatively few experienced and trained staff is a major challenge. Where families have a positive experience they will continue to support the development of palliative care and this underpins the importance of clinical governance to palliative care.

Ethical questions

What of ethics? At an earlier stage in planning this book there was to be a chapter on Irish ethics in which we intended to visit some of the ethical debates. Pressure of space has led to its demise but there are many challenging ethical dilemmas facing both health care professionals working in Irish palliative care and all stakeholders. One of these is how monies either allocated by state agencies or donated directly by the public does not always end up exactly where it was intended.

Statutory funding for palliative care services is initially determined by the Department of Health and Children and filters down through the health boards to the clinical service providers. Ensuring that all identified funding reaches its intended destination is a major challenge. Leakage of palliative care funding results in patients and families not receiving the level of care intended and deserved. Pressure on financial controllers to balance budgets and competing services results in some palliative care funding being an easy target. Currently the system is not transparent and there is minimal involvement of clinicians in the financial decision-making process. A government initiative to respond to these criticisms has been implemented in some settings and is in the process of being developed in Our Lady's Hospice, Dublin (Office for Health Service Management, 2000).

The voluntary hospice sector also needs to have fully transparent accounting to retain the confidence of the Irish public who donate so generously. Families should have some influence in determining how donated monies are spent, particularly if they wish to acknowledge the care and support received from a particular unit or service. Spending monies donated by a family cared for by one service, in another unrelated area, without the donor's consent, is at best a dubious practice!

Our multiculturalism and societal change have been discussed at length by Geraldine Tracey and Julie Ling and alluded to in several other chapters. As a nation with a young population, can we expect more traditional views and Catholic teaching to hold sway or will issues such as the legalization of euthanasia be called for? Certainly, well developed palliative care services are a strong response to the request for euthanasia but there are always going to be a small number of people who wish to end their lives at a time and manner of their choosing. The individual's rights versus the greater good of society is a much travelled debate. In the UK, some health care professionals express the view that it is only a matter of time before public opinion and political will changes the law on euthanasia. How would such a change impact on Irish palliative care? Currently, abortion is illegal in Ireland and many young Irish women travel to the UK each year for abortions. Would legalization of euthanasia in the UK result in a similar situation for people who wish for euthanasia in the Republic of Ireland? It would certainly put the debate back on centre stage and the palliative care community would need to be represented clearly in the debate.

Report of the National Advisory Committee on Palliative Care

The *Report of the National Advisory Committee on Palliative Care* (Department of Health and Children, 2001) was a serious attempt by both the then Minister for Health, Mr Micháel Martin and the professionals, charities and voluntary groups to try to agree a blueprint for future development of palliative care services. This *Report* is now over three years old and has been partially implemented as discussed in Chapter 1 by Tony O'Brien and David Clark. While much has already been achieved, whether the political will is there fully to implement this report remains to be seen. Palliative care is not cheap and there are many competing services clamouring for funding.

To date, there has been a significant increase in the number of consultant and clinical nurse specialist posts. Needs assessments have been commenced in all health board areas. However these have not been standardized and vary in content. Since publication of the *Report*, while services across Ireland have developed, regional variations in job specifications and roles are causing confusion. The need for an overall co-ordinating body in the form of a representative National Palliative Care Forum was identified in the *Report* but has yet to come to fruition, which remains a key issue.

Education and research

Education is the key to both setting and maintaining standards of care and best practice. Without this investment, the new and expanded services outlined as necessary in the National Advisory Committee Report, will lack the necessary skill mix and knowledge base to provide specialist palliative care. The establishment of academic departments of palliative care with chairs in both palliative medicine and palliative nursing has been highlighted as essential by Phil Larkin and Stephen Higgins. To resource these departments will require an injection of funding but the benefit will be seen in the provision of a well-educated, specialist workforce to fill the new posts being developed throughout the country.

Currently consultants and some community clinical nurse specialists carry a large clinical workload and work in single-handed practice. Their ability to undertake useful research is limited and their involvement in education at undergraduate and postgraduate levels limited. To date, opportunities for nurses to pursue further education have been limited to undertaking a higher diploma in palliative nursing or a generic Masters programme. No palliative care Masters programme is currently offered in the Republic of Ireland.

The development of a research ethos in palliative care in the Republic of Ireland is overdue and can only be achieved by promoting research as a means to providing improved patient and family care. The Republic of Ireland is a relatively small country and this provides the opportunity for the development of good collaborative research work. The first step on the research journey is to develop audit and to support this with the use of information technology. The development of a minimum data set is a recommendation of the *Report*.

To date the universities, particularly the medical schools, have benefited from involvement of palliative care consultants in undergraduate teaching. It is now critical that the universities use their knowledge and influence to support the academic development of this new specialty. No consultant in the Republic of Ireland currently holds an academic appointment with protected time for teaching and research. The initiative by Our Lady's Hospice in partnership with both University College Dublin and Trinity College Dublin to develop the first academic department of palliative care, deserves full support.

Collaborative working

In palliative care most patients will remain under the care of the team until their death. Referrals are received from many sources. General practitioners have a central role in referring patients in the community to specialist palliative care services. For patients who remain at home a shared model of care is more effective. Most general practitioners have genuine interest in improving their own knowledge and skills in palliative care and it is important for specialist teams to acknowledge their skills and to support the general practitioner.

Community services are critical to palliative care in that most patients wish to be at home during their illness and a strengthening of these services and relationships is vital to ensure this outcome for as many people as possible.

With the development of cancer services many patients are referred at an earlier stage in their disease trajectory by oncologists. In the Republic of Ireland many medical oncologists have undertaken training in their speciality in the United States. The hospice movement in the United States is a very different model to that practiced in the Republic of Ireland and this can lead to different expectations. As more patients are referred to palliative care, collaborative working has increased significantly and deserves full support.

One major structural change in the Irish health care system is the proposed establishment of cancer super-centres in a small number of geographical locations. The thinking behind this is that a comprehensive cancer service will be provided from one geographical location with all the necessary facilities and support services available on site. This would replace the current system where surgery, radiotherapy and chemotherapy are not necessarily provided in the same location. The implications for palliative care are interesting as the 2001 *Report* preceded this development. The existing specialist in-patient units are largely independent of acute general hospitals. Should there be the full range of palliative care services including in-patient beds, available on site if these super-centres develop?

International dimension

The development of palliative care services in Ireland may serve as a model for other countries where palliative care services are in the process of being developed. There has always been a strong missionary ethos among many of the religious orders in Ireland and it is not surprising to see the development of new projects, for example the twinning of Our Lady's Hospice, Dublin with Our Lady's Hospice, Zambia. The palliative care community in Ireland have a great deal to share with emerging services world-wide. They also have an important voice to represent these countries where for many palliative care is not within reach and where our level of development is an impossible dream.

Conclusion

It is possible to develop an excellent specialist palliative care service in the Republic of Ireland, building on the foundations laid by religious orders, the voluntary hospice movement, supportive charities, health care professionals and a responsive and creative Department of Health. Much has been achieved, services have developed and public awareness and expectations have been raised. The challenge now for palliative care in Ireland is to fulfil this promise. To do so will require not only resources but imagination and creativity together with a practical approach to strategic problem solving. Collaboration and communication are the keys to achieving a world class palliative care service.

References

Department of Health and Children (2001), *Report of the National Advisory Committee on Palliative Care*. Dublin: Stationery Office.

Office for Health Service Management (2000), Clinicians in Management (1): Introduction and Case Studies, Discussion Paper No 1; Clinicians in Management (2): A Framework for Discussion, Discussion Paper No 2.

Index

population changes 56
priorities, timeframes and costs
16–17
recommendations 10–17
research 14
scale of unmet need 11
settings for palliative care 11–12
specialist palliative care nurses
48–9
specialist palliative care services
13
staffing levels 167
standards in palliative care 15
structure of palliative care
settings 12
teamworking 87, 88–9
*Report of the National Task Force
on Medical Staffing* 181
research 14, 198, 209–10
hospital-based teams 68–9
respite care 74, 75, 76
response shift 126
Rest for the Dying, The 4
Reynolds, Albert 24
Riper, H. 50
rituals 105, 106
around death 150–1, 156–7,
159, 169, 199, 201
Travellers 137–9, 141–4
see also traditions on dying and
death
Robinson, Mary 166
rosary 151, 156–7
Royal College of Nursing 173
Royal College of Paediatrics and
Child Health (RCPCH) 72
rural areas 22–3
infrastructure 57–8
rural home care 54–60
access to medication 59
communication with patients
59
development of 54–5
first visit 58
patient profile 55–6
role of rural home care nurse
56–7
support structure for nurses 57

satellite palliative care units 55
Satterly, L. 113
Saunders, Cicely 19, 31, 120, 123,
124, 128–9, 185
'saying hello again' 97, 98–9
scale of unmet need, quantifying
11
Scudder, J.R. 186
secondment to palliative care team
182
service demands *see* demand for
services
settings for palliative care 11–12
Seymour, J. 186
Shaping a Healthier Future 7, 25,
36, 86
Sheehan, Siobhan 199
Sherman, D. 171
Silverman, P. 96
Sisters of Charity 3–4, 6, 27, 34,
61, 65, 111, 123
Sisters of Mercy 34
Sjernsward, Jan 25
Skeel, R.T. 37
Sligo Champion 24
smoking, ban on 205
Sneddon, M. 186
social support 105
social workers 47, 85, 88–9
specialist palliative care services
12–13
specialist palliative care units 55
specialist registrars (SpRs) 182–3
specialization, levels of 12–13
Speck, P. 91
Spencer, D.J. 77
Spilker, B. 37
spirituality 171
of hospice staff 120
Irish predisposition to whole-
person care 122–3
religion, faith and 109–21
Spruyt, O. 173
St Bartholomew's Hospital,
London 67
St Brigid's Hospice, Kildare 63
St Christopher's Hospice, Cavan
63

Tse, C.Y.   170
Tsilika, E.   90
tuberculosis (TB)   6, 61
Tuberculosis Bill of 1945   6
Tunney, Carmel   23
Tyler, M.K.   164, 174

unconscious processes   91
undergraduate medical education
   180–1
United States   210
University College Dublin
   academic department of
      palliative care   179, 188, 210
   Department of Irish Folklore
      150
unmet need, quantifying the scale
   of   11
urban home care   45–53
   challenges   48–51
   education   48
   evolution   45–8
   quality   51–2

Vachon, M.L.   50
value for money   124, 207
Van Doorslaer, O.   138, 141
vigil   153
vision   40–1
voluntary bereavement support
   services   101–2
voluntary hospice movement   7,
   19–22, 62
voluntary hospital movement
   33–4
voluntary sector   19–32, 35, 205
   accountability   208
   Irish Cancer Society   24, 26–8,
      31, 45, 65
   Irish Hospice Foundation   24,
      29–31, 62, 66, 71, 95

North West Hospice   20, 22–6,
   62, 63, 207
   supporting families with sick
      children   74, 76
   voluntary-statutory
      partnerships   16, 21–2
volunteering   20
Vose, C.   173

wakes   138, 174
Waldron, D.   37, 131
Walsh, Declan   25
Walter, T.   169
Ward, Chrissie   138
welcome   194
White, M.   97, 100
whole person care   122–33, 168–9
   attitudes and caregiving   128–9
   implications for Irish palliative
      care   130–1
   intervening to solve problems
      128
   key constructs   124–5
   medical education   129–30
   palliative care and healing
      125–6
   promoting healing   126–7
   therapeutic relationship   127
   who caregivers are as persons
      127
   working directly with the healing
      principle   128
Wiles, R.   50
Wilkes, E.   50
Wilson, I.   126
Winslade, J.   97
Wolfelt, A.   101
Worden, W.   96–7, 99–100
World Health Organization   9, 122
wounded healer   127
Wyndgard, B.   100